New York:
SONGS OF THE CITY

THE CITY OF NEW YORK

Lyric and Music by
THOMAS G. MEEHAN

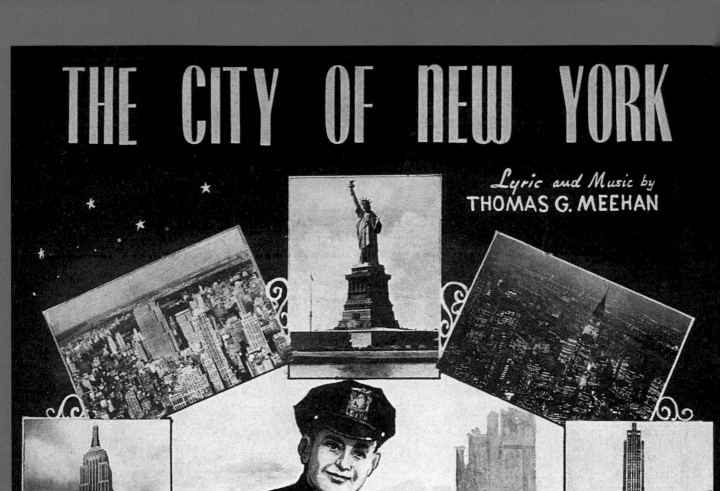

JAMES MUSIC, INC.   149 Broadway, New York

NEW YORK:
SONGS OF THE CITY

Nancy Groce

WATSON-GUPTILL PUBLICATIONS/NEW YORK

ILLUSTRATION CREDITS

Those images not otherwise credited are in the author's personal collection.

Courtesy of The Estate of Irving Berlin. Used by Permission: 154.

Harper's New Monthly Magazine, March 1887: 127.

Courtesy of Don Meade: 109.

Courtesy: Museum of the City of New York: 18, 19, 24 bottom, 25, 39, 49, 59, 64 bottom, 86, 156 top; Gift of Mr. J. Omar Cole: 18; Mills Artists, Inc. Gift of E.B. Marks: 86.

Courtesy of The Zimmerman Collection: 1, 6 top, 7 top, 12, 14 both, 16, 17, 32, 34, 36, 37, 38, 41, 42 bottom, 45, 46, 47, 51 left, 52, 53, 54, 90, 95, 97 right, 98, 99, 100 left, 112, 119, 128, 129, 130 top, 135, 139, 149, 150, 158 both, 159, 161 left, 162, 163 bottom, 168, 172.

PAGE 1: Stylized skyline of New York graces the cover of George C. Durgan's "The New York Rag" (1911).

PAGE 2: Thomas G. Meehan's "The City of New York" (1948) featured a policeman with a child wearing a Police Athletic League shirt surrounded by city landmarks. The first verse begins *"An enchanting little Isle / Better known as Old New York / It was bought with beads and guile / From some boys with tomahawks. . . ."*

PAGE 5: The Philadelphia-based Mr. Lincoln, who both composed and published this march-two step in 1919, has graphically stranded Miss Liberty in mid-ocean. Lincoln was either going for the fully metaphorical treatment, or—more probably—he wished to ignore the fact that Miss Liberty resided in New York.

Senior Editor: Bob Nirkind
Editor: Margaret Sobel
Editorial Assistant: Sarah Fass
Book and cover design: Areta Buk
Production Manager: Hector Campbell

NB: The author has made a good faith effort to locate, identify, and properly credit all songwriters, artists, and publishers whose work appears in this text, and to obtain necessary rights and permissions from all copyright owners. Any inadvertent omissions or errors will be corrected in future editions.

First published by Billboard Books,
an imprint of Watson-Guptill Publications,
a division of BPI Communications, Inc.,
1515 Broadway, New York, N.Y. 10036.

Library of Congress Cataloging-in-Publication Data

Groce, Nancy.
    New York, songs of the city / Nancy Groce.
        p.   cm.
    Includes bibliographical references (p.   ) and index.
    ISBN 0-8230-8349-7
    1. Popular music—New York (State)—New York—History and criticism. 2. New York (N.Y.)—Songs and music—History and criticism. I. Title.
    ML3477.8.N48G76   1999
    782.42'156—dc21   99-11122
                                           CIP

Manufactured in Italy

First Printing, 1999

1 2 3 4 5 6 7 8 / 04 03 02 01 00 99

For my New York parents
Raymond and Marian Groce and
my New York grandparents
Pauline and Solomon Pearlman.

Where the Hudson River meets the sea
There's a peculiar community
All the citizens agree
Anything can happen in New York

"Anything Can Happen in New York" (1947)

CONTENTS

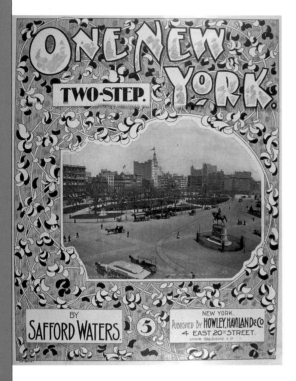

PREFACE

This book is an exploration of New York City's history and culture through the poetry of its music.

No American city has inspired more music than New York. For more than three hundred years, composers have sought to capture the sounds, energy, and sophistication of New York life in song. Through these songs, New York's complex urban landscape developed a soundscape all its own. Today, few New Yorkers "Take the 'A' Train," walk "The Sidewalks of New York," or go "Up on the Roof" without hearing a faint echo of a song. Since very early in its history, New York songs have provided a musical backdrop as the city grew from a small provincial outpost to a world-class metropolis. This book celebrates the songs that celebrate New York. It also tells the stories of the colorful men and women who composed and performed this music and poetry to express their fascination with the city.

To date, I have found almost one thousand songs dealing with all aspects of life in New York. With so many examples and points of view to choose from, it is hard to make many sweeping generalizations about New York City songs. Many of the earliest songs—as well as some of the later ones—are out-and-out celebrations of city life. From 1831, when J.A. Gairdner composed "New York, O! What a Charming City," to 1985, when Mayor Ed Koch declared John Kander and Fred Ebbs's "New York, New York" the city's official anthem, enthusiastic, if sometimes naïve boosterism found a receptive audience among local residents. Not all songs about the city were celebratory, however. Beginning in the early nineteenth century, songwriters also started to paint a nuanced, multifaceted picture of their city, and at their best, these songs provide listeners with an aural slice of contemporaneous urban life. As the city changed, so did its music: mid-nineteenth-century pastoral idylls with lyrics proclaiming, *"I love the Heights of Brooklyn with its green and shady bowers"* (1854), gradually gave way to songs that reflected less pleasant realities of the modern cityscape. These include one of my personal favorites: William Slafer's 1907 "The Brooklyn Daily Eagle Bridge Crush March, Descriptive," a musical tribute to the

travails of commuting, which begins with the immortal lyric: *"Say au revoir but not good bye / We won't get home till morning."*

The experiences of immigrants and migrants greatly enriched the city's musical landscape. Wave after wave of immigrants, many coming directly from tradition-bound rural cultures to an increasingly complex urban environment, turned to music for comfort, for entertainment, and to explain themselves to their fellow New Yorkers. Few lyricists did a better job of capturing the spirit or describing life in the crowded tenements of nineteenth-century New York than Edward Harrigan (1844–1911). Part of the famous Irish-American vaudeville team of Harrigan & Hart, Harrigan is best remembered today because of George M. Cohan's 1908 tribute song that began *"H, A, double-R, I, G, A, N spells Harrigan."* It would be hard to overstate the impact he and his creative partner, the composer David Braham (1838–1905), had on the American theatre during the 1870s and 1880s. Although not an immigrant himself (he was born on the Lower East Side), Harrigan drew inspiration for his work from the daily lives of New York City's newest residents.

Immigrants wrote songs both for home consumption and for performances at theatres, social clubs, beer gardens, and music halls. Many songs were written in languages other than English such as German, Yiddish, and Spanish, as well as Gaelic, Chinese, Slovak, and Arabic. Nor does this trend show any signs of stopping. For example, although we tend to think of Irish immigration as a nineteenth- or early-twentieth-century phenomenon, during the 1980s a wave of semi-legal young Irish immigrants flooded the city. Within a few years, songwriters among them were combining traditional Irish folk music, British rock, American rap, and their personal experiences in America to create "Green Card Rock" songs about the Bronx. Even now, Dominican musicians in Washington Heights are busily composing merengues about their new hometown, and a recently composed Yiddish song about New York's pooper-scooper law written by a Russian Jewish immigrant in Brighton Beach is rumored to be spreading like

OPPOSITE: This 1907 sheet music, illustrated by respected artist and songwriter Gene Buck, features a view of the New York Times building in Times Square.

Hollywood meets Broadway in the 1929 film *Broadway Melody.*

established black community had flourished since the seventeenth century. In the 1910s, improvements in urban transportation and changes in the real estate market enticed many black New Yorkers to move to Harlem. By the 1920s, the critical mass of artists, writers, philosophers, and musicians living in this uptown neighborhood threw off enough artistic heat and intellectual fervor to ignite the Harlem Renaissance. Chapter Five includes a few of the many great songs that were written about Harlem during this era. But African-American contributions to New York's musical history certainly did not end in the 1920s. Through the big-band era of the 1930s and 1940s, the urban doo-wop craze of the 1950s, the rock revolution of the 1960s, and the explosion of that ultra-urban art form, hip hop, in the 1980s and 1990s, black New Yorkers have continued to enrich our shared musical landscape.

The other great influx of migrants to influence New York's music was neither regional, ethnic, nor racial—instead, it was composed of the culturally gifted from America's hinterlands seeking a haven from what they considered the boredom and conformity of mainstream American life. Perhaps no song better sums up the hopes and dreams of these cultural refugees than the 1977 theme from the film *New York, New York,* which states:

> *If I can make it there, I'd make it anywhere,*
> *It's up to you, New York, New York.*

Before beginning our musical tour, a few logistical notes: To facilitate the narrative, full citations for many songs have been omitted in the text; however, bibliographic information for each piece can be found in the Song Index at the end of the book. Also, due to space constraints, I have often taken the liberty of omitting some verses or portions of verses. Throughout the text, missing verses are noted by a row of tildes (~ ~ ~); missing words with ellipses (. . .). Over the years, some of the most colorful songs were either never printed or printed with the blandest of covers. Conversely, some of the most spectacular sheet music covers have promoted the most uninspired of songs or lackluster instrumental compositions. I have therefore selected the best of both lyrics and cover illustrations to illuminate our musical journey, and readers are advised that they will sometimes find one without the other. Reproducing actual music in the text was not possible due to space limitations; however, most of the sheet music discussed in the text

wildfire through Brooklyn. Chapter Seven highlights songs written specifically about the experience of immigration, but songs composed by immigrants can be found throughout the text.

In addition to immigrants from overseas, the city has been a magnet to other Americans who saw in New York opportunities, freedom, glamour, and excitement that were lacking in their hometowns. Despite a deep-seated Jeffersonian distrust of cities, Americans have been flocking to New York since the days of the Dutch. This book focuses on two special groups of American-born "urbanites by choice" that had a disproportionally large impact on the city and its songs. First, it focuses on the contributions of the hundreds of thousands of African Americans, largely from the southern United States, who began arriving in New York in great numbers during the latter half of the nineteenth century. Drawn by job opportunities and hopes for greater personal freedom, these migrants initially settled in neighborhoods such as San Juan Hill (now West 57th Street between Eighth and Ninth Avenues), Greenwich Village, and parts of Brooklyn, where New York's already

can be found in research libraries throughout America and most of the twentieth-century songs are available on recordings. If I have not included your favorite New York song, I hope that I have at least touched on a few runners-up. Choosing which songs to include was difficult.

The ability of lyricists to punctuate their works in standard English has varied widely. Written punctuation was often not critical when the pieces were sung since musical phrasing reinforced and/or clarified the meaning of the lyrics. Reading lyrics, however, is a different kettle of fish. Therefore, throughout this book, I have occasionally made minor changes in spelling or punctuation when needed for the sake of clarity. When it is obvious that songwriters purposely used antiquated or dialect spellings, I have omitted "[sic]" to avoid clutter. Over the last two hundred years, musical terms such as "vamp," "verse," "chorus," and "refrain" have often been used loosely and interchangeably by composers of popular songs. Rather than take sides, I have opted to use the same term as that used in the piece under discussion. Throughout the lyrics double slashes appear to separate verses from choruses, or in some cases, to demarcate one musical section from another.

Finally, let me address the thorny question of copyrights and permissions. Many songs written after 1923 are still under copyright. The author has made a good faith effort to locate, identify, and properly credit all songwriters, song publishers, and copyright holders and to obtain necessary rights and permissions. The author apologizes in advance for any inadvertent omissions or errors, which will be corrected in future editions.

For the sake of consistency, when teams of songwriters are mentioned, the name of the lyricist is given first, the name of the composer second, and the date of publication last, as in (w. Edward Harrigan/m. David Braham: 1879). I have, however, occasionally made an exception to this rule, particularly in the case of Richard Rodgers and Lorenz Hart, who preferred to be listed as Rodgers and Hart.

The author would like to thank several institutions and individuals without whom this project would have been nearly impossible. First, my thanks to the staff of the Brooklyn Historical Society, especially Head Librarian Michell Hackwelder; the staff of the Museum of the City of New York, especially Marty Jacobs, Jan Ramirez, Peter Simmons, and Marguerite Lavin; Dr. Paul F. Wells, Director of the Center for Popular Music at Middle Tennessee State

University; the staff of the Music Division at the Library of Congress, especially Nancy Seeger; and the staff of the New York Society Library. The New York Public Library is one of the world's great research institutions and the Music Library and Special Collections divisions at the New York Public Library at Lincoln Center were particularly helpful in the course of my research. My heartfelt thanks go to John Shepard and George Boziwick for their interest and encouragement.

Thanks are due also to Brooklyn Borough Historian John Manbeck, who was more than generous in sharing his unpublished research on Brooklyn songs and providing me with additional advice and information. I am most grateful to Dr. Maureen Buja, Dr. Martin Burke, Marian Groce, Dr. Nora Groce, Don Meade, Berthe Schuchat, and Carol Selman, who were kind enough to read the manuscript before it was in a readable condition. Friends and colleagues Dr. Ray Allen, Gene Bruck, Kathleen Condon, Fred Nesta, Laura Maestro, Dr. Michael Taft, Dr. Lois Wilcken, Mary Ann Wurlitzer, and Dr. Steve Zeitlin helped with various aspects of the research and were of invaluable assistance. Editors Margaret Sobel and Robert Nirkind of Billboard Books deserve praise for helping me fashion my rough draft into a readable text, as does Areta Buk who put a great deal of time and thoughtful effort into the design. A special thanks to Liam Reilly, John Strauss, Don Wade, Terence Winch, and the other songwriters who responded so warmly to this project and generously permitted use of their songs. And I am very grateful to record collector extraordinaire Pat Conte who took time to help me with the earliest stages of this project. Professor Philip Furia of the University of North Carolina/Wilmington and attorney Jack Handler were both extremely gracious about helping me to sort my way through the labyrinthine world of copyrights and permissions. I owe my book agent Katharine Sands of the Sarah Jane Freymann/Stepping Stone Literary Agency sincere thanks for her faith and advice in bringing this project to fruition.

Lastly, a profound thanks to two individuals who have been more than generous with their time and expertise. First, photographer Martha Cooper, who did such an excellent job of capturing the images which illuminate these pages. And second, thanks to Larry Zimmerman, an expert on nineteenth-century New York City sheet music who generously gave me access to his magnificent collection and was most helpful in helping me prepare this manuscript for publication.

OUR NEW YORK

OFFICIAL EDITION
Approved by
MAYOR LA GUARDIA

FAIRCHILD AERIAL SURVEYS, INC. N

Words and Music by SIGMUND SPAETH

WHEN PERFORMING THIS COMPOSITION KINDLY GIVE ALL PROGRAM CREDITS TO
EDWARD B. MARKS MUSIC CORPORATION · RCA BUILDING · RADIO CITY · N. Y

Chapter 1

"I'll Take Manhattan"

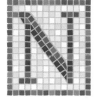ew York City has always been a unique place. It might have been its Dutch ancestry or something in the Hudson River water, but from its earliest days visitors from New England, Philadelphia, and the South complained about the noise, bustle, and pace of the city. Worse, it was

inhabited by New Yorkers—a polyglot jumble of different nationalities, races, and religions from all corners of the globe who, the outsiders said, were more interested in making money and entertaining themselves than in keeping the Sabbath and establishing a "proper" society.

Since the consolidation of Greater New York in 1898, New York City has encompassed five boroughs: Manhattan, Queens, Brooklyn, the Bronx, and Staten Island. Yet even today, when New Yorkers talk about "The City" or "New York" they are usually referring only to the smallest of the boroughs, Manhattan. Thirteen miles long and only two miles across at its widest point, the 22.6 square miles of Manhattan are home to 1.5 million people, hundreds of skyscrapers, and thousands of taxicabs. The excitement of Broadway, the fashions of the Garment District, the advertising campaigns of Madison Avenue, and the wealth of Wall Street are all created within a few shorts blocks of each other. Yet at the same time, Manhattan also boasts many quiet neighborhoods and peaceful parks.

Early City History and Music in the City

"Manhattan" was a European interpretation of a Lenni-Lenape word used by the Munsee tribe. Some scholars contend that the original Native American word might have been *manahactanienk*—

Munsee for "place of general inebriation,"[1] but we don't know for sure. We do know that the first permanent European settlement was established in 1624 by members of the Dutch West India Company who built Fort Amsterdam at what is today Battery Park on the southeastern tip of the island. By 1653, feeling increasingly threatened by the British, the Dutch thought it advisable to build a protective wall along what is now Wall Street and generally fortify the colony. It didn't work. In 1664 New Amsterdam fell to the British, who promptly renamed the young city in honor of James Stuart, Duke of York (1633–1701). Peter Stuyvesant (1610–1672), the last Dutch Governor of New York, who was legendary both for his peg leg and short temper, was not amused. He retired to his farm in what is today Stuyvesant Town near First Avenue and 14th Street, and the four thousand or so newly named "New Yorkers" began to learn English.

Unfortunately, we know very little about music in seventeenth-century New York. As early as 1659, the directors of the Dutch West India Company did ship some "drums . . . drumskins, snares, and strings" for the colony's military band.[2] Period accounts confirm that New Yorkers enjoyed music, dance, theatre, and public amusements under both Dutch and British rule, and by the mid-eighteenth century, New York newspapers carried advertisements for numerous concerts, plays, music teachers, and music stores. Pleasure gardens—privately

OPPOSITE: New York from the air in 1939 graced the cover of "Our New York." Intended to serve as the city's anthem, this was the "*Official Edition Approved by Mayor La Guardia.*"

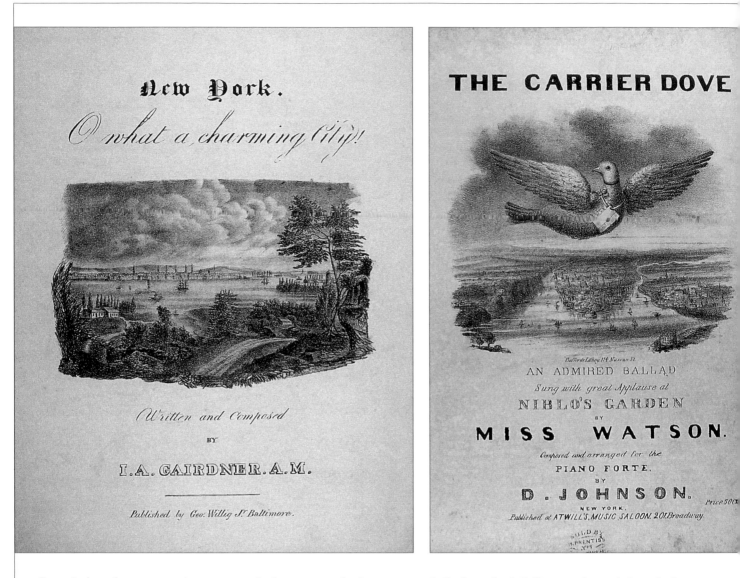

Two early views of Manhattan Island on sheet music covers.

owned open-air parks featuring paths for strolling, refreshments, dancing, entertainment, and fireworks within their fenced perimeters—were extremely popular during the late eighteenth and early nineteenth centuries. Reservations about the propriety of public performances and the Sabbatarian laws, which hampered the development of musical culture in cities such as Boston and Philadelphia by forbidding Sunday performances, were largely absent in New York.

During the Revolution, New York remained firmly under British control. In fact, from November 1776 until the signing of the Treaty of Paris in 1783, the city served as the center of British military operations in North America. Thousands of British troops, joined by large numbers of camp followers and loyalist refugees, swelled the city's population to a new high of perhaps thirty-three thousand. Far from the front lines, and faced with long periods of calm between military operations, residents of New York had both the time and money to pursue cultural activities, and theatres and concert

halls flourished. Following the withdrawal of the British, the selection of New York as the nation's first capital from 1785 to 1790 also encouraged New York's cultural preeminence.

New Yorkers have always been proud of their city. Like other colonial Americans, New Yorkers probably "localized" songs by including local references in folk and popular songs from the Old World soon after their arrival on these shores. By the early nineteenth century, as the city became a major center of music publishing, hundreds of songs and instrumental pieces specifically about New York were composed.

America's Sheet Music Industry

There is no better place to start our musical journey than with a quick overview of songs and instrumental pieces that celebrate the very idea of New York. Before setting off, a few words might be in order about the American music industry, and particularly the sheet music publishers, whose beautifully illustrated wares illuminate these pages. During the eighteenth and early nineteenth centuries, song texts or parodies written to be sung to well-known tunes, were popular. Published without musical notation on large sheets of inexpensive "broadside" paper and occasionally illustrated with crude woodblock prints, these "broadside ballads" usually focused on crimes, scandals, political issues, disasters, and confessions. Serving as the tabloid newspapers of their day, broadside ballads flourished in New York from the early eighteenth century through the 1880s. At the beginning of the nineteenth century, broadside ballad publishers—who frequently doubled as broadside lyricists—would festoon the fence around the newly built City Hall with their wares. For a penny, New Yorkers could learn—and sing—the latest news, neatly packaged in rhyme. In the 1880s, one of New York's last broadside publishers, Michael Creganeteine, organized pairs of indigent alcoholic hawkers and sent them out to sell his wares for a few pennies apiece. They were, one observer wrote, "colorful figures in an expressive town."[3]

Public interest in buying the latest songs to play at home dates from the mid-eighteenth century and was strongly tied to the rise of parlor music and the popularity of the piano. Illustrated or lithographed sheet music flourished throughout the nineteenth and early twentieth centuries, and it has been estimated that 2.5 million songs were published in American during that period.[4] Lithographed sheet music covers functioned the same way that CD and record covers do today—they served as a marketing device to advertise the music and entice customers.

Lithography (a printing process that used specially prepared stones to transfer an image) was invented in Austria in 1798. It was an inexpensive and comparatively rapid way of reproducing images and music. By the 1820s, American sheet music manufacturers were employing lithography, as well as older techniques such as copperplate and wood engraving, to produce eye-catching illustrations on the front or "cover" pages of sheet music. Songs about the city usually appeared in four- to eight-page packages of music and lyrics fronted by an attractive illustration selling for between ten to fifty cents. One of America's pioneering lithographers, John Pendleton, set up a music publishing shop in New York, where, in 1831, he produced one of the earliest illustrated songs about the city: J.A. Gairdner's

"New York, O! What a Charming City." The cover illustration, executed by an artist named Lopez, features an overview of Manhattan Island, viewed across the bay, possibly from Weehawken, New Jersey.[5] Inside, Gairdner's delightful melody is matched by equally charming lyrics:

> The ardent, romantic / The charming God of song, / Cross'd lately th' Atlantic / Nor thought the journey long, / He tripped along in shoes of cork, / Singing many a ditty, / But he chang'd his song when he reach'd New York, / To what a charming city.
>
> In Bowery, in Broadway, / He rambled up and down, / The byway and odd-way, / Resolved to see the town, / And as he went, he sung this song, / "Now, is it not a pity, / I should have stayed away so long / From such a charming city."

From the 1820s to the 1950s, it is possible to trace the physical development of New York and learn about its most significant events solely by studying the illustrations and lyrics that appeared in period sheet music. After the 1950s, with the rise of long-playing records and television, and a concomitant decline in the popularity of printed sheet music, the importance of illustrated sheet music waned.

Pianos and Home Music-Making

During the nineteenth century, American composers and American music publishers, both eager to make a profit, produced millions of attractively packaged pieces of sheet music. But who was buying it? Much of the nineteenth- and early-twentieth-century music discussed in this book was written for the rapidly expanding ranks of amateur musicians who, accompanied by that newly fashionable instrument, the piano, indulged in the fad for parlor music. The ability to sing and play the piano were seen as marks of gentility and few middle-class families—or those that aspired to be middle-class—could resist. Both men and women were actively involved in home music-making. Piano builders flourished. By the 1820s, musical instrument manufacturing was one of the largest industries in New York City—only sugar refining, shipbuilding, metalworking, and furniture building exceeded it in size and economic impact. By 1890, New York was home to 131 piano makers—including some of the country's most noted firms such as Steinway & Sons, Haines Brothers, and Sohmer & Company. According to that

RIGHT: A fashionably dressed woman plays an upright piano in this advertisement for piano makers and sheet music publishers Firth, Hall & Pond, circa 1843.

BELOW: Scenes of early Dutch New York based on the stories of Washington Irving. Note one-legged Peter Stuyvesant on upper right and the depiction of early New Amsterdam in the center. The waltzes advertised the Irving House, a hotel on the corner of Broadway and Chambers Street.

OPPOSITE: Father Diedrich Knickerbocker, the legendary literary figure, capers in front of the Flatiron Building in 1907.

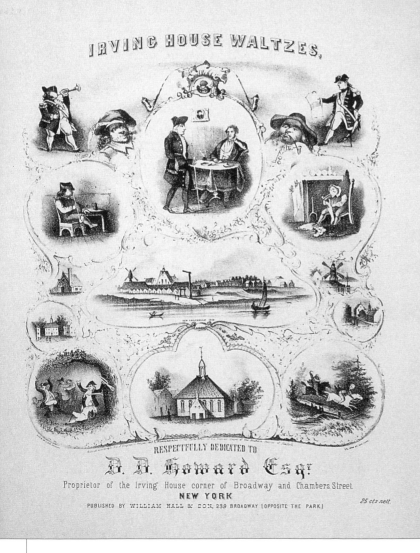

IRVING HOUSE WALTZES,

RESPECTFULLY DEDICATED TO

B. B. Howard Esq.

Proprietor of the Irving House corner of Broadway and Chambers Street.
NEW YORK

PUBLISHED BY WILLIAM HALL & SON, 239 BROADWAY (OPPOSITE THE PARK.)

25 cts nett.

year's Federal census, New York's musical instrument makers employed 5,958 craftsmen and produced $12,824,451 worth of instruments. By the early years of the twentieth century, decreasing piano prices and the introduction of monthly payment plans made pianos common even in the most modest of homes and tenement houses.

The surge in sheet music sales reflected increased musical literacy on the part of the general public, and also marked the commodification of music in an entirely new way. By World War I, the fashion for home music-*making* was beginning to wane. It was replaced over the next decades—thanks to such technological breakthroughs as radios, record players, and tape decks—with the idea of *consuming* music at home. Yet, despite massive technological and social changes over the last 150 years, some of the business structures and practices that drive today's music industry can trace their roots back to the nineteenth century.

Celebrating Manhattan

Songs celebrating Manhattan have taken several forms: Most early songs combine an uninhibited love of New York with an endearing sense of boosterism, pledges of undying loyalty, an engaging melody, and mediocre poetry. Over the years, however, some of the hundreds of celebratory songs have included truly memorable lyrics—lyrics that manage to capture one or more aspects of the multifaceted city.

In 1904, Tin Pan Alley[6] composer William "Billy" Jerome and Jean Schwartz wrote "Dear Old Manhattan Isle" for the musical *Piff! Paff!! Pouf!!!* Jerome, who began his career on the minstrel stage, was a prolific lyricist of music for Broadway shows, and also authored such classic songs as "Mr. Dooley," "Rip Van Winkle Was a Lucky Man," and "Bedelia." He begins "Dear Old Manhattan Isle" with the time-tested approach of comparing New York favorably with other beautiful spots. The next verse is particularly interesting, since the city's first subway line, the Interborough Rapid Transit (IRT), had just opened in October of 1904. Like many New Yorkers, Jerome believed that the subway would alleviate the overcrowding on the streetcars and provide an escape from the omnipresent advertising posters that plastered the city at the turn of the century. (Little did he know that subway advertising loomed in the future.) In 1904, Harlem was the city's newest middle-class suburb, and Long Acre Square,

Cole Porter (1940). This is the only portrait for which Porter is known to have posed.

live in style, / But for Harlem I don't care / Give me good old Long Acre Square, / In the little town they call Manhattan Isle.

Cole Porter was both a uniquely gifted composer and an example of a cultural refugee drawn to the city by his interest in the arts and his desire for a sophisticated lifestyle. Born in 1893 to a wealthy family in Peru, Indiana, Porter attended Yale, where he spent an inordinate amount of time writing football songs and organizing theatrical productions. He then briefly studied music at Harvard before leaving to tour Europe, teach gunnery to American soldiers during World War I, and marry an American heiress. After the war, he settled in Paris, where he and his wife were known for throwing sumptuous soirées and wild parties. Porter returned to New York in 1924, and quickly established a reputation as both a lyricist and a composer of witty, ultra-sophisticated music for Broadway shows. Among these was his paean to his adopted hometown, "I Happen to Like New York," from the 1930 musical *The New Yorkers*, in which he cited a number of reasons, including:

> I like the city air, I like to drink of it. / The more I know New York, the more I think of it. / I like the sight and the sound and even the stink of it. / I happen to like New York.

As the song progresses, the narrator speaks of visiting Battery Park to watch the ocean liners *"booming in."* Why, he asks, have they come so far across the sea? *"I suppose it's because they all agree with me / They happen to like New York."* In fact,

> When I have to give the world a last farewell / And the undertaker / Starts to ring my funeral bell / I don't want to go to heaven / Don't want to go to hell. / I happen to like New York / I happen to love New York.

"If you want to write about New York you don't have to be as naive as 'East Side, West Side,'" the twenty-four-year-old lyricist Lorenz Hart assured the seventeen-year-old composer Richard Rodgers when they first met at the house of a mutual friend in 1918. It was just the sort of remark a brash young Columbia University graduate with a string of well-received college varsity shows to his credit might make, but this young man soon proved his point in a spectacular way. Over the next quarter century, the team of Rodgers and Hart produced some of the most sophisticated and complex music ever written for the American theatre.

the newest center of the theatre district on "Dear Old Manhattan Isle," had yet to be renamed Times Square:

> They may sing in praise of farms, / Country life and rustic charms; / They may sing about the meadows and the hills; / Of their old Kentucky home, / Or of lands across the foam, / The babble of the brooks and rippling rills, / But to me there is a spot / Dearer, yes, than all the lot, / And I'm sure it beats all others by a mile; / For the sun shines night and day / On a road they call Broadway / In the little town of old Manhattan Isle.

> Chorus: Dear old Manhattan Island, / Sweet Manhattan Isle; / Where the sidewalks seem to greet you with a friendly smile. / Where pleasure reigns supreme, / And life's a golden dream; / It's no idle talk / There's but one New York / It's dear old Manhattan Isle.

> In the future we'll be found / Riding swiftly underground, / For we have too many overcrowded cars. / For that day my poor heart pines, / Safe away from all the signs, / Omega Oil and Jackson Square Cigars. / To Harlem is the cry / In the sweet, sweet bye and bye, / Where for little money you can live in

Their collaborations included such blockbuster shows as *The Boys from Syracuse, Pal Joey,* and *On Your Toes.*

In 1920, Rodgers and Hart wrote one of the greatest of all New York songs, "Manhattan." It was introduced to the public several years later as part of the first *Garrick Gaieties,* a revue which opened on May 17, 1925. Performed by the younger members of the Theatre Guild to raise money for new theatre curtains, the revue was an unexpected success. Even the formidable critic Robert Benchley praised it as "the most civilized show in town." The song itself, sung by performers June Cochrane and Sterling Holloway, stopped the show and assured Rodgers and Hart's success in the years to come.

Today, this song is often called "I'll Take Manhattan," and few people are aware that the clever first verse is followed by some even wittier later verses. It opens with a vamp, a short introductory section to set the scene:

First edition of "Manhattan" from the 1925 *Garrick Gaieties.*

Summer journeys to Niag'ra / And to other places aggra- / Vate all our cares. / We'll save our fares! / I've a cozy little flat in / What is known as old Manhattan, / We'll settle down / Right here in town!

The songs then relaxes into an elegantly paced, jazz-tinged melody:

We'll have Manhattan, / The Bronx and Staten / Island too. / It's lovely going through / The zoo; / It's very fancy / On old Delancey / Street, you know. / The subway charms us so / When balmy breezes blow / To and fro. / And tell me what street / Compares with Mott Street / In July? / Sweet pushcarts gently gliding by. / The great big city's a wondrous toy / Just made for a girl and boy. / We'll turn Manhattan / Into an isle of joy.

In the following verses, the plot thickens and things start to become a bit more risqué. By the last verse the couple has been arrested at "Inspiration Point" on, it is broadly hinted, a public morals charge:

A short vacation / On Inspiration Point / We'll spend, / And in the station house we'll end. / But Civic Virtue cannot destroy / The dreams of a girl and boy. / We'll turn Manhattan / Into an isle of joy.

Although only Manhattan, the Bronx, and Staten Island are mentioned in the chorus, references to Jamaica Bay in Queens, and Brooklyn's Canarsie and Coney Island in the verses make this one of the very few songs to mention all five boroughs. Hart, it was said, was the first lyricist "to make any real assault on the intelligence of the song-listening public." Who else would think to rhyme "onyx" with "Bronnix," as in the line from verse four: "*As black as onyx / We'll find the Bronnix / Park Express.*"

The songwriting team of George and Ira Gershwin was one of the most influential and talented of all time. Ira, the lyricist, was born to Russian immigrant parents in a building on the corner of Hester and Eldridge Streets on the Lower East Side in 1896. The family moved often, and George, the composer, was born in 1898 in the East New York section of Brooklyn. Ira was always a serious student, but George paid little attention to school and showed only a slight interest in music, until the family acquired a piano when he was about twelve. His talent quickly became apparent, and by the age of fifteen he was working as the youngest song demonstrator ("plugger") on Tin Pan Alley; his first published song appeared in 1916. Although the brothers occasionally worked with other collaborators, the popular songs they wrote as a team dominated and enlivened musicals, films, and revues throughout the 1920s and 1930s. George's interest in classical as well as popular composition led him to write such important works as *Rhapsody in Blue* (1924), *Piano Concerto in F* (1925), *An American in Paris* (1928), and the opera *Porgy and Bess* (1935). In 1936, the brothers moved to Hollywood to write music for the movies, but their collaboration was cut short by George's tragically early death from a brain tumor in 1937 at the age of 38. Ira continued to work as a lyricist with composers such as Harold Arlen, Jerome Kern, Burton Lane, and Kurt Weill, and coauthored a string of successful musicals and films. When he died in 1983, he left behind an astounding body of lyrics and an indelible contribution to American culture. Throughout their careers, the Gershwins wrote many songs that expressed their love for the city. In "New York Serenade" from the 1928 musical *Rosalie,* for example, they focused "*on the serenade you hear / When you land on a New York pier*":

Ten thousand steamboats hootin'— / A million taxis tootin'— / What a song! What a song! / That dear old New York Serenade! / Just hear those rivets rattling— / And hear that traffic battling— / Come along, come along and hear it played. . . .

The year 1977 was a good one for songs about New York. First, Steve Karmen wrote "I Love New York," which Governor Hugh Carey named the official New York State song in 1980. Karmen, who dropped out of an NYU pre-med program to become a calypso singer, was a successful advertising jingle writer (his other hits include "When You Say 'Budweiser', You've Said It All"). Despite its catchy tune, the lyrics to "I Love New York" bordered on the mundane.

A more successful attempt to write the great New York song was Fred Ebb and John Kander's "New York, New York," which appeared in Martin Scorsese's 1977 film of the same title, starring Robert De Niro and Liza Minnelli. The film did well, but the song took on a life of its own. A Frank Sinatra version of the song recorded soon thereafter transformed it from a hit into a classic. Recognizing this fact, Mayor Ed Koch selected it as the city's official theme song in 1985. Nevertheless, it should be noted that the person singing the song is not actually a New Yorker, even though he (or she) is arriving soon:

Start speadin' the news, I'm leaving today, / I want to be a part of it—New York, New York. . . .

Anxious to lose his "little town blues," the singer looks forward to the competitive challenge of the city:

I wanna wake up in the city that doesn't sleep, / To find I'm king of the hill, head of the list, cream of the crop, at the top of the heap.

Also in 1977, Martin Charnin and Charles Strouse's Tony Award–winning musical *Annie*

included the character Daddy Warbucks singing about his love-hate relationship with the city in the song "N.Y.C." Warbucks begins by asking:

N.Y.C., What is it about you? / You're big, you're loud, you're tough. / N.Y.C., I go years without you, / Then I can't get enough, / Enough of cab drivers answering back in language far from pure, / Enough of frankfurters answering back. / Brother you know you're in N.Y.C. / Too busy, too crazy, too hot, too cold; / Too late, I'm sold again on N.Y.C.

One of several musical bright spots for New York City in 1977 was the Martin Charnin and Charles Strouse musical *Annie*.

Some of the songs that celebrate New York are slightly wistful and just a touch nostalgic, such as Vernon Duke's "Autumn in New York" (1934) from the musical *Thumbs Up* and Robert Lamm's "Another Rainy Day in New York City" (1976). Among the best of these is "New York State of Mind" (1975), a lovely impressionist poem about needing the *"give and take"* of the city, by singer/songwriter Billy Joel:

> *Some folks like to get away, take a holiday from the neighborhood / Hop a flight to Miami beach or to Hollywood / I'm takin' a Greyhound on the Hudson River line / I'm in a New York state of mind. . . .*

Tourists

New York is America's number one tourist destination—today some forty million people visit New York annually. That works out—very roughly—to five tourists for every New York native; however, since very few tourists venture beyond Manhattan Island, the ratio is actually closer to 26.6 tourists to every Manhattanite. New Yorkers are very hospitable—really!—but occasionally there have been some sarcastic songs about tourists.

In the old days, New Yorkers called out-of-towners "hicks" (from hickories), "yaps" (rustics), "rubes" (from "Ruben," a name that urbanites thought was disproportionately common among residents of small country towns), or "rubberneckers" (because they had to bend their necks back to look up at the tall buildings). As George M. Cohan noted in 1905, just "Forty-Five Minutes From Broadway" in New Rochelle was the *"place where real rubens dwell."* Today, among themselves, Manhattanites sometimes dismissively refer to tourists, particularly those from other boroughs, as "b and t [bridge and tunnel] people."

Open-roofed carriages and buses were popular with tourists, and even found their way into a 1904 song, "Seeing New York in the Rubber-Neck Hack":

> *Up, down, all over town, 'way up to Harlem and back, / The things I observed, got me twisted and curved, / While seeing New York in the rubber-neck hack . . . On the front was a feller who talked thro' a horn, / Never heard such a cuss since the day I wuz born, / He pointed out places and houses and folks, / He'd make a clown laugh with his comical jokes. . . .*

In a 1908 novelty song, songwriters Will Cobb and Melville Gideon wrote of a *"sunburned farmer's sunburned son"* who was coming to New York to make his fortune and advised him to "Take Plenty of Shoes":

> *It's a good old town that New York town, / It's the farm where the fortunes grow. / All you need to do is pick yourself a few / And that feller, Rockefeller, won't have anything on you. / When your feet slam down on that Amsterdam town / You can fill your trunk with all the plunks you choose; / But it's a long roam, back home, take plenty of shoes.*

Being in New York transformed some people. Take, for example, Hiram Gruben, the church elder in the 1914 song "When He Goes to New York Town." According to songwriters Joe Goodwin and Ted Snyder, *"At home he never swears, he always says his prayers: / And tho' he says it's shocking to see a girlie's stocking, when he comes to New York / He's right besides the other men, he's on a windy corner. . . ."*[7]

The little girl in pink is Marie.

SCENE OF NEW YORK, STARTING 23RD. STREET.

LEFT: Seeing New York in a Rubber-Neck Hack, circa 1905.

OPPOSITE: Fashionable Fifth Avenue crowd strolling past the Flatiron Building in 1903.

ABOVE: Three sailors setting off to see "New York, New York" in the 1945 Comden, Green, and Bernstein musical *On the Town.*

RIGHT: Cohan, "The Yankee Doodle Comedian," giving his regards to Broadway in 1904.

In 1945, Leonard Bernstein, Betty Comden, and Adolph Green wrote the quintessential tourist song for *On the Town,* a landmark musical about the adventures of three sailors on a one-day leave who are determined to see all of New York—as well as find and romance the elusive "Miss Turnstiles." (And, yes, there was a monthly "Miss Turnstiles" beauty competition.) The show's wonderful opening song, "New York, New York (It's a Helluva Town)," has also become one of the most famous of all New York City songs:

> *New York, New York, a helluva town, / The Bronx is up but the Battery's down, / And people ride in a hole in the ground; / New York, New York, / It's a helluva town!*

"Give My Regards to Broadway": New York From Afar

If celebrating and visiting New York inspired many songs, so too did thinking about New York from a distance. This distance could be either spatial or temporal: travelers sang about the city they had left behind, the old longed for the city of their youth. There is a spate of songs in which homesick travelers come across fellow New Yorkers on their travels and ask to be remembered to their beloved city and their friends back home. These meetings usually took place somewhere in Europe, which inevitably allowed city songwriters to compare their city favorably to older, more established cities such as London or Paris. This sentiment was neatly summed up in Will Cobb and Gus Edwards's 1907 hit "Bye, Bye, Dear Old Broadway" with the lines: *"And no matter where I wander, to you I will ever be true. / For the more I see of other towns the better I like you."*

In the course of his long career, the versatile composer, lyricist, actor, playwright, and producer George M. Cohan wrote numerous songs about being away from New York, including "Too Many Miles From Broadway" (1901), "Forty-Five Minutes From Broadway" (1905), and "Too Long From Long Acre [Times] Square" (1908). However, none of them enjoyed the popularity of his 1904 instant classic, "Give My Regards to Broadway." First featured in Cohan's Broadway musical *Little Johnny Jones,* the song is still beloved by New Yorkers. Its title has become a catch phrase:

> *Did you ever see two Yankees part upon a foreign shore; / When the good ship's just about to start for Old New York once more? / With tear-dimmed eyes*

*they say goodbye, they're friends without a doubt; /
When the man on the pier / Shouts, "Let them clear,"
as the ship strikes out.*

*Chorus: Give my regards to Broadway, / Remember
me to Herald Square. / Tell all the gang at Forty-
Second Street, that I will soon be there. / Whisper of
how I'm yearning, / To mingle with the old time
throng. / Give my regards to old Broadway and say
that I'll be there e'er long.*

*Say hello to dear old Coney Isle, if there you chance
to be, / When you're at the Waldorf have a smile and
charge it up to me; / Mention my name ev'ry place
you go, as 'round the town you roam, / Wish you'd
call on my gal, / Now remember, old pal, when you
get back home.*

Perhaps inspired by Cohan's success as much
as by their own love for New York, several
well-known Tin Pan Alley songwriting teams
also composed songs about longing for the city
from afar. For example, there was Andrew B.
Sterling and Harry Von Tilzer's catchy 1907
waltz, "Take Me Back to New York Town,"
which was popularized by the songstress Lillian
Shaw. Harry Von Tilzer (1872–1946), a prolific
composer and powerful music publisher, is best
remembered today for his 1899 song, "A Bird
in a Gilded Cage." Born plain Harry Gumm in
Detroit, Von Tilzer changed his name and made
his way to New York where he became a major
player in the world of Tin Pan Alley.

*Chorus: Take me back to New York town, New York
town, New York town, / That's where I long to be, /
With friends so dear to me, / Coney Isle down the
bay, / And the lights of old Broadway, Herald
Square, I don't care, anywhere, New York town. . . .*

Then there was the 1905 hit "Good-Bye,
Sweet Old Manhattan Isle" by the successful Tin
Pan Alley songwriting team of William Jerome
and Jean Schwartz. Its snappy upbeat melody
makes it sound like a slightly dated high school
fight song, but many contemporary New Yorkers
would still agree with the sentiments:

*Though cramped for space, it's quite a place, why
Paris can't compare, / Our buildings high flirt with
the sky, we're all up in the air. / And underground we
ride around all night as well as day, / And now you
know the reason why when leaving home, I'll say:*

*Chorus: Good-bye, sweet old Manhattan Isle, good-
bye dear old Broadway / My heart belongs to you old
town, no matter where I stray. / That I'll be true to you,
to you / There's not the slightest doubt / For when you
leave old New York town / You're only camping out.*

GEORGE M. COHAN (1878–1942)

Perhaps the ultimate Broadway song-and-dance man, Cohan,
the son of two performers, was born and raised on the vaudeville
circuit. As an infant he served as a human prop in some of his
parents' sketches, at nine he was an official member of the act,
and at thirteen he was writing his own material. With his parents
and his older sister Josephine, he formed part of the Four Cohans,
a headline vaudeville act. About 1900, he began the transition
from the world of vaudeville sketches to the "legitimate stage"
of Broadway musicals. His first major Broadway success was the
1904 musical comedy *Little Johnny Jones*, for which he single-
handedly wrote the book, lyrics, and music, and also starred in
the leading role. For most of his career Cohan really was, to
quote the title of his 1909 musical, *The Man Who Owns Broadway*.
Although he is best remembered for patriotic songs, he also had
an abiding love and fascination with New York City and wrote
songs about it throughout his career.

A jaunty and successful young George M. Cohan.

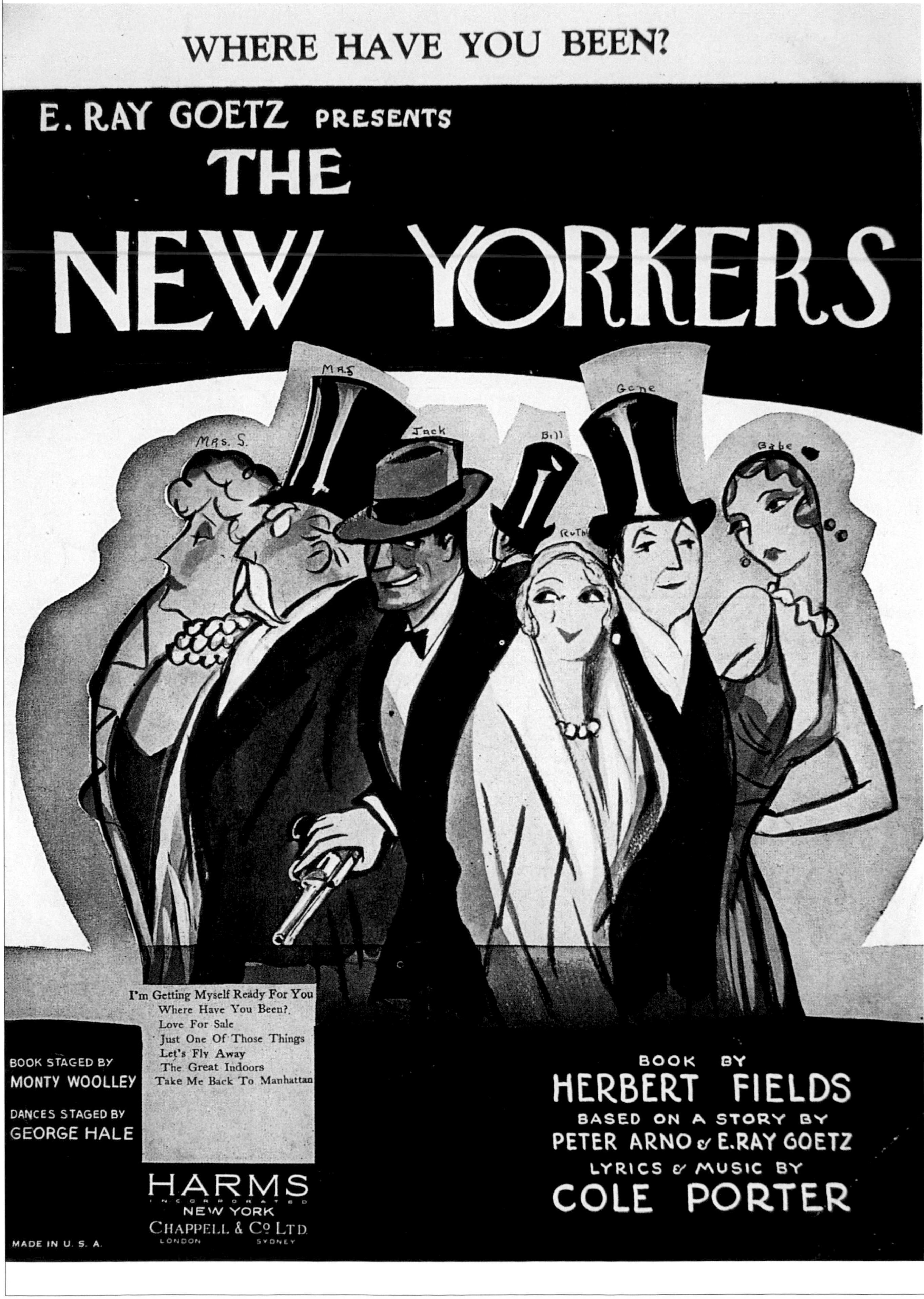
WHERE HAVE YOU BEEN?
E. RAY GOETZ PRESENTS
THE
NEW YORKERS
MRS. S.
MRS
Jack
Bill
Gene
Ruth
Babe
I'm Getting Myself Ready For You
Where Have You Been?
Love For Sale
Just One Of Those Things
Let's Fly Away
The Great Indoors
Take Me Back To Manhattan
BOOK STAGED BY
MONTY WOOLLEY
DANCES STAGED BY
GEORGE HALE
BOOK BY
HERBERT FIELDS
BASED ON A STORY BY
PETER ARNO & E. RAY GOETZ
LYRICS & MUSIC BY
COLE PORTER
HARMS
INCORPORATED
NEW YORK
CHAPPELL & Co LTD.
LONDON SYDNEY
MADE IN U. S. A.

A generation later, the team of Lorenz Hart and Richard Rodgers wrote another great "I miss New York" song for the Depression era film *Hallelujah, I'm a Bum*. Adapted from a Ben Hecht story, the 1933 United Artists film starred Al Jolson, but the songwriters also put in cameo on-screen appearances: Rodgers played a photographer and Hart a bank teller. In the film, their song, "I Gotta Get Back to New York," was sung by Jolson, one of several hobos stranded *"A hundred and twenty-one miles, / Maybe twenty-two. / From Central Park . . . A hundred and twenty-six miles / From Lenox Avenue"*:

> *Way up North the sun'll / Always shine—That lovely Hudson tunnel / Is my Mason-Dixon Line. / Where the tempo races, / Let me be. / The great wide-open spaces / Are places that smother me. . . .*

> *Refrain: I'll climb up that Woolworth and kiss every floor. / The subway makes music for me with a roar. / I'm dying to feel that I'm living once more. / I gotta get back to New York. / There's only one statue, I know you'll agree. / The dame with the torch looking over the sea. / The smell of the Bronnix is perfume to me. / I gotta get back to New York.*

Even the ultra-sophisticated Cole Porter contributed an "I miss New York" song, which appeared in his 1930 score for *The New Yorkers*. Billed as "a Sociological Musical Satire," the show's plot featured a tour of the city's high and low life, with stops at Park Avenue ("where bad women walk good dogs"), a bootleg liquor factory (where comedian Jimmy Durante presided as a gangster), a street in Harlem, Reuben's Restaurant on Madison Avenue, and Sing Sing Prison. Among the show's songs—which included the hits "Just One of Those Things" and "Love for Sale"—was "Take Me Back to Manhattan," in which the New York–deprived narrator explains:

> *The more I travel across the gravel, / The more I sail the sea, / The more I feel convinced of the fact / New York's the town for me. / Its crazy skyline is right in my line, / And when I'm far away / I'm able to bear it for several hours, / And then break down and say:*

> *Take me back to Manhattan, / Take me back to New York, / I'm longing to see once more / My little home on the hundredth floor. / Can you wonder I'm gloomy? / Can you smile when I frown? / I miss the East Side, the West Side, / The North Side and the South Side, / So take me back to Manhattan, / That dear old dirty town.*

"When Gramercy Square Was Up-Town": Little Old New York

Like most things, New York improves with hindsight. "Little Old New York," an idealized view of the pre-twentieth-century city, began to be celebrated by songwriters in the 1910s. The nostalgic view of the city would be more persuasive if we did not also have Jacob Riis's photographs from the 1890s to remind us how "the other half" really lived. Nevertheless, tuneful reminiscences of the older city proved popular with the song-buying public and produced such hits as "New York Ain't New York Any More" (1925), "When Broadway Was a Pasture" (1911), Irving Berlin's "Where Is My Little Old New York?" (1924), and the Isadore Kornblum and Zeke Meyers hit, "When Gramercy Square Was Up-Town," from the 1921 musical *Blue Eyes* staring Lew Fields and Mollie King:

> *When grandpa was a lad, / Oh, what a time he had . . . No taxi bills to pay / No dry laws to obey / Nothing to do but chase a chicken or two / Down the cowpaths of Broadway: / / Chorus: When Gramercy Square was up-town, / Each Saturday night would see, / Grand-pa in his ruffles and his frills / Dancing the schottische[8] and quadrilles; / It only remains in fancy / This New York that used to be. / The whispered vow, the quaint old fashioned ways, / We need them now / We need the good old days / For romance was theirs, / When Gramercy Square was way up-town.*

In 1937, toward the end of his career, George M. Cohan wistfully remembered the New York of his childhood through heavily rose-tinted glasses in the song "When New York Was New York (New York Was a Wonderful Town)," which advised:

> *If you want a real breath of fresh air / Take a stroll around Washington Square / For it's there you can see what New York used to be, / Before all of its glamour and glare. / And then for a bit of a lark / Take a turn around Gramercy Park, / And while you are on tour, / If you listen you're sure to hear some good old timer remark:*

> *Chorus: When New York was New York, the town we used to know . . . When your dad and my dad, and this lad and that lad, / Were all gay and all glad, / What real friends we all had, before we went jazz mad / New York was a wonderful town.*

Cohan concludes his last verse with a warning:

> *It's a much great town on the whole, / "Greatest of all" is its goal, / But to me it appears, / With the passing of years / That it's losing its heart and its soul.*

Chapter 2

NEW YORK LANDMARKS IN SONG

Streets and Sidewalks

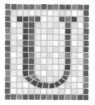sing only songs for our road map, we can take a rather complete tour of New York past and New York present. Our musical tour begins with that most accessible and public urban institution, the street. Except for Broadway and a few other lanes that followed early Indian paths,

OPPOSITE: Father Knickerbocker shows off a bustling Herald Square in 1914.

early Manhattan streets resembled those of any other early modern Dutch city: they were narrow, poorly paved—if paved at all—and haphazardly laid out. As the city grew larger and more complex, so too did the difficulty of finding one's way around. A commissioner of streets was not appointed until 1798—more than 150 years after the city was founded, and a very long time to wait for potholes to be repaired.

At the beginning of the nineteenth century, a commission was formed to survey Manhattan Island and plan for the city's future transportation needs. The commissioners submitted an innovative plan that called for the remaining undeveloped portions of Manhattan to be neatly segmented into a series of more than two hundred evenly spaced, consecutively numbered east-west streets. When this "grid plan" was enacted in 1811, the commission believed that the heaviest traffic would flow between the docks that lined the East and Hudson Rivers, so they included far fewer north-south avenues and spaced them wide apart. In 1811, almost no buildings exceeded three stories in height, and mechanical transportation of any kind was a generation away. The grid plan worked beautifully in the early nineteenth century; however, almost two hundred years later, in a radically altered urban landscape, it is somewhat more problematic.

Today, streets in the older neighborhoods of Manhattan still retain names, not numbers. In 1865, a Dr. W.J. Wetmore celebrated these old names by stringing them together in a song entitled "The Streets of New York." The good doctor, who obviously knew the city well, was not above some very bad puns. Here are several of the least painful verses. By the way, most of the streets named still exist, although some of the occupations have vanished:

All you who've been around the town, / Or travelled through the city, / Just list to what I've noted down, / And strung into my ditty. / Perhaps you've never thought of what I've got in my narration / How "every street is fitted for / A certain occupation."

The Butchers live in "Market Street," / The Boatmen in "Canal Street"; / The Masons live in "Stone Street," / And the Builders live in "Wall Street"; / The Hatters live in "Beaver Street," / The Jewelers in "Gold," sirs; / The Virgins live in "Maiden Lane" / At least so I've been told, sirs.

"Attorney Street" and "Sheriff Street" / Suite Lawyers to a T, sirs; / And, as for Blind men, they, of course, / Must live in "Avenue C," sirs; / Fruit-dealers live in "Orchard Street"; / In "Read Street" the School-teachers; / There's "Dey Street" for the Doctors, / And there's "Church Street" for the Preachers.

In New York, strolling around town has always been a popular form of recreation. New Yorkers, many of whom still do not own cars—or even know how to drive—regularly walk the streets and avenues of their city just to "check out" what's going on. Not much has changed since 1868 when William H. Lingard and Charles Pratt wrote the hit song "Walking Down Broadway":

> The sweetest thing in life (And no one dare say nay) / On a Saturday afternoon, Is walking down Broadway; / My sisters in the Park, Or at Long Branch wish to stray, / But I prefer to walk / Down festive, gay, Broadway. / Walking down Broadway, The festive, gay Broadway, / The O.K. thing on Saturday / Is walking down Broadway. . . .

The song's lyricist, William H. Lingard, was a famous female impersonator. In the 1870s, he and his brother Dick had a popular act that was regularly featured at Jim Fisk's Grand Opera House on Eighth Avenue and 23rd Street. The Lingards specialized in farces and light after-pieces following the evening's main show, and apparently it was their ability to mimic women sashaying up and down Broadway that drove audiences wild.

W.H. Latham's 1835 song "Broadway Sights" is remembered today primarily by sheet music collectors because of the striking cover executed for it by the engraver J.H. Bufford. The lyrics are none-too-subtle plugs for the shops and stores that lined Broadway just south of St. Paul's Chapel at Fulton Street. Atwill Music Saloon—which just coincidentally also published the song—fared particularly well in the lyrics. Today, this block lies in the shadow of the 110-story towers of the World Trade Center; St. Paul's Chapel, however, is practically unchanged.

Although some songwriters like Jule Styne and Bob Hilliard would later argue that "Every Street's a Boulevard in Old New York" (1953), most composers knew that each street and avenue had a distinctive character all its own. The lilting 1906 hit song "Streets of New York" from Victor Herbert and Henry Blossom's smash musical *The Red Mill* suggests that some local men had an interesting way of navigating around town:

> In dear old New York it's remarkable very! / The name on the lamp-post is unnecessary! / You merely have to see the girls to know what street you're on! / Fifth Avenue beauties and dear old Broadway girls! / The tailor-made shoppers, the Avenue "A" girls, / They're strictly all right, but they're different quite, / In the diff'rent parts of the town.

For example, one of the verses describes girls from the Bowery, a tough neighborhood on the Lower East Side:

> What ever the weather is, shining or showery, / That doesn't "cut any ice" on the Bowery / Every night till broad daylight, they dance and sing and talk! / The girls are all game and they're jolly good fellows, / They're not very swell but they're none of them jealous, / They go it alone in a style of their own / On the Bowery, New York.

> Chorus: In old New York! / In old New York! / The peach crop's always fine! / They're sweet and fair and on the square! / The maids of Manhattan for mine! / You cannot see in gay Paree, in London, or in Cork! / The queens you'll meet on any street in old New York.

Although they don't often admit it, New Yorkers are as amazed by their magical metropolis as out-of-towners. Hence, just walking around is a popular local sport. This attitude was captured beautifully in "Let's Take a Walk Around the

"As Sung with great Applause by Mr. Latham, at the Grand Concerts, at Niblo's Garden" in 1835.

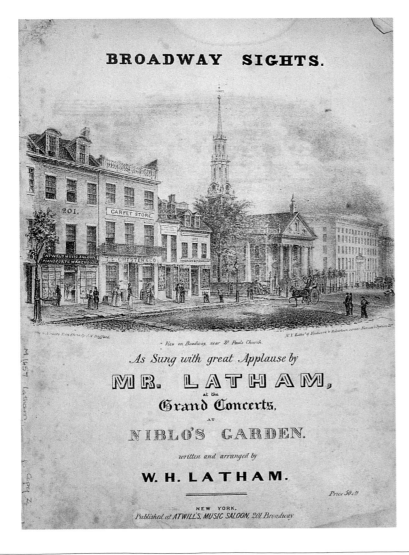

Block," a song with lyrics by Ira Gershwin and Yip Harburg, and music by Harold Arlen, that appeared in the 1934 revue *Life Begins at 8:40*:

> *I've never traveled further north / Than old Van Courtlandt Park, / And never further south than the Aquarium. / I've seen the charm of Jersey City— / But first, let me remark— / I saw it from the Empire State Solarium. / Still I've been putting nickels / In the Postal Savings Bank . . . But while we are flat in / Old Manhattan— / Gangway, let's walk around the block!*

Years before, "Walking Down Broadway," a German dialect song from the 1880s (which seems, in turn, to have been a parody of William Lingard and Charles Pratt's 1868 hit of the same title) also reflected New Yorkers' love of strolling:

> *De sveetest ting in life, vat odder peoples say, / Iss Samstag afternoon, a-walkin' down Broadway. / Mein schwester in der lager beer saloon vill stay. / But I should always make a valk / Right down dot pretty Broadway.*

If the streets of New York were not sufficient inspiration, songwriters could always turn to sidewalks. The most famous of these songs, James Lawlor and Charles Blake's "Sidewalks of New York" (1894), is discussed in Chapter Nine about neighborhood life; however, there are numerous other examples of songs celebrating these pedestrian refuges in the urban landscape. In 1933, for example, Joe Young and J. Fred Coots, inspired by Lawlor and Blake, wrote "The Sidewalk Waltz," which includes references to the old neighborhood, the old organ grinder (playing an old tune), and golden-haired children waltzing on the sidewalks of long ago. In New York songs, the street and sidewalk often become metaphors for urban life itself.

Real life in New York was the theme for the lovely song "In a Sidestreet Off Broadway" written by Edgar Fairchild and Henry Meyers for the 1927 musical *The New Yorkers*:

> *Some people may say / That the Great White Way, / Is the soul of old New York. / But run down heels and ten-cent meals / Speak louder than popping cork. / And far from the glitter and glare / New York's great soul lies bare.*
>
> *New York is found in the modest ground, / Of a sidestreet off Broadway. / In brownstone fronts that were famous once, / In a sidestreet off Broadway // For Broadway's life is a life of art, / Its people are actors, all playing a part, / But you'll find the City's aching heart, In a sidestreet off Broadway.*

THE SIDEWALK WALTZ

WORDS BY JOE YOUNG
MUSIC BY J. FRED COOTS

Irving Berlin, Inc.
MUSIC PUBLISHERS
1607 Broadway New York

MADE IN USA

Sidewalk and skyline frame an organ grinder and waltzing children in this 1933 song.

Finally, before we leave the general topic of streets, it would be remiss not to mention New York's most popular competitive sport— jaywalking! It is easy to spot tourists because they are the only people in Manhattan who obey the traffic signals. Jaywalking—crossing busy streets mid-block with little regard to traffic or personal safety—comes as second nature to most New Yorkers. Unfortunately, this also means that a large number of New Yorkers are injured or killed annually by cars, trucks, buses, and bicycles. In 1961, to try to combat this dangerous behavior pattern, the New York State Department of Safety introduced a musical jingle composed by Vic Mizzy that ran incessantly on local media for years. Given the number of New Yorkers who still jaywalk, the media campaign could hardly be considered a success, but nonetheless,

The Flatiron "appeared to be moving toward me like the bow of a monster ocean steamer—a picture of new America still in the making." Alfred Stieglitz, Photographer

story Flatiron Building on 23rd Street and Fifth Avenue. When it opened in 1903, it was the tallest building outside the financial district. Officially titled "The Fuller Building," it was built on a triangular piece of land and almost immediately acquired the nickname "flat iron" because local wags thought it looked like an old-fashioned three-sided pressing iron. And, because of its odd shape and its location at the edge of Madison Square, local men soon noticed that a strong wind often whipped around the base of the building, raising skirts and dresses of passing women well above ankle height. In an era long on hemlines and short on opportunity, crowds of men would assemble on 23rd Street to watch the free show. According to a local legend (apocryphal), the era's famous catch phrase, "Twenty-three Skiddoo," was what New York policemen would shout to break up lounging voyeurs. The situation inspired a number of composers: in 1903 Herbert Walter wrote an instrumental march and two-step entitled "A Breezy Corner," which he "dedicated to 'THE CORNER' of 23rd Street, Broadway, and 5th Ave." Another march and two-step, "The Flatiron," by J.W. Lerman appeared the same year.

At least one Broadway musical, *Skyscraper* by Sammy Cahn and James Van Heusen (1965), highlighted the impact of skyscrapers on the urban landscape. And Gordon Jenkins' popular oratorio *Manhattan Tower* (1945) related the story of life, love, and loss in a skyscraper. Early in the piece, the easily excitable narrator, who has recently arrived in New York, tries to explains the impact of his new high-rise home on his imagination:

> My heart beats faster than the raindrops as I looked up and saw it painted against the sky. The outside of the building was as beautiful as the outside of anything can be . . . but the inside was pure enchantment. The elevator operator was Merlin . . . my feet touched the Magic Carpet as I ran down the hall.

Years before, Rodgers and Hart had also tried to express their fascination with the New York skyline in the song "Sky City," which was unfortunately cut from the 1929 musical *Heads Up* before opening night. The song reflects the pride Jazz Age New Yorkers took in their rapidly expanding town: "*Sky city, my city, climbing through, Heaven's blue; proud and free, rising from the sea . . .*"

To get to one's "city in the sky," elevators were extremely useful. New Yorkers still debate the finer points of elevator etiquette, but to

embedded deep in the memory banks of all New Yorker over the age of thirty-five is the jingle "(Don't Cross the Street) In the Middle, In the Middle, In the Middle of the Block."

The Skyline and Skyscrapers

New York has more skyscrapers than anywhere else in the world. They began to sprout in lower Manhattan in the 1860s when the demand for space—and the development of reliable elevators—pushed new office buildings to the unheard-of heights of seven and eight stories. By the 1890s, New Yorkers were referring to their crop of towering buildings as "sky-scrapers." (The word had previously been used to refer to the topsail on clipper ships.)

In Manhattan's forest of tall buildings, a few stand out as local favorites. One of these is architect Daniel Hudson Burnham's twenty-one-

several turn-of-the-century songwriters, the novelty of close, unchaperoned proximity to members of the opposite sex was too good to ignore. Elevators were the setting for several surreptitious romances—or at least golden opportunities for "mashers."[1] Among elevator songs from this period are "Going Up (The Elevator Man's Love Song)" by Gordon and Roth (circa 1900), and Irving Berlin's 1912 song "The Elevator Man, Going Up, Going Up, Going Up!":

> *Andy Gray, young and gay, was an elevator man / Like an aviator, in his elevator / All day long he was on the job, taking people up and down. / Mandy Brook, as a cook, started working in the place, / And they found her later in the elevator / With Andy, so handy, said Mandy, "It's dandy!"*

Andy marries Mandy, and, the song continues, *"We discovered later that the elevator / Was the place where the knot was tied."* In an unexpected twist, the last verse tells how Andy was later discovered in his elevator with a *"gal known as Sal [who] came to work in Mandy's place / With Andy, so dandy, and handy, like Mandy!"*

Composers soon discovered that in addition to being sung about in their own right, skyscrapers proved a perfect stage set for interpersonal dramas—which, like the giant buildings that housed them, were usually portrayed as unhappy, stark, and depersonalized. Then, in the 1920s, penthouses came to symbolize the essence of New York sophistication. Songwriters celebrated this ultramodern lifestyle with such songs as Eddie Dowling and James F. Hanley's "Play-Ground in the Sky" (1927); Duke Ellington's "Sugar Hill Penthouse" (1945); and Will Jason and Val Burton's "Penthouse Serenade" (1931). Of course, as we all know, choosing money over true love leads to unhappiness, as composer/lyricist Gene LaBarre recognized in 1935 when he self-published "Repenting in a Penthouse," a "Throat-Lumping Ballad" which began:

> *He pictured a penthouse high up on the roof, / She fell for his line. My! How he could "spoof." / She thought she'd have love and on it surely thrive, / All she really got was a good view of the Drive [Riverside] . . . Repenting in a Penthouse—High up in the sky.*

A more musically successful celebration of penthouse living was presented in Will Jason and Val Burton's "Penthouse Serenade" (1931), a duet which was also known by the title "When We're Alone." It begins with the male singer alluding to a cottage by a stream, but his aspirations, he assures his lover, are different.

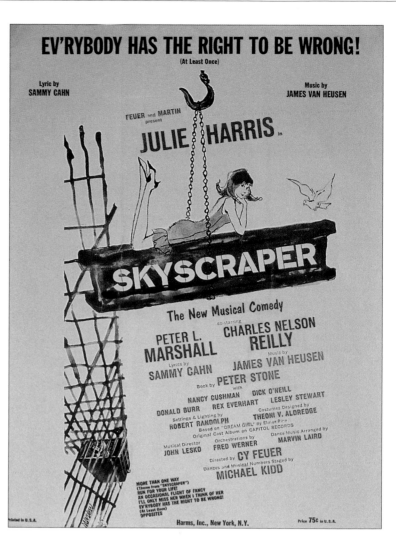

ABOVE: Julie Harris starred in this 1965 tale of an antique shop owner who dreams of saving her historic Manhattan building from an encroaching skyscraper.

LEFT: Artist's vision of "Future New York: The City of Skyscrapers" circa 1915.

He dreams instead of being a millionaire, and can imagine only one place for their future life together:

> Just picture a penthouse 'way up in the sky, / With hinges on chimneys for stars to go by, / A sweet slice of heaven for just you and I, When we're alone. / From all of society we'll stay aloof, / And live in propriety there on the roof, / Two heavenly hermits we will be in truth, When we're alone. / We'll see life's mad pattern, As we view old Manhattan, / Then we can thank our lucky stars, That we're living as we are. / In our little penthouse, we'll always contrive / To keep love and romance forever alive, / In view of the Hudson just over the Drive, When we're alone.

She responds with enthusiasm to a life "on modern lines expressed" where "love alone will be the architect." And, if they are lucky:

> In a little while, dear, maybe I'll wait, As a normal wife should do. / Keeping the tradition, not by the gate, / But with perambulator, By the elevator.

Leave it to Cole Porter, however, to capture the essence of sophistication, love gone wrong, and isolation in a Manhattan high-rise. "When the only one you've wanted wants another," it is easy to be "Down in the Depths (on the 90th Floor)":

> With a million neon rainbows burning below me / And a million blazing taxis raising a roar / Here I sit, above the town / In my pet pailletted gown. / Down in the depths on the ninetieth floor. / While the crowds at El Morocco punish the parquet / And at Twenty-One, the couples clamor for more, / I'm deserted and depressed / In my regal eagle nest / Down in the depths on the ninetieth floor.

Hotels

Hotels have always had a prominent place in New York life. In the nineteenth century, some hotels, like contemporaneous shops, began to advertise through sheet music. When major events took place at hotels, these, too, were duly recorded in music. Modern songwriters have tended to concentrate more on the few residential hotels that still survive in Manhattan—especially that legendary home to artists, the Chelsea Hotel on Eighth Avenue and 23rd Street, which has figured prominently in a number of rock songs. Long before Sid Vicious, Lou Reed, and Leonard Cohen made the Chelsea famous, New York composers were celebrating other local hotels.

Before the introduction of apartment houses in the late nineteenth century, those New Yorkers who did not own their own homes, or were too "respectable" to inhabit a tenement, lived in residential hotels, a sort of middle-class boarding house. They were often run by women, especially widows, who would establish their own rules and regulations over these mini-fiefdoms. The imaginary "Misses Doyle" from Edward Harrigan and David Braham's 1878 farce *Mulligan Guard's Picnic* were particularly ruthless according to the song "Locked Out After Nine":

> I'm stopping at a house that's kept by Misses Doyle / The rules and regulations forninst [against] us all the while / Three meals a day we get, we sit all in a line / It's ev'ry man in bed by eight or locked out after nine. // Chorus: There's Slattery McGormigle, McGilligan and Dan O'Burke / A Scandinavian fisherman, a Norwegian and a Turk / Oh, two ladies and a child that's christened Baby mine / It's ev'ryone in bed at eight or locked out after nine.

> The six-day walking match was up at Madison Square / The boarders all determined in a body to go there / We shouted hip-hooray! O'Leary walked so fine / But Murphy's watch it stopped at eight, we were locked out after nine. // Chorus: Then Slattery

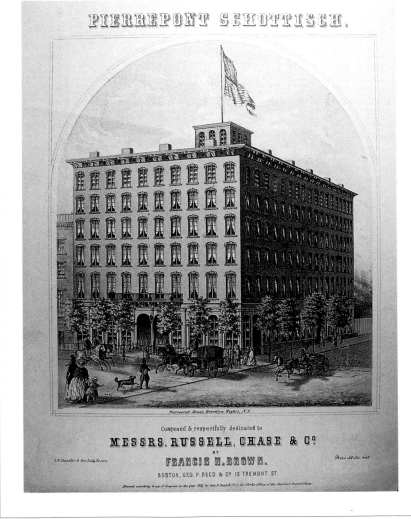

Not all the fine hotels were located in Manhattan. This schottisch promoting the Pierrepont House in Brooklyn Heights shows the active neighborhood in 1855.

PIERREPONT SCHOTTISCH.

Composed & respectfully dedicated to
MESSRS. RUSSELL, CHASE & Cº.
BY
FRANCIS H. BROWN.
BOSTON, GEO. P. REED & Cº 13 TREMONT ST.

McGormigle kept kicking the hall door, / The ladies and the babies, oh! for Misses Doyle did roar. / We woke the neighbor up; the tailor Rubenstein / Said: "Walk away my Irish friend, you're locked out after nine."

There was a row the next day, the boarders all got drunk; / Miss Doyle got excited and threw out ev'ry trunk; / Hat boxes and valises, the shirts from off the line / Came out with all the lodgers; cause we were locked out after nine. / / Then Slattery McGormigle, McGilligan and Dan O'Burke / They whaled the Scandinavian and ostracized the Turk / The Policeman did appear, the tailor Rubenstein / Said: "Take 'em in! What a sin, you're off your beat at nine."

For those who wanted classier quarters and had the means to pay for them, an increasingly elegant parade of fashionable hotels opened during the latter half of the nineteenth century. As New York grew uptown, the fashionable hotels followed, introducing guests to such sybaritic novelties as running hot water, bathtubs in every room, electric lights, and room service. The ultimate in elegance was achieved in 1893, when William Waldorf Astor decided to build a state-of-the-art hotel where his house had stood on the corner of Fifth Avenue and 33rd Street—just to spite his aunt and next-door neighbor, Mrs. Astor, with whom he was feuding. The first Waldorf Hotel opened on March 14, 1893. After a year of living next door to a thriving commercial establishment, his ultra-snobby aunt—who was then *the* leader of New York society—fled the area for the more refined, less commercial precincts of the Upper East Side. Her son, John Jacob Astor IV, grudgingly agreed to tear down his mother's mansion and construct a hotel on his site. It would be taller and more elegant than the Waldorf, but run in conjunction with his cousin's property. The complex was renamed "The Waldorf-Astoria." To connect the two, a 300-foot-long passageway was built which was almost immediately nicknamed "Peacock Alley" because of the constant parade of the city's most elegantly dressed socialites and important out-of-town guests. At the height of the Gilded Age, it was the place to be seen. Of course, like today, not everybody seen there was actually a guest or a patron of the hotel's extremely expensive restaurant, the Palm Garden. Many, like the poseur in the 1897 song "Waldorf 'Hyphen' Astoria," simply hung around for a glimpse of the rich and famous. The Oscar mentioned in the lyrics was Oscar Tschirky, the Waldorf-Astoria's powerful and punctilious headwaiter:

Waldorf-Astoria Hotel, New York City.

Early postcard of the Waldorf-Astoria.

We have all met those guys who affect to patronize / The hotel with the hyphenated name. / But if it should befall that on them we'd try to call, / It would be hard to find them just the same. / After hunting long and well through each separate hotel, / Without result, a fellow must decide, / They may be on the square, but if they are living there, / It must be on the "hyphen" they reside.

Chorus: At the Waldorf "Hyphen" Astoria, / No matter who or what you are, / Be sure you nod to Oscar as you enter. / Just speak to him by name, / And for "ten" he'll do the same— / That's the proper thing at the Waldorf "Hyphen" Astoria.

Stores, Shops, and Emporiums

Advertising has long played a part in American life. In early New York, vendors used "street cries"—an early form of the advertising jingle—

to hawk their wares. As early as 1848, "Shopping: A Comic Song," with lyrics supposedly written "by a Lady of this City" and "published for A.F. Stewart's Department Store," contained the less-than-subtle suggestion, *"Go child and get your bonnet on; / To Stewart's we will go!"* By mid-century, many store owners turned to sheet music elaborately illustrated with pictures of their establishments or their products to lure customers. These advertising pieces, commissioned from local composers and given away as gifts to customers or potential customers, tended to be instrumental compositions of mediocre musical merit. However, their beautifully detailed cover sheets give us glimpses of what shopping was like in the stores, shops, and emporiums of early New York:

As the modern department store, bursting with ready-made goods, began to replace old-fashioned dry-good emporiums, shop "girls" began to take the place of male clerks. By the 1890s, thousands of young, single women found work in New York stores. They were such a novelty that they inspired songs, like

"Cash! Cash! Cash!" by Harrigan and Braham about a hardworking cashier with no time for "mashers." When it was written in 1882, Macy's was still located on 14th Street:

> *At Macy's grand Emporium I met a charmer fair. / Oh, she was selling neckties, To the swells that gathered there; / I stepped up to the counter, / I said: My name is Frash / Said I: My pretty little girl—she simply holler'd: Cash! / / Chorus: It was Cash! Cash! Cash! with a smash, smash, smash, / Oh, she hammered on the counter for number Forty-nine; / It was Cash! Cash! Cash!, / I thought I had a mash, / But when I went to speak to her 'twas Cash! Cash! Cash!*

As the pace of advertising picked up in the early twentieth century, so did the number of places anxious to sell space to advertisers. In 1917 the Brooklyn Rapid Transit Company decided to hold a contest to find a song to promote the advertising space on its subway cars. If the concept was slightly bizarre and the music unmemorable, the sheet music cover was a graphic tour de force celebrating a dizzying array of World War I era consumer products.

BELOW: The owner of the fashionable Belgian Gallery at 547 Broadway commissioned the well-known musician Harvey B. Dodworth to write a polka for the store. On the cover, illustrator Otto Boetticher carefully recorded the interior in 1853.

OPPOSITE: The "cake walk" dance craze was too much for the Brooklyn-based Drake Brothers bakery to resist. In 1890, years before their Ring Dings were even a cake-batter concept, they commissioned this instrumental piece by Edwin Kendall.

BELGIAN GALLERY POLKA,

Interior of the Belgian Gallery, 547, Broadway

Lith of Otto Boetticher 337 Broadway

BY
HARVEY B. DODWORTH.
NEW YORK, PUBLISHED BY H.B. DODWORTH & Cᵒ 493, BROADWAY,
Wᵐ HALL & SON, 239, BROADWAY.

25 Cⁿ nett.

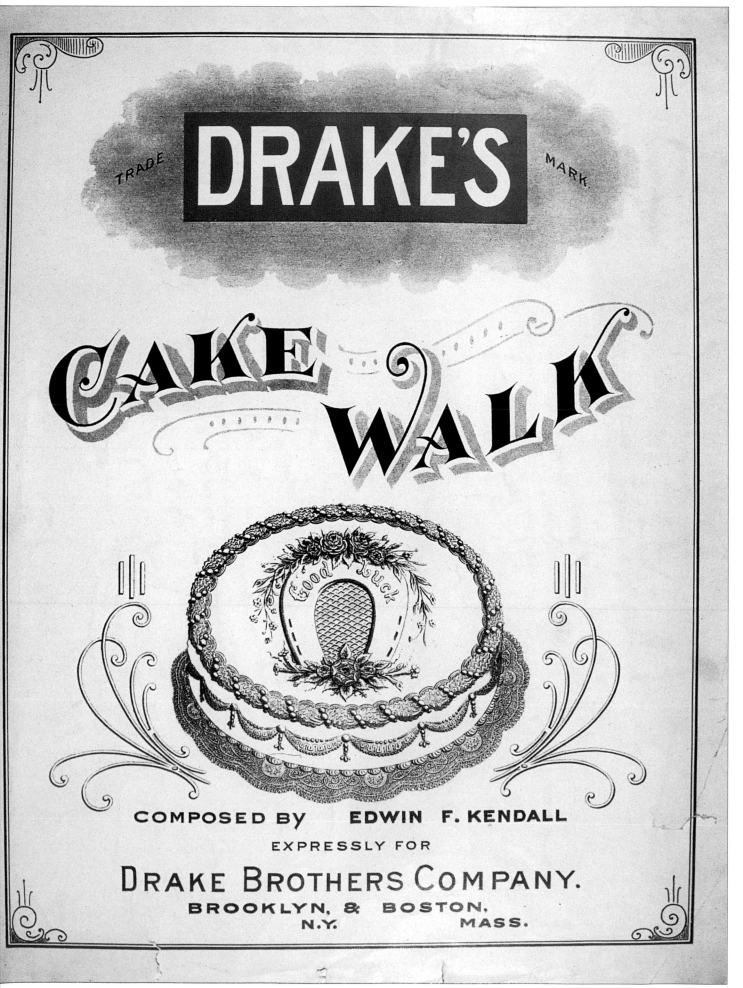

Despite the song, the BRT declared bankruptcy in 1918. Reorganized, it reappeared in 1923 as the BMT.

Today, New Yorkers are deluged with jingles and musical ads singing the praises of local stores and businesses. This attitude was neatly satirized years ago by a song in *The Little Show*, a sophisticated 1929 revue that contained an Arthur Schwarz and Howard Dietz song purporting to be the theme song for what was then a well-known local hardware store: It was entitled "Hammacher, Schlemmer, I Love You."

Restaurants

Ever since Swiss immigrants John and Peter Delmonico opened the first modern restaurant on William Street in 1827, New Yorkers have enjoyed some of the finest and most diverse eateries in the world. It was inevitable that some of these dining experiences would make their way into song.

Songs celebrating famous New York restaurants include "Lüchow's" (1955), "Schrafft's" (1947), and the 1913 Ziegfeld Follies hit "If a Table at Rector's Could Talk." At the time, Rector's was one of New York's most fashionable "lobster palaces." These large, ostentatiously ornate establishments specialized in gargantuan late-night dinners and attracted everyone from the more daring members of "established society," to the nouveau riche, to theatre people. Having a midnight "bird-and-bottle" date with a "chorine" from one of the Broadway shows

was quite the thing in the decades before and after 1900. Rector's, located on Broadway between 43rd and 44th Streets, was at the heart of it all, and, the songwriting team of Hubble and Conn suggested in 1913, "If a Table at Rector's Could Talk":

> *You would hear what someone's Adam said to someone else's Eve / You would hear that men don't have to wear a moustache to deceive . . . A lot of men would pony up a lot of alimony . . . some good old reputations would start off on long vacations, / If a table at Rector's could talk . . .*

For the less well heeled, there were plenty of other eating options. Street food has always been popular, and in the late nineteenth century, the ancestor of the modern diner, inspired by that era's railroad dining cars, made its appearance. As noted in the 1891 Harrigan and Braham song "Up in the Tenderloin," in that less-than-glamorous West Side neighborhood, *"You eat your meals a-top of wheels inside the banquet wagon."*

When the Childs Brothers opened their new restaurant at 130 Broadway in 1898, they introduced New Yorkers to an entirely new concept in dining—the cafeteria. The public, intrigued by industrial production lines and newly conscious of the dangers of germ-laden back kitchens, was delighted and patronized this early cousin of modern fast-food joints in great numbers. Childs' success encouraged Messrs. Horn and Hardart, two restaurateurs from Philadelphia, to go the cafeteria one better and open the city's first "automat" in 1912.

LEFT: Horn and Hardart's Automat, "As famous as the New York Skyline itself," starred as the epicenter of unlimited gastronomic wonder in this 1930s postcard.

OPPOSITE: Like many companies in that era, the BRT supported an employee-run band. Its members are almost lost among the flurry of advertisements, trolleys, commuters, and subway cars.

By inserting a nickel, hungry New Yorkers could select buns, beans, fish cakes, or coffee from behind spotless glass doors. Automats soon became synonymous with inexpensive food and unpretentious dining. Irving Berlin and Moss Hart, in their Depression era musical *Face the Music* (1932), opened the show with an amusing sketch in which the newly impoverished Mrs. Astor (still sporting a pearl necklace) and "her girlfriend" Woolworth heiress Mrs. Hutton (then the world's richest woman) dine among the hoi polloi at an automat-like cafeteria and then split the check.

The very clever 1947 revue *Make Mine Manhattan* contained a particularly funny song about that New York culinary institution, Schrafft's. A bastion of American-style cuisine and "ladies' lunches," it was obviously not a favorite of the songwriting team of Arnold Horwitt and Richard Lewine, who wrote about a restaurant *"Where all the help are so well bred . . . you should be serving them instead"*:

> *In Schrafft's! There is a tingle in the name / Schrafft's! Where all the dishes taste the same / Your heart will sing, Your soul will feel exalted ordering a double frosted chocolate malted! / / Schrafft's! Where you can eat right off the floor / Schrafft's! And you'll enjoy it even more / Take off your shoe, and possibly your girdle too, / In Schrafft's, Schrafft's, Schrafft's!*

> *There's a hostess to greet you, and a hostess to seat you, and a hostess who's giving commands / There's a girl who brings the water and a girl who takes your order, and a girl who don't do nothin', she just stands . . .*

Today, most of us take background music for granted. From elevators to airports, mechanically reproduced music infuses our daily lives. However, before radios became commonplace in the 1920s, whenever you heard music, a live person was performing it. Better restaurants throughout America often enticed diners by providing background music in the evening, but only in a truly up-to-date cosmopolitan city like New York could a patron find a restaurant that offered music *during* the day. Childs' cafeteria introduced daytime music, played by a five-piece orchestra, as early as 1898, but in 1911, dining to music in the daytime was still such a novelty that Seymour Brown and Nat Ayer actually wrote a song about it for their musical *A Million* entitled "Gee, I Like the Music With My Meals":

> *There's a little restaurant on old Broadway / Where they keep the music going night and day; / Oh, even in the morning or the afternoon, / Anytime you wander in you hear a tune. / I think the man who owns it has the right idea / He feeds the empty stomach and he pleases the ear / The only reason that I eat there ev'ry night / Is because the music seems to help my appetite. / / Chorus: Oh when that orchestra starts in a-playing you can see ev'rybody present swinging and swaying, / You can hear knives and forks beating time on the dishes; / See the waiters running with the steaks and fishes . . . Gee! but I like music with my meals.*

Bridges

Of New York's five boroughs, only the Bronx is located on the North American mainland. Manhattan and Staten Island are on islands of their own; Brooklyn and Queens share the western end of Long Island. The first

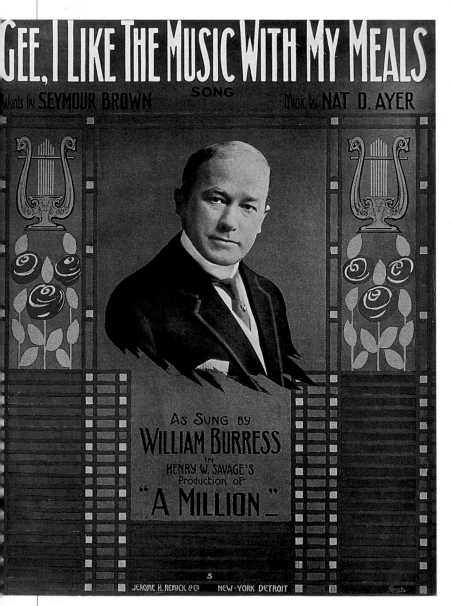

Novelty song from the 1911 musical *A Million*.

BROOKLYN BRIDGE

GRAND MARCH.

By E. MACK.

NEW YORK.

Published by **C.H. DITSON & CO.**, 867 Broadway

ST. LOUIS, J.L.PETERS.   BOSTON, O.DITSON & CO., 451 WASHINGTON STREET   CHICAGO, LYON & HEALY.   BOSTON, J.C.HAYNES & CO.   PHILADA., J.E.DITSON & CO., SUCCESSORS TO LEE & WALKER.   SAN FRANCISCO, SHERMAN, CLAY & CO.

COPYRIGHT 1883 BY OLIVER DITSON & CO.

Manhattan bridge, King's Bridge, which connected the northern end of the island to the Bronx across Spuyten Duyvil ("in spite of the Devil") Creek, was built in the late 1600s. However, the King's Bridge was of little use to most New Yorkers because they lived at the opposite end of the island and usually wanted to go south to Brooklyn, Queens, Staten Island, or New Jersey. For years, New Yorkers relied on dozens of different ferries to cross the Hudson River, the East River, and New York Harbor. Then, in 1883, John Augustus Roebling, ably assisted by his son Washington Roebling, his daughter-in-law Emily Warren Roebling, and several thousand construction workers, completed the Brooklyn Bridge. Today, there are seventy-six major water-spanning bridges in New York City, but the Brooklyn Bridge remains the favorite of both natives and songwriters. True, there are a few songs that mention other New York bridges—most

notably Paul Simon's 1966 "feelin' groovy" hit "59th Street Bridge Song"—but as an icon for the city, nothing comes close to the Brooklyn Bridge.

When the Brooklyn Bridge opened on May 24, 1883, it was truly, to quote one songwriter, a "19th Century Wonder." An engineering marvel in its day, its distinctive gothic arches and graceful loom of cables immediately became a symbol of pride for both the city and the nation. Songwriters rushed to join the celebration.

After the celebrations ended, New Yorkers quickly discovered that in addition to easing travel, their new bridge was also a great place for two of their favorite urban activities: strolling and meeting members of the opposite sex. Before the end of 1883, songs such as the metaphorical "The Highway in the Air: A Ballad of the Brooklyn Bridge" and "Strolling on the Brooklyn Bridge" were published.

Perhaps the most beautiful of all sheet music pieces to celebrate the 1883 opening of the Brooklyn Bridge.

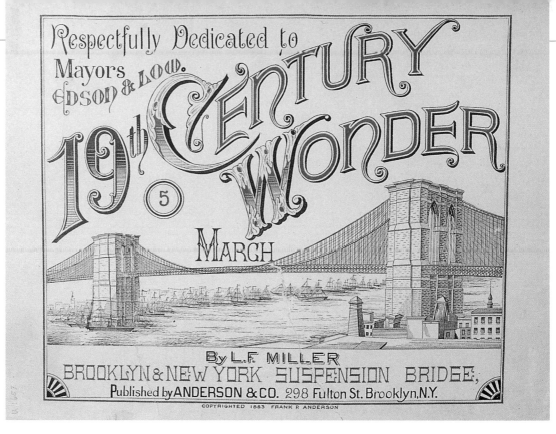

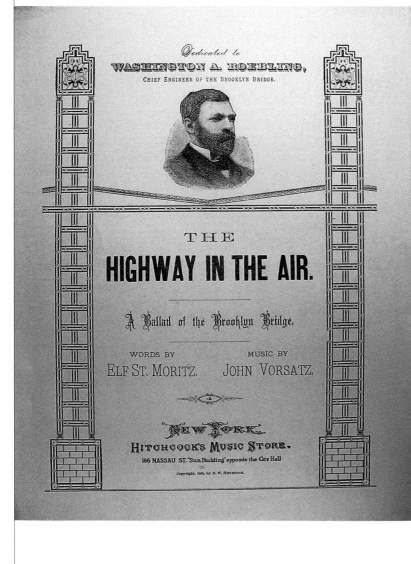

"The Highway in the Air: A Ballad of the Brooklyn Bridge" (1883)

At the union of the city by the Highway in the air, / I met a pretty, witty little girl. / "Good Evening, Cousin Brooklyn," I said with laughing eye; / "Good evening," she answered with a tender sigh; / And we strolled along the pathway, beneath the twinkling stars, / And agreed to meet again when we parted on the cars.

I firmly hope and trust, that the Highway in the air, / Will unite the two cities by the sea, / In interest and affection and that the wedded pair, / Will give a loving Brooklyn Bride to me.

And that when our pretty first-born is in its cradle curled, / The one great town will be the metropolis of the world; / That the union of the cities by the Highway in the air / Will end 'fore many years have passed with a wedding firm and fair.

"Strolling on the Brooklyn Bridge" (1883)

It's gay to ramble out at night with some nice girl so true; / Then in the lovely pale moonlight, To care we bid adieu! / The ferry boat once took us home, My little girl and me; / Now o'er the Brooklyn Bridge we roam, When moonlight tints the sea!

Chorus: Strolling o'er the Brooklyn Bridge, Dreamy hours go by! / Whisp'ring words of fond delight 'neath the starry sky! / Happy as the dancing waves, Hearts are lost and won; / We fondly stray with hearts so gay upon the Brooklyn Bridge!

CROTON WATER

In addition to celebrating bridges, New York composers occasionally wrote music to honor other water-related portions of the urban infrastructure. One of the factors that allowed nineteenth-century Manhattan to expand as it did was the unlimited supply of clean, fresh water. Through one of the largest and most elaborate engineer projects of its day, water from Croton in upstate New York was channeled forty-one miles via a series of tunnels, bridges, and reservoirs into a giant aqueduct at Fifth Avenue and 42nd Street. (Today, it's the site of the New York Public Library.) The aqueduct was officially opened with mammoth citywide celebrations on July 4, 1842. Like everyone else, local composers gushed with enthusiasm and marked the event with several beautifully illustrated, if musically undistinguished, instrumental marches such as the "Croton Jubilee Quick Step" by a composer surnamed von Volte (1843). At the event itself a mass choir assembled in City Hall Park to sing "Croton Water Celebration 1842" with words by the respected poet George P. Morris and music by Sidney Pearson:

Gushing from your living fountain, / Music pours with falling strain, / As the Goddess of the Mountain / Comes with all her sparkling train. ~ ~ ~ Ever sparkling bright, and single / Will this rock-ribbed stream appear, / When prosperity shall mingle / Like the free gathered water here.

CROTON WATER CELEBRATION 1842

Firemen, horse-drawn firetrucks, marching bands, soldiers, and what appears to be the entire population of New York march past a giant fountain at the southern end of City Hall Park. Looking uptown from Ann and Vesey Streets: to the right is present day Park Row; to the left, Broadway.

In 1891, one of the most poignant of the Brooklyn Bridge songs, "With Danny by My Side," had its premiere in the Harrigan & Hart musical *The Last of the Hogans.* Years later in 1932, when former New York governor and ex-presidential candidate Al Smith was asked to sing a song at celebrations marking the fiftieth anniversary of the Brooklyn Bridge, this is the one he chose:

> *The mothers with the children, go out to take the air. / From tenement and alley, a pleasure oh so rare; / It's there the poor and lowly, all watch the river glide. / What joys to me such sights to see, with Danny by my side.*

> *The Brooklyn Bridge on Sunday is known as lovers' lane. / I stroll there with my sweetheart, oh, time and time again; / Oh, how I love to ramble; oh, yes, it is my pride, / Dressed in my best, each day of rest, with Danny by my side.*

It is important to remember that when it was built, the Brooklyn Bridge connected two separate cities—New York and Brooklyn. Some songwriters have concentrated on the Brooklyn side of the span, such as "Just Over the Brooklyn Bridge" (1991) from a short-lived television series of the same name. But perhaps the greatest of all the Brooklyn Bridge songs is Jule Styne and Sammy Cahn's lyrical 1947 classic, "The Brooklyn Bridge." Written for the film *It Happened in Brooklyn,* the ballad was sung by that sensational young heartthrob, Frank Sinatra:

> *Isn't she a beauty? Isn't she a queen? / Nicest bridge that I have ever seen! / Her paint's a little tattered, Where age has left its touch; / Still, I guess I'll always love her very much.*

> *Like the folks you meet on, Like to plant my feet on The Brooklyn Bridge. / What a lovely view from, Heaven looks at you from The Brooklyn Bridge. / I love to listen to the wind through her strings, The song that it sings for the town. / I love to look at the clouds in her hair, She's learned to wear like a crown. ~ ~ ~*

> *If you've been a rover, Journey's end lies over The Brooklyn Bridge. / Don't let no one tell you, I've been trying to sell you The Brooklyn Bridge. / You'll miss her most when you roam, 'Cause you'll think of her and think of home, / The good old, Brooklyn Bridge.*

THE BROOKLYN BRIDGE

Lyrics by SAMMY CAHN   Music by JULE STYNE

Metro-Goldwyn-Mayer presents

FRANK **SINATRA** · KATHRYN **GRAYSON**

PETER **LAWFORD** · JIMMY **DURANTE**

IN

"It Happened in Brooklyn"

Screen Play by
ISOBEL LENNART
Based On An Original Story by
JOHN McGOWAN
Directed by   Produced by
RICHARD WHORF   JACK CUMMINGS

Lyrics by   Music by
SAMMY CAHN   JULE STYNE
♪ IT'S THE SAME OLD DREAM
♪ TIME AFTER TIME
♪ I BELIEVE
♪ THE BROOKLYN BRIDGE
♪ WHOSE BABY ARE YOU
♪ THE SONG'S GOTTA COME FROM THE HEART

SINATRA SONGS, INC.
1619 BROADWAY · NEW YORK 19, N. Y.

ABOVE: Sammy Cahn and Jule Styne's 1947 classic "The Brooklyn Bridge."

OPPOSITE: This 1930s tribute to bridge builders is one of the few to celebrate another New York bridge—in this case, the Bayonne Bridge in Staten Island.

SELLING THE BROOKLYN BRIDGE

At an early date, possibly before it was even completed, a local folktale developed about how fast-talking con men were selling the Brooklyn Bridge to gullible tourists and newly arrived immigrants. "Selling the Brooklyn Bridge" soon became a byword for a swindle, and over the years the legend has made its way into several songs, including "That Man Could Sell Me the Brooklyn Bridge" by Webster and Fain, which was sung by Pat Boone in the 1958 film *Mardi Gras;* and "Brooklyn Bridge," a 1954 song by Leon René that begins with the traditional line, *"Anyone wanna buy the Brooklyn Bridge?"* Perhaps the old vaudeville comedians had a point when they jokingly remarked, "All that trouble, just to get to Brooklyn?"

BRIDGEBUILDERS

A Song of the Oxford Group

Words by
JOHN M. MORRISON

Music by
GEORGE M. FRASER

The Statue of Liberty

More than a few songwriters have yielded to the temptation of writing about "The Lady in the Harbor." Created by sculptor Frédéric-Auguste Bartholdi to commemorate a century of friendship between the French and American people, the 394-foot statue was dedicated with much fanfare on October 28, 1886. (Actually, Bartholdi had originally wanted to build his colossus at the entrance of the Suez Canal. New York was his second choice—but that's another story.) Like the Brooklyn Bridge, completed only three years before, the Statue of Liberty soon became both a local and national icon. Although the French generously paid for the 151-foot statue, funds for the 244-foot pedestal were raised, with some difficulty, from the American people. As part of these fundraising efforts, schoolchildren and newspaper readers, led by the *New York World*, contributed their pennies, and artists created and sold their works. It was for the pedestal fund that Emma Lazarus penned her famous poem, "The New

Colossus" (1883), which contains the immortal lines, *"Give me your tired, your poor, / Your huddled masses yearning to breathe free . . ."*

The patriotism ignited by the Spanish American War led to the use of the Statue of Liberty as the female counterpart of Uncle Sam—preeminent symbols of home and freedom. The cover of the World War I song, "The Statue of Liberty Is Smiling," (1918) shows Liberty's torch illuminating streams of troop ships returning from France. World War II inspired such songs as "Ten Million Men and a Girl" (1942) and "She Will Still be Standing in the Harbor" (1943)—*"While we fight for ev'rything she stands for . . ."*

In 1949 Irving Berlin wrote *Miss Liberty*, a musical comedy about a young woman who is brought to America under the mistaken assumption that she was Bartholdi's model for the statue. In addition to setting the Lazarus poem to music ("Give Me Your Tired, Your Poor"), Berlin wrote several clever songs, including "The Most Expensive Statue in the World," and "Miss Liberty," a spoof on those who would commercialize the icon to sell such mundane products as pimple ointments.

Fairs and Expositions

Over the years, New York has been the site of numerous expositions and three world's fairs. The first North American World's Fair, the "Exhibition of the Industry of All Nations," opened in 1853 in what is today Bryant Park. More than one million people flocked to see the four thousand exhibits celebrating industry, crafts, and arts from all corners of the globe. Equally impressive was the "Crystal Palace," the enormous cast-iron and glass building in which it was housed. Unfortunately, the Crystal Palace's reputation as a fireproof structure was vastly overrated, and when it caught fire on October 5, 1858, it reportedly took only fifteen minutes to burn to the ground.

New York's second World's Fair took place from 1939 to 1940 in Flushing Meadow Park, a city park reclaimed from the huge tidal expanse that had previously served as the Corona Dumps. (F. Scott Fitzgerald in *The Great Gatsby* had dismissed this part of Queens as "a valley of ashes.") Opening in April 1939 on the 150th anniversary of George Washington's inauguration, the fair's futuristic theme, "Building the World of Tomorrow," was symbolized by two enormous sculptures: the Trylon and the Perisphere. At singer Kay Swift's request, Ira Gershwin created

BELOW: In 1884 composer Harry Kennedy printed and donated one hundred thousand copies of "Liberty" to the *New York World*, "in aid of the Bartholdi Pedestal Fund."

OPPOSITE: The enterprising Mr. Rothstein composed a march, waltz, galop, gavotte, lanciers, quadrille, and song to mark the statue's arrival. Note Manhattan Island and the Brooklyn Bridge in the background of this beautifully executed lithograph.

the fair's official theme song, "Dawn of a New Day," by writing lyrics to a tune he found among his late brother George's music manuscripts. (George had died unexpectedly in 1937.) Ira came up with a passably good tune, to which he set passably good lyrics, exhorting listeners to:

> Leave those cares and furrows! / Come, come where Five Boroughs / Join to fulfill a dream! / Where all creeds and races / Meet with smiling faces, / Democracy reigns supreme! / Let the New York Fair proclaim the story! / Orange, blue and white[2] beside old Glory!

In 1940, following the outbreak of hostilities in Europe and Asia, the fair's theme was changed to "For Peace and Freedom." Eugene LaBarre (composer of "Repenting in a Penthouse") took on the task of composing a new theme song, "Peace and Freedom: The Official Song of the World's Fair of 1940 in New York," which included such grammatically challenged lyrics as: *"Peace and Freedom is [sic] the emblem of our nation, / May it always, like our flag, wave high. / We can never bring upon it degradation, / We'll keep its standards raised up to the sky."* Non-official efforts included "souvenir songs" such as Arthur Salzer's "From Old Broadway to the Fair Grounds" (1938); Tommy Martin's "The Gates of Old New York Swing Open to the Fair" (1939); "Meet Me at the New York Fair" (1937) by lyricist Bob Randolph and composer Joseph E. Howard

(better remembered for his earlier hit, "I Wonder Who's Kissing Her Now"); and the memorably entitled "I'll Be You're [sic] Trylon If You'll Be My Perisphere" (1939). Written by Bill Bush and John W. Kellette (who also wrote the near classic "I'm Forever Blowing Bubbles"), the song's first verse tells of two happy little love birds who flew to New York to see the fair *"and as they gazed on the Perisphere, / These words chirped out on the air"*:

> I'll be your Trylon if you'll be my Perisphere. / Ever together and I'll always love you dear. / In the wonderful world of tomorrow, / We'll never know a care or sorrow. / I'll be your Trylon if you'll be my Perisphere.

Several classical composers contributed compositions for the 1939 World's Fair. William Grant Still, for example, composed "Song of a City (Trylon and Perisphere)," and Aaron Copland wrote the soundtrack for a featured documentary entitled *The City.* Even Trinidadian calypso master Wilmoth Houdini, then living in Manhattan, marked the event by composing the calypso hit "Roosevelt Opens the World's Fair" (1939).

The World's Fair of 1964–1965 was also held in Flushing Meadows Park. Although it featured a new symbol, the Unisphere, and a catchy new theme, "Peace Through Understanding,"

RIGHT: The New York Crystal Palace, inspired by a structure built two years earlier for the 1851 London Exposition, dazzled both locals and out-of-town visitors.

OPPOSITE: The cover of Ira and George Gershwin's official 1939 World's Fair anthem featured the Trylon and the Perisphere in high art deco.

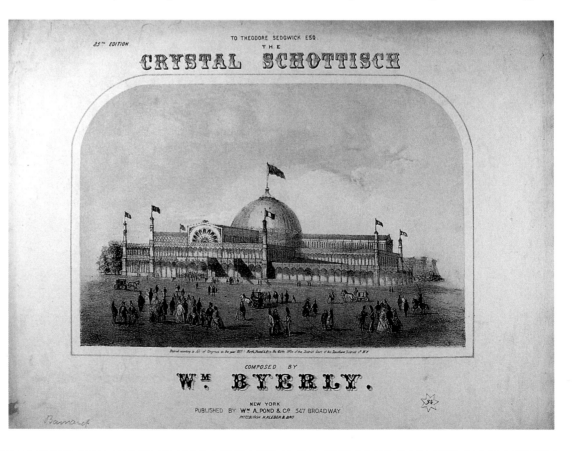

TO
Mrs. George Holland

That Little Church Around the Corner

REV. G H. HOUGHTON'S CHURCH, N.Y.

SONG AND CHORUS.

WORDS BY DEXTER SMITH. MUSIC BY

C. A. WHITE.

BOSTON.
White, Smith & Perry.
298 & 300 Washington St

the 1964–1965 World's Fair, like the two before it, was a financial disaster. Musically, it didn't fare much better, although it did inspire "Queen of the New York World's Fair" (1964), and the annoyingly jingle-like official song "Take Me to New York, Take Me to the Fair" (1964).

Churches and Schools

New York abounds with houses of worship, but few of them have inspired songs. The notable exception is the Church of the Transfiguration, a small Protestant Episcopal Church on 29th Street. In December 1870, a popular comedian named George Holland died in New York. A delegation of his friends, headed by the famous actor Joseph Jefferson, approached the pastor of the Church of Atonement, a prominent Fifth Avenue "society" church, and asked him to perform Holland's burial service. The Reverend William Sabine, horrified at the idea of associating with actors, immediately declined, but informed the delegation that "there was a little church around the corner that did that sort of thing." Jefferson indignantly rose to his feet, announced "God bless the little church around the corner," and swept out of the room. Dr. George Houghton, rector of the Church of the Transfiguration gladly obliged and "The Little

Church Around the Corner" became famous as "the actors' church." As the story spread, the Church of the Transfiguration also became an exemplar of Christian piety and a congregation's openness to serve even God's lowliest creatures (i.e., actors). Between 1870 and 1913, no less than six songs were written about the incident, several based on George Cooper's poem, which was *"Respectfully dedicated to Rev. Geo. H. Houghton"*:

> *God bless the little church around the corner / The shrine of holy charity and love / Its doors are ever open unto sorrow, / A blessing fall on it from above. / The rich and poor are equal 'neath its portals, / And be our path in life what e're it may, / No heart that needed comfort in affliction / Was ever turned uncomforted away. . . .*

Any self-respecting school needs an anthem, or at least a fight song. Despite some valiant efforts, none of those celebrating local schools have become classics, although a few might be fondly remembered by alumni. City high schools have inspired such efforts as the "Brooklyn Tech Marching Song" (1933), "Erasmus Hall" (1898), and "Cheer for Erasmus Hall" (1908), "Marching Song of the Washington Irving Girls," and "Hurrah for Bushwick High" (1912). Columbia was lucky to have the very young Rodgers and Hart write "College on Broadway"

OPPOSITE: This 1870s retelling of the Little Church Around the Corner's story was thoughtfully dedicated to Mrs. George Holland, the actor's widow.

BELOW LEFT: It is not known why Curtis chose a French title, but this 1857 piece, based on two student songs, was *"composed expressly for the annual commencement"* at the Brooklyn Collegiate & Polytechnic Institute. Renamed the Polytechnic University, the school still thrives in downtown Brooklyn.

BELOW RIGHT: The Brooklyn Collegiate Institute in Brooklyn Heights in 1831. Note the passing man and dog.

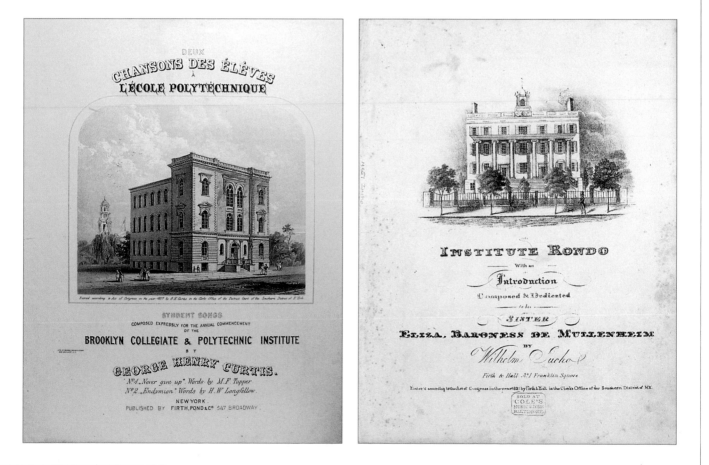

for their 1920 student revue, *Fly With Me*, but other songs, such as "I Wanna Go to City College" (1946), have sunk without a trace. Two dramas set in New York City schools—the movie *Fame* (1980) and the television series *Welcome Back, Kotter* (1976)—provided, by far, the best New York school-related songs.

Landmark Events: Consolidation 1898

On January 1, 1898, present-day New York City was born when Manhattan, Queens, the Bronx, Staten Island, and Brooklyn incorporated themselves into a single giant metropolis. Although consolidation had been approved by a majority of New York voters in 1894 in a non-binding referendum, the action did not enjoy universal support. Citizens of Brooklyn, led by the League of Loyal Citizens of Brooklyn and *The Brooklyn Eagle* newspaper, were particularly unhappy. (During centennial celebrations in 1998, some Brooklynites were still referring to consolidation as "the Anschluss.")[3] As usual, local songwriters rushed to celebrate the event with music.

To mark the actual 1898 incorporation ceremony, W.F. Easton and band conductor Francesco Fanciulli composed an "Ode to Greater New York," designed "to be played by Fanciulli's band of eighty pieces and sung by a chorus of two thousand voices in the City Hall Plaza, New Year's Eve." If Easton's lyrics weren't so weak, "Ode to Greater New York" might have become the city's official anthem:

> Hail thee, city, born today! / Commercial monarch by the sea, / Whose throne is by the Hudson's way; / 'Mid thousands' homesteads join'd to thee. / On terrace race, plain and mountainside, / Where countless millions shall abide. / Let the bells in triumph ring, / Let the thundering cannon say, / Let a million voices sing: / Hail, our city, born today.

Also expressing their musical support for consolidation were composers such as Safford Waters, who wrote the "One New York Two-Step" (1896), and Charles Miller, who contributed "The Belle of Greater New York" (1897)—actually a reworking of the earlier hit, "East Side Belles." And, in the opposite musical corner, were the diehard Kings County separatists, led by the League of Loyal Citizens of Brooklyn. In 1898 the League published a two-in-one piece of musical propaganda which began with Alfred D. Fohs "Greater Brooklyn Two-Step March" and then segued into John

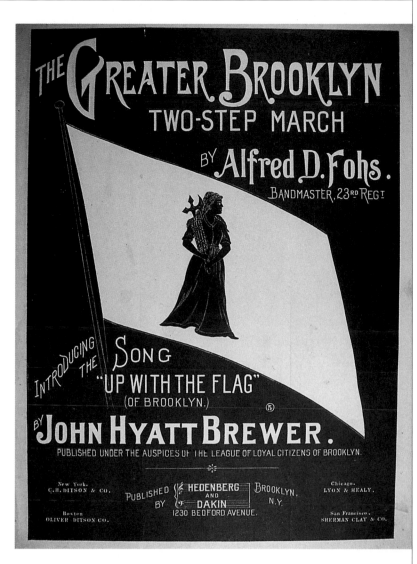

Brewer's blood-stirring cut-time song "Up With the Flag of Brooklyn."

> Up with the flag! the flag that long, / Has waved over Brooklyn's city fair, / To keep her sons in union strong. / To bid them heed the motto there— / "Right makes might" / Then up with right and down with wrong. / Up with the flag and let it wave, / Unhurt by factions with'ring blast. / Oh, Brooklyn's loyal sons be brave, / And nail it to the mast!

> Rise, flag of independence, rise, / For mercenary foes are near, / To steal away in friendship's guise, / The treasures that we hold most dear. / Right makes might. / But now our right in peril lies, / Our civic charter in the grave / Of ruin would these tricksters cast. / Up with the flag our fathers gave. / And nail it to the mast! ~ ~ ~

> Dear city of our native home, / Where justice rules in court and hall, / We see thy sons in myriads come / To save thee from the hated thrall [i.e., Manhattanites] / "Right makes might." / They will not to thy call be dumb, / Be deaf to all thy ancient fame; / To all that crowns thy glorious past / Their flag they'll raise in honor's name / And nail it to the mast.

ABOVE: Fohs's "The Greater Brooklyn Two-Step March" segued into Brewer's song "Up With the Flag of Brooklyn."

OPPOSITE: A pro-consolidation piece by Safford Waters. The cover shows Union Square at 14th Street looking north toward what is today Park Avenue South. Although Union Square has been enlarged over the years, the photo is confusing to contemporary New Yorkers because the statue of Washington, which originally stood near the end of present-day Fourth Avenue, was later moved half a block west to the center of Union Square.

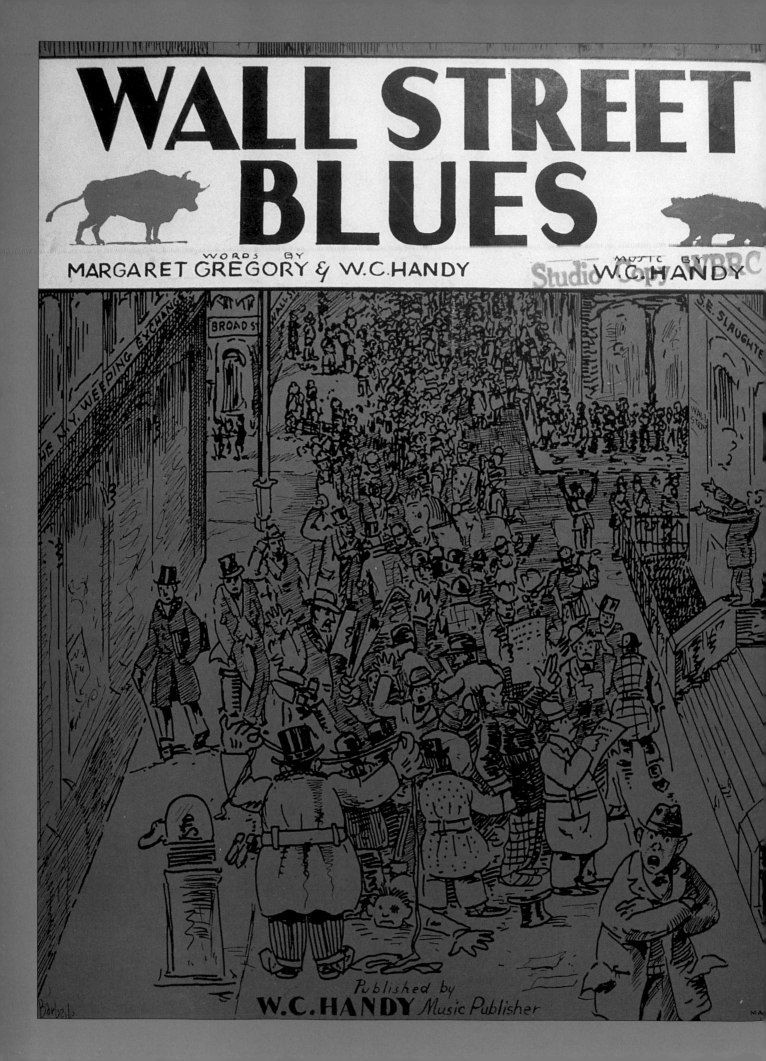

Chapter 3

MANHATTAN NEIGHBORHOODS

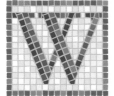

Whwhen New Yorkers think about New York, they rarely think of the entire city. Rather, they mentally compartmentalize the city into different neighborhoods that function almost as adjoining villages, each with a distinctive look, history, and character of its own.

To the natives, the cafes of Greenwich Village or the tree-lined streets of the Upper West Side are light years away from the pandemonium of midtown or the palatial elegance of Park Avenue. If pressed, most New Yorkers will tell you (confidentially) that their neighborhood is really the best and then proceed to give you a list of reasons. Songwriters are much the same. Here, then, is a quick musical tour of some of Manhattan's most distinctive neighborhoods, beginning at the southern end of the island.

The Battery

If Manhattan begins anywhere, then most New Yorkers would agree it begins at Battery Park, the southernmost tip of the island. Now an eighty-acre park, the Battery was originally on a small island that housed New Amsterdam's first fortification, a battery of guns. In 1811, when the present fort, Castle Clinton, was built, a bridge connected the island to the mainland. The new fort was deemed obsolete almost as soon as it was completed, so in 1823 the United States ceded it to the city, which constructed a roof over it and had it refurbished as a public auditorium. Renamed "Castle Garden," it was the city's leading entertainment venue for more than thirty years. It was here in 1850 that P.T. Barnum first presented Jenny Lind, the "Swedish Nightingale," to America. Castle Garden served as the main

federal immigration center on the East Coast from 1855–1890, before it was replaced by larger facilities on Ellis Island. Still later, it was connected to Manhattan by landfill and housed the New York Aquarium from 1896–1941; then it stood empty for many years before being restored as a national monument in the 1970s.

From the founding of the city until the early 1900s, Battery Park was one of the most fashionable sites in the city for strolling, summer evening band concerts, and outdoor public dancing, and there are numerous songs and dances celebrating it. As early as 1770, a broadside ballad appeared entitled "A New Song, or, Castle Island Song." In 1819, Edward Riley published "The Castle Garden March," and then there was the "Castle Garden Schottisch" (1852), the "Kayydid Polka or Souvenirs of Castle Gardens" (1852), and "The Opera Schottish" (1853), with a beautifully illustrated cover showing the inside of the hall.

John Watson's "Light May the Boat Row" (1836), which was "set to a Northumbrian Melody" and dedicated to "the New York Boat Clubs," commemorated a rowing race off the Battery. The song's lyrics are of less interest than the important early view of New York Harbor on its cover.

At the close of the nineteenth century, outdoor public dancing in city parks was all the rage. Murphy and Mack, a well-known music

CASTLE GARDEN SCHOTTISCH.

NEW YORK, PUBLISHED BY JAQUES & BROTHER 385 BROADWAY
W? HALL & SON 289 BROADWAY.

hall team of the 1880s, had a hit with a song about the popular open-air dances held during the summer in Battery Park. Despite the lyric's protestations of propriety, at the time these outdoor dances were considered slightly risqué because they attracted groups of unescorted shopgirls who liked to "spiel" (dance) with strangers at "The Dance at Battery Park":

> You never saw such a happier lot / In the course of all your life, / Young men of twenty with their girls, / The working man and his wife. / They're happy as if they were kings and queens, / They're bound to have a lark; / Would set you wild, the music would, / The dance at Battery Park.

> All classes are represented there, / Every Tuesday and Friday night, / The best of order is maintained, / And not a single fight. / It is always crowded, yes, / From six till after dark, / The pivoters and spielers are always there, / To dance at Battery Park.

A decade later, the songwriting team of Paul Dresser and Leo Evans composed "The Battery" (1895), another interesting aural snapshot of turn-of-the-century New York life. Dresser was a gifted composer and lyricist who is best remembered today as the author of Indiana's state song "On the Banks of the Wabash." Ability with words seems to have run in his family—his brother was the novelist Theodore Dreiser. In "The Battery," Dresser describes straying down to the Battery,

Where the summer winds are blowing, / When the sun has sunk in grandeur in the West; / And the shining stars come peeping, their nightly vigil keeping, / And the great ships in the harbor are at rest. / When behind the steamboat speeding, the billows swift receding, / In the moonlight, chase each other to the land: / I love, on Friday evening, when the shades of night are deep'ing, / To listen at the Batt'ry to the Band.

Wall Street

Once the northern boundary of New Amsterdam, the Wall Street neighborhood has been the heart of New York's financial district ever since the 1790s. Although classical composer Charles Ives wrote a piece about nearby Ann Street in 1921, most of the musical interest in this part of town has focused on the ups and downs of the stock market. For example, there were Scott Joplin's "Wall Street Rag" (1909), Duke Ellington's "Wall Street Wail" (1930), Richard Whiting and B.G. DeSylva's post-Crash "Humpty-Dumpty" (1932), and W.C. Handy's classic "Wall Street Blues" (1929):

I can sing the blues from the bottom of my heart, / I can sing the blues from the bottom of my heart, / All my profits gone 'fore I even got a start. ~ ~ ~ Oh Wall Street you've got me depressed, / Down-hearted, you can guess the rest, / River's East end, [Trinity] Graveyard's at the West. ~ ~ ~ / / I used to be a bull, wolves got me there, I used to be a bull, wolves got me there, / Now I'm just a little sheep without no hair.

In 1896, songwriters William Jerome and D. Fitzgibbon wrote a parody of the international hit "The Man Who Broke the Bank at Monte Carlo" and called it "The Man That Broke the Brokers Down on Wall Street":

A happy individual without a single care / With an independent air, causing ev'ryone to stare: / The brokers and the bankers they are pulling out their hair, / In Wall Street I have raised an awful flare, / Among the famous little Bulls and Bears . . . Every since that day I chanced to call the ducky turn. / The day I broke up each concern / And now I've lots of money, boys, to burn . . . I'm the man that broke the brokers down on Wall Street. . . .

The Bowery

Originally an Indian path, today the Bowery runs from Chatham Square in Chinatown to Cooper Square in the East Village. Seventeenth-century Dutch New Yorkers began calling it the *bouwerij* because it led to "bowers" or farms just north of the city. During the eighteenth century, it served as the first leg on the main route to Boston, and by 1800, as the city expanded northward, the Bowery developed into a broad, elegant street lined with fine homes and ornate theatres. (When the Great Bowery Theatre opened in 1826, it was hailed as the largest public hall ever built in North America.) At the time of the Civil War, the Bowery was the heart of New York's entertainment district, but as the century progressed, the area fell into decline. In the late nineteenth century, as Broadway and Fifth Avenue became the city's major thoroughfares, the Bowery's once-famous theatres were turned into nickel museums, vaudeville houses, and low-class concert saloons; its fine homes were partitioned into cheap boarding houses (many of them brothels). Less-refined establishments, such as McGurk's Suicide Hall (managed by Eat-'Em Up Jack McManus) and Chick Tricker's

Wall Street looking west toward Trinity Church from Federal Hall. The third church built on this site since 1698, Trinity's steeple was the tallest structure in New York until well after the Civil War.

THE BOWERY, BY NIGHT, NEW YORK CITY.

"The Bowery at Night," circa 1915.

Flea Bag, sprang up to service the thirsty. By 1900, the Bowery had become New York's answer to skid row, a neighborhood full of dilapidated buildings and forlorn people, and it has only recently begun to recover. During its heyday, few New York neighborhoods inspired more songs than the Bowery. The popularity of "Mose The Bowery B'hoy," the area's entertainment industry, and the presence of colorful characters from the surrounding slums made the Bowery exotically urban, slightly dangerous, and quintessentially New York.

During the first half of the nineteenth century, the neighborhoods surrounding the Bowery were some of the most dangerous in the city, and warfare between marginally employed, criminally inclined street gang members posed a serious threat to public law and order. Things got so out of hand that on July 4, 1857, open gang warfare broke out in the Sixth Ward. It seems that the Dead Rabbits, a Catholic Irish-American street gang, had trashed the Green Dragon, a saloon at 47 Bowery which was the unofficial club house for their rivals, a Protestant gang of pro-Nativist thugs who called themselves the Bowery Boys. For two days, police and residents of the Sixth Ward watched helplessly as the rival gangs (joined by members of other area gangs such as the Plug Uglies, the Atlantic Guards, and the Roach Guards) maimed, clubbed, and shot each

other after closing down the streets with hastily erected barricades. Most of the fighting took place on Bayard Street. By the time the militia was finally called in to help the police on the third day, at least twelve people were dead. A broadside ballad, set to the spiritual, "Jordan Is a Hard Road to Travel," appeared almost simultaneously with the events, and described in detail the "Dead Rabbits' Fight With the Bowery Boys":

> *They had a dreadful fight, upon last Saturday night, / The papers gave the news accordin', / Guns, pistols, clubs, and sticks, hot water, and old bricks, / Which drove them on the other side of Jordan. / / Chorus: Then pull off the old coat and roll up the sleeve, / Bayard is a hard street to travel. / Pull off the old coat and roll up the sleeve, / The Bloody Sixth is a hard ward to travel, I believe.*[1]

After the nadir of the 1857 riot, the image of Bowery b'hoys began to improve—perhaps because it had nowhere to go but up. By the end of the nineteenth century, songwriters were portraying Bowery boys as tough but basically decent; more interested in dancing than fighting—although not averse to the latter, should the situation arise. Nevertheless, the songwriting team of Charles Ward and Gussie L. Davis were probably overly generous in their assessment of the neighborhood youth when they wrote "Only a Bowery Boy" in 1894:

I was born down on the Bowery, right between Spring Street and Prince / My old man and my mother have lived there ever since; / I has a crippled sister, I works hard to support, / But when we knocks off Saturday, till Monday I can sport. / My mother goes out washing, my sister minds the place, / The old man he ain't working, the can [liquor] he likes to chase; / I makes my little eight a week, I'm satisfied with dat. / On Saturday night I takes home six and dumps it in my mother's lap.

Chorus: I'm only a Bowery boy, not a bad feller at all. / I can sing, I can dance, I'm a spieler, I take in ev'ry party or ball: / Down in the Fourteenth Ward all the pleasures of life I enjoy. / And the roundsman he says to the copper, "He's all right, he's only a Bowery boy."

The Bowery b'hoys were well-matched with their Bowery g'hals, who also attracted the attention of numerous nineteenth- and early-twentieth-century songwriters. Bowery girls were characterized as tough, loud, unpretentious, loyal, and—much like inner-city girls today—possessing an inimitable style all their own in songs like William Jerome and Belle Stewart's 1894 "The Bowery Girls":

The uptown girls are jealous of our own peculiar style / Instead of Saratoga we go down to Coney Isle. / Champagne it cuts no figure, for it really is too dear. / The Bowery girls are satisfied with good old lager beer. // Chorus: For we're the Bowery girls, oh! yes, the Bowery girls / To sing and dance is our delight, and we could keep it up all night; / We don't stay out late, or dine with Lords and Earls, / Hey! Hey! Clear the way for the rollicking Bowery girls—

One of the interesting things about Bowery songs is that from the 1840s on, songwriters attempted to capture local color by including New York slang words and using spellings that reflected the local accent. These songs provide us with some of the earliest indications about how lower- and working-class New Yorkers actually spoke. So, for example, in "My Beau's a Bowery Boy," an 1894 parody-ballad written by William Delaney under the alias of "William Wildwave," we have a sound bite from the inner city of a century ago preserved in the amber of poetry:

Of course ev'ry dame has a lover, / An' so has dis chick, I believe; / Of all dat's dead square in der city / Dere's none "in it" wid my "blokie" Steve. / He runs a swell joint on der Bowery. / Where hard gents der pictures enjoy; / Der "chippies" around all are jealous, / For my beau's a Bowery boy.

MOSE THE BOWERY B'HOY

America's first urban folk hero was based on a real Robin Hood character named Moses Humphreys. Like many other young "loafers" and "dandies" who grew up in the tougher neighborhoods of New York during the 1830s and 1840s, Humphreys was said to be a brawler, a slangy talker, and a flashy dresser, whose main interest and only allegiance in life was his local volunteer fire company. (These companies served as neighborhood social clubs while also providing much-needed protection against conflagrations.) In 1848 playwright Benjamin Baker used Humphreys as his model for the hero in his wildly successful melodrama, *Mose, A Glance at New York*. The leading actor, Francis Chanfrau, distinctively clad in the style then popular with local toughs—shiny stovepipe hat, bright red shirt, heavy pearl-buttoned pea jacket, rolled-up trousers tucked into boots, and sporting a "long nine" cigar—was immediately recognized and appreciated by New York audiences. Mose's surly manner, rolling gait, and New York accent ("Get off dem hose or I'll hit yer wid a spanner") became legendary. With a supporting cast of local character types that included his best "gallus g'hal" Lizey and his sidekick Skyesy, Chanfrau starred in dozens of sequels over the next twenty years. Mose was the first of the stereotypical New York wise guys: a tough talker with a heart of gold. The real Mose supposedly fled to Hawaii after being publicly humiliated in a brawl, but almost a century later, legends persisted around the Bowery of a twelve-foot giant named Mose who led his gang into battle against the East Side gangs, the Plug Uglies and the Dead Rabbits. Mose, they said, was last seen about 1900 brandishing an uprooted lamppost in one hand, throwing paving blocks with the other, and smoking a two-foot cigar.

MR. F. S. CHANFRAU AS "MOSE." (BY PERMISSION, AFTER LITHOGRAPH DRAWN BY JAMES BROWN.)

Francis Chanfrau as "Mose."

This 1935 edition of "The Bowery" proves the song, and the stereotypes about the neighborhood, were still popular with radio audiences.

"living picture" during which *"May McNulty will rise from the sea, / As Venus so sweet and fair / Her dress will consist of a beautiful smile and a silver comb in her hair."* Like many others, this Bowery Ball ultimately ends with a brawl. Yet, despite the area's many problems, New Yorkers had a deep love for the neighborhood. As the entertainment industry gradually moved to Broadway, nostalgia began to fill the empty spaces. Songs appeared like Edward Harrigan's, "The Old Bowery Pit" (1882), a musical salute to the Bowery's once elegant theatres, and Charles Van and George Johnson's 1905, "Give My Regards to the Bowery," a parody of George M. Cohan's 1904 hit:

You may sing out in praise of old Broadway, / Of its splendor, its glitter, its glare. / Grand opera and dining at Shanley's / And friends around old Herald Square / Millionaires, pretty show girls, and clubmen / Congregate there each night to shine: / Though I've lived all my days in old Gotham, I'll say / There is only one place, boys, for mine:

Give my regards to the Bowery, that's where I long to be. / My home, sweet home's on the East side, but the Bowery is Broadway to me. / At night the sights you see there would turn old Broadway upside down / So give my regards to the Bowery in New York town.

The increasing seediness of the area was more realistically noted in such songs as Henry Sayers' parody "I've Been to the Bowery" (1894):

I went to a museum, the funny sights to see, / I saw a big fat lady nursing a tattooed baby; / Mermaids milked the two-headed cow, the monkeys they all wore pants / The legless and the ossified man did a breakneck song and dance. . . .

Today, one song remains strongly associated with the neighborhood: "The Bowery" was one of several hit songs from Percy Gaunt and Charles Hoyt's phenomenally successful 1891 musical, *A Trip to Chinatown*. Hoyt, a prolific writer of plays and farces and a one-time Boston drama critic, initially set the story in San Francisco's Chinatown. Gaunt, the play's musical director, had previously worked for Harrigan & Hart. The play opened in the Madison Square Theatre on November 9, 1891, to mixed reviews. After a few shaky weeks, Hoyt asked actor Harry Conor ("who never failed to get a laugh") to "interpolate" (add) a humorous song about the nearby Bowery to give it more appeal to New York audiences. The song, a catchy waltz, saved the show, which went on to run

Dancing was always popular on the Bowery. Working-class dance halls lined the street, and for a modest entrance fee enthusiastic patrons participated in rowdy "receptions" and "balls" that often lasted all night. Fights were not uncommon, and the participants' trend-setting fashions were frequently mentioned. Joseph P. Galton's song, "The Bowery Ball" (1895), describes an event that was probably a bit more risqué than most:

There's going to be a reception tonight at Michael Casey's hall / For months it has been all the talk of the East Side. / The annual Bowery Ball . . . Oh, all the fellows and girls in the gang, / For "certain, sure" will be there. / And all the big swells of Fifth Avenue, at our costumes and style will stare. . . .

The lyrics go on to inform listeners that the music will be "up to date," and at 9:30, as a special treat, there will be a "stage tableau" or

for 650 performances—a phenomenal run in that era. Although it was a sensational hit, the song was later blamed for single-handedly ruining the reputation (and real estate values) of the entire neighborhood. The song tells the story of a country rube who comes to New York one night and goes "out for a quiet walk." Despite being warned by folks who are *"on to"* the city to *"take Broadway,"* he strolls down *"the Bow'ry ablaze with lights,"* where he is taken advantage of by dishonest merchants, belittled by local wiseguys, and ultimately mugged. Most New Yorkers can still recall its catchy chorus:

The Bow'ry, the Bow'ry! / They say such things, and they do strange things on the Bow'ry! / The Bow'ry! I'll never go there anymore!

In between the choruses, the rube gets himself into a number of scrapes:

Verse 2: I had walk'd but a block or two, / When up came a fellow and me he knew; / Then a policeman came walking by, / Chased him away and I asked him why? / "Wasn't he pulling your leg?" said he; / Said I "he never laid hands on me!" / "Get off the Bow'ry, you Yap!" said he, / I'll never go there anymore!

Verse 3: I went into an auction store, / I never saw any thieves before; / First he sold me a pair of socks, / Then said he, "how much for the box?" / Someone said "two dollars," I said "three!" / He emptied the box and he gave it to me. / "I sold you the box, not the socks," said he, / I'll never go there any more!

Verse 6: I struck a place that they called a "dive," / I was in luck to get out alive; / When the policeman heard my woes, / Saw my black eyes and my batter'd nose, / "You've been held up!" said the copper, "fly!" / "No, sir, but I've been knocked down!" said I; / Then he laughed, tho' I couldn't see why! / I'll never go there any more!

Greenwich Village and Washington Square

If bohemians, hippies, and pursuers of alternative lifestyles could ever agree on a national capital, it might well be Greenwich Village. Since the first decade of the twentieth century, the Village has served as a sort of an urban safety valve for non-conformists, iconoclasts, revolutionaries, and the doggedly eccentric. It didn't start that way: located two miles north of the Battery, the Village was once a favorite hunting and fishing spot for the Carnarsee Indians who came over from Brooklyn for occasional visits. In the 1630s, Dutch settlers cleared land around Minetta Brook (from *manetta*, Indian for "devil water") and established farms and a tobacco plantation. Soon, a rural farming hamlet developed, and for the next 150 years or so, Greenwich Village was largely self-contained and removed from the bustle of lower Manhattan.

In the early nineteenth century, several severe outbreaks of cholera and yellow fever in downtown New York encouraged those who could flee (the wealthy) to relocate temporarily to the healthier climes of the Village. After the 1821 epidemic, many of these refugees settled permanently in the neighborhood, building fashionable houses and business offices along the narrow, winding village streets. Eventually, as fashionable New York moved relentlessly uptown, the picturesque neighborhood became home to an increasing number of impoverished Irish, German, and Italian immigrants. By 1900 Greenwich Village had become an ethnically diverse slum. Although a backwater, its low rents and quirky charm began to attract "bohemians"— painters, actors, writers, and musicians who laid the groundwork for generations of talented but starving Greenwich Village artists. From the Beats in the 1950s, to folk musicians in the 1960s, punk rockers in the 1970s, and gay rights activists in the 1980s, the Village has seen it all. Today, exorbitant rents make the West Village too expensive for struggling artists, but the East Village continues to attract pre-celebrities seeking their big break. Both East and West Villagers retain rather relaxed, laissez-faire attitudes about lifestyles and behaviors that would draw considerable attention elsewhere. Of course, these things have been duly noted by songwriters.

Just after World War I, a host of songs celebrating the Village's bohemian lifestyle appeared. Among these were "Down in the Village" (1928), "My Greenwich Village Sue" (1920), "Down Greenwich Village Way" (1922), and "Come to Bohemia" from the 1920 show *Greenwich Village Follies*, which recommends running away to the Village as an antidote to quotidian ennui:

If you find nothing in life / But disappointment and strife; / If ev'ry new day is just one more blue day, / The same old sensations / With no variations: / Why don't think the world is all wrong, / But come where you really belong. / Care will forsake you / If you let me take you / Where life is just laughter and song . . .

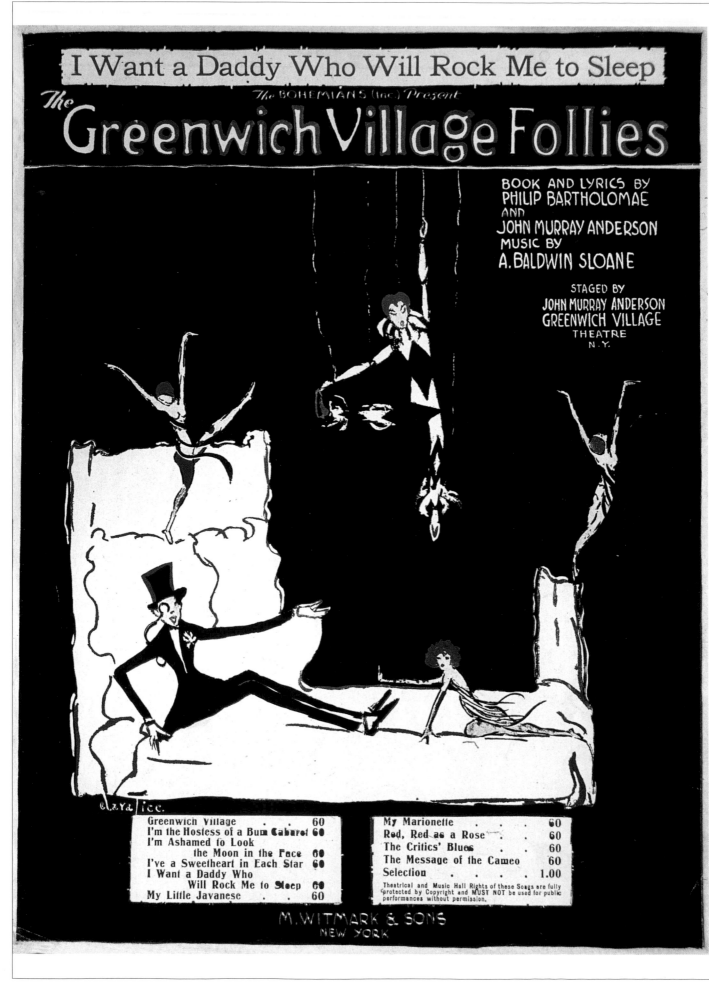

Song collector Frank Shay in his 1928 book *More Pious Friends & Drunken Companions* included the folk song "Down in Dear Old Greenwich Village," which, he claimed, was widely sung in the neighborhood during the 1920s. He collected this version from Bobby Edwards, "the last of the troubadours," who accompanied himself on a homemade cigar box ukulele and sang regularly at Polly's, that era's bohemian dive of choice. With a few minor changes, "Down in Dear Old Greenwich Village" could describe today's neighborhood equally well:

> *Way down South in Greenwich Village, / That's the field for culture's tillage. / There they have artistic ravings, / Tea, and other awful cravings: / But the inspiration stops and they start silly little shops. / You'll find them anywhere 'round Washington Square.*

> *Down in dear old Greenwich Village, / There they wear no fancy frillage. / And the ladies of the Square / All wear smocks and bob their hair. / There they do not think it shocking to wear stencils for a stocking, / That saves the laundry bills in Washington Square.*

> *Way down South in Greenwich Village, / There the spinsters come for thrillage, / There they talk of "sex relations," / With the sordid Slavic nations. / 'Neath the guise of feminism, Dodging social ostracism, / They get away with much in Washington Square.*

> *Way down South in Greenwich Village, / There they all consume distillage, / Where the fashion illustrators / Flirt with interior decorators. / There the cheap Bohemian fakirs, And the boys from Wanamaker's / Gather "atmosphere" in Washington Square.*

> *Way down South in Greenwich Village, / Where the brains amount to nillage, / Where the girls are unconventional, / And the men are unintentional, / There the girls are self-supporting, There the ladies do the courting. / The ladies buy the "eats" in Washington Square.*

> *Way down South in Greenwich Village / Comes a bunch of Uptown Swillage, / Folks from Lenox Subway stations / Come with lurid expectations. / There the Village informalities are construed as abnormalities / By the boobs that visit Sheridan Square.*

Other musical references to the Village are found in song titles such as Melvin Van Peebles' "Tenth and Greenwich" (1971) and Bob Dylan's "Positively 4th Street" (1965). Another good description is found in Betty Comden and Adolph Green's lyrics for Leonard Bernstein's 1953 musical *Wonderful Town*, which was based on Ruth McKenney's book, *My Sister Rose*. Set in 1935, the musical's plot revolves around the adventures of two sisters from Ohio who come to New York looking for fame, success, and romance. They wind up living in a Greenwich Village basement apartment surrounded by colorful local characters. To set the stage, the musical opens with a tour guide's musical description of one of the Village's main arteries, "Christopher Street," as quaint, sweet, pleasant, and peaceful. But perhaps P.G. Wodehouse and Jerome Kern defined it best in their song "Greenwich Village" (1918) from the show *Oh, Lady! Lady!*:

> *Oh, down in Greenwich Village, there's something 'twould appear demoralizing in the atmosphere. / Quite ordinary people who come and live down here, / Get changed to perfect nuts within a year! / They learn to eat spaghetti (That's hard enough you know!) / They leave off socks and wear greek smocks and study Guido Bruno. / / Chorus: For there's something in the air of little Greenwich Village / That makes a fellow feel he doesn't care! . . . When he hits our Latin Quarter, / He'll do what he didn't oughter / It's a sort of . . . kind of something in the air!*

Washington Square

If the Village has a heart, it is Washington Square Park, one of New York City's great public spaces. Originally a potter's field (some claim one hundred thousand people are buried there), the Square was also used for public hangings. In 1827, the city turned it into a military parade ground, but this didn't work too well—the heavy artillery kept collapsing into the graves below—so instead, the city laid out a spacious park, ready-made for strollers and those who liked to "hang out." The well-known triumphal arch, designed by Stanford White after the Arc de Triomphe in Paris, was erected in 1892. Like the Village itself, Washington Square soon became synonymous with alternative lifestyles.

In 1920, at the dawn of the nightclub era, nothing was more up-to-date or sophisticated than attending a late-night revue at one of New York's roof-top supper clubs, such as the one "atop the New Amsterdam Theatre" on 42nd Street. Theatrical producer Florenz ("Flo") Ziegfeld, in his risqué *Ziegfeld Midnight Frolic*, had the famed comedian and singer Fanny Brice introduce a song about an artist's model from the Village. Interestingly, the original sheet music

Fanny Brice posing as "Rose of Washington Square" on the 1920 sheet music cover.

includes both an inoffensive "ballad version" ("A garden that never knew sunshine / Once sheltered a beautiful rose . . ."), and a "comedy version" with lyrics that would make even a nude Village model blush:

> I'm Rosie, the queen of the models / I used to live up in the Bronx / But I wander'd from there down to Washington Square / And Bohemian Honky Tonks. / One day I met Harrison Fisher / Said he, "You're like roses—the stems / I want you to pose for a picture / On the cover of Jim Jam Jems." / And that's how I got my start / Now my life is devoted to art, I hey call me:

> Chorus: Rose of Washington Square / I'm withering there / In basement air I'm fading, / Pose, with plain or fancy clothes, / They say my Roman nose / It seems to please artistic people, / Beaux, I've plenty of those / With second hand clothes, And nice long hair. / I've got those Broadway vampires lashed to the mast, / I've got no future but Oh! what a past / I'm Rose, of Washington Square.

> I'm terrible good as a model / The artists are stuck on my charms / Once a feller said he would paint Venus from me / Only Venus ain't got no arms. / Rube Goldberg my figure admires / He dresses me up in a veil / And uses my shape for the pictures / That he draws in the Ev'ning Mail. / He promises some time when he's free / That he'll model a statue of me, They call me. . . .[2]

FANNY BRICE (1891–1951)

Born in New York in 1891, Fanny Brice was one of the first female comedians from the Yiddish theatre to make a successful transition to Broadway and the commercial mainstream. Singing songs such as "Rose of Washington Square," "Second Hand Rose (from Second Avenue)," and "My Man," Brice became a staple of Florenz Ziegfeld's *Follies* between 1910 and 1923, and a star of numerous Broadway musicals during the 1930s and 1940s. She later gained national renown playing Baby Snooks on the radio. The 1964 musical *Funny Girl* is based on her life.

Autographed photo of a young Fanny Brice.

In the 1950s and 1960s, Washington Square served as the heart of the folk music revival. In 1963, a New York–based, Dixieland-inspired band had an unexpected hit with an instrumental rendition of Bob Goldstein's song "Washington Square." Although many New Yorkers remember the quirky modal tune, few are aware that it also had lyrics inviting folk musicians from across the country to come to Washington Square:

> From Cape Cod light to the Mississip' to San Francisco Bay, / They're talkin' 'bout this famous place down Greenwich Village way. / They hootenanny all the time with folks from everywhere, / Come Sunday mornin' rain or shine, right in Washington Square.

Bob Dylan in "Talkin' New York Blues" (1961) had a less-romanticized view of the Village's folk music scene. In it, he tells of riding a rickety subway to the Village and auditioning for a disinterested coffee house owner, only to be told that he sounds too much like a hillbilly and the club is really only looking to book folk singers.

On the Avenues: Fifth, Park, and Madison

Early on, Manhattanites decided it was preferable to live as far as possible from the noise, dirt, and confusion of the waterfront docks. Since docks lined both sides of the narrow island, New York's better, more prestigious neighborhoods developed along the avenues that ran along the central spine of Manhattan. Fifth Avenue, which runs up the center of Manhattan Island and serves as the dividing line between the East Side and the West Side, Madison Avenue, and, later, Park Avenue were where those who could afford to choose, chose to live.

In the nineteenth century, some of New York's finest mansions were built along Fifth Avenue. It is still one of New York's most fashionable addresses, especially the residential stretch facing Central Park from 59th to 110th Street, even though today many of the free-standing mansions have been replaced by large, luxury apartment buildings. Among composers, Fifth Avenue became a shorthand way of connoting class. Early examples include the "Fifth Avenue Polka" (1852), "A Fifth Avenue Belle" (1895), and female impersonator William H. Lingard's 1868 song "Fifth Avenue."

Recorded by THE VILLAGE STOMPERS on Epic Records

WASHINGTON SQUARE

Words & Music by BOB GOLDSTEIN

SHOWBOAT SONGS, INC.

Sole Selling Agents:
Cimino Publications Incorporated
479 Maple Avenue • Westbury, L. I., N. Y.

Stanford White's arch forms the gateway to Washington Square on the cover of Bob Goldstein's 1963 hit.

Among later efforts we find "The Lady From Fifth Avenue" (1937), "Teatime on Fifth Avenue" from the 1940 revue *Two Weeks, With Pay*, and the 1945 hit song "Fifth Avenue," by Saul Chaplin and Eddie DeLange about the street that *"sets the beat"* of New York. These were balanced with songs such as "The Fugitive From Fifth Avenue" (1949) from the revue *Along Fifth Avenue*, and "Lament on Fifth Avenue" (1957) from another revue, *Shoestring '57*.

In an earlier age, Madison Avenue also carried connotations of upper-class refinement. The area near Madison Square was particularly fashionable, and it was here that songwriter Will S. Hay set his 1868 comic song "Mistress Jinks of Madison Square," a parody of the enormously popular British hit "Captain Jinks of the Horse Marines":

I'm Mistress Jinks of Madison Square, / I wear fine clothes and I puff my hair. / And how the gentlemen at me stare / While my husband's in the army! / Where e're I go I'm talked about, / I'm talked about, / I'm talked about. / I wear the latest fashions out / While the Captain's in the army.

A year after "Mistress Jinks," the songwriting team of George Cooper and Sidney Franks wrote of another upper-class twit named Fred Fitz Noodle who was afraid to venture into the less-refined adjoining neighborhoods in "I Never Go East of Madison Square" (1869):

I'm a "gentleman's son," / And the barber he curls my hair! / I was always taught to shun things "low," / And dress "just so," from top to toe; / And

View of Park Avenue in the 1920s.

View of Park Avenue, Taken from N. Y. Central Bldg., New York City.

though I have often been asked to go, / I have never left Madison Square! . . . // Chorus: I never go east of Madison Square! / Of Madison Square! / Of Madison Square! / You see I was born in Fifth Av'nue-ar, / And I never go east of Madison Square! / Spoken: Just fancy this elegant shape of mine being seen over in the Bowery! Why the very thought of it shocks my nerves.

The Murray Hill neighborhood, located just north of Madison Square and built on what was once the Murray family's farm, received several mid-nineteenth-century musical tributes such as the "Murray Hill Waltz" (1868), the "Murray Hill Gallop: Dedicated to Officers & Men of the Murray Hill Sociable" (1866), "The Belle of Murray Hill" (1899)—"*She's causing much talk in Greater New York*," and the Harrigan and Braham song, "She Lives on Murray Hill" (1882). In 1925, the young songwriting team of Rodgers and Hart wrote *Dearest Enemy*, a musical based on a well-known local legend about Mrs. Robert Murray of Murray Hill. According to the story, Mrs. Murray was a celebrated hostess and enthusiastic patriot, despite being married to a wealthy and powerful loyalist. At the beginning of the Revolution, the American army under Washington's command was soundly beaten at the Battle of Long Island (1775), which took place in what is now Brooklyn's Prospect Park. The remnants of the Continental Army retreated northward through Manhattan, only minutes in front of the British—who were not in a good mood. Mrs. Murray morosely watched the dispirited Americans cross her estate, but when General Gage and the British high command marched by a few minutes later, she ran out of her house and insisted that they stop for tea. Even though her husband was away, she said, it was her duty to entertain such distinguished visitors. A beautiful woman who would not take no for an answer was too much temptation; the hungry and tired British officers were enticed inside. While His Majesty's troops waited outside, Mrs. Murray and her household proceeded to ply the British officers with food and a great deal of drink, and amuse them with songs, stories, and gossip. The officers were so charmed that they lingered for the rest of the afternoon—allowing General Washington and the remnants of the Continental Army to slip away across the Hudson River to Valley Forge. Thus, locals believe Mrs. Murray can be credited with single-handedly saving the Revolution.

Today's Park Avenue actually came into existence only in the early twentieth century, when the open railroad tracks that ran north from Grand Central Station along industrial Fourth Avenue were sunk below ground and replaced with an attractive strip of greenery. No longer marred by the noise and smoke of the trains and optimistically renamed "Park Avenue," the street experienced a real estate boom as developers rushed to construct elegant apartment houses. In the 1920s and 1930s, Park Avenue became synonymous with elegant urban living. A fad for putting the most expensive apartments on the tops of the new buildings introduced New Yorkers to "penthouses"—the last word in urban sophistication. Songwriters have not overwhelmed Park Avenue with their attentions, but there have been a few memorable attempts: for example, there was "Park Avenue Strut" (1929) from the musical *Pleasure Bound*; "Park Avenue Fantasy" (1935); "Park Avenue's Going to Town" (1936); Jerry Herman's 1958 class-conscious "Confession to a Park Avenue Mother (I'm in Love with a West Side Girl)"; Harold Rome's "Yuletide, Park Avenue" (1946) from *Call Me Mister*; and "Movie House in Manhattan" from the 1947 revue *Make Mine Manhattan*, which describes a Park Avenue cinema so exclusive that even Minnie Mouse's spouse is known as "Michael Mouse."

But leave it to the ever-creative Irving Berlin, writing at the height of the Depression, to call attention to the then-popular pastime of "slumming" by reversing the usual order of things. Instead of the wealthy visiting less fortunate neighborhoods, in "Slumming on Park Avenue," written for the 1937 film *On the Avenue*, Park Avenue residents are themselves being "slummed":

Put on your slumming clothes and get your car / Let's go sightseeing where the high-toned people are. / Come on, there's lots of fun in store for you, / See how the other half lives on Park Avenue. // Chorus: Let's go slumming, take me slumming / Let's go slumming on Park Avenue.

Midtown

Midtown, the central business district of Manhattan between 34th and 59th Streets, is home to many of New York's best-known attractions. The Empire State Building, the Chrysler Building, Grand Central Station, Saint Patrick's Cathedral, and the New York Public Library all lie within its boundaries. Among the most famous of midtown sites is Rockefeller

Center, a giant complex of office buildings, restaurants, shops, studios, and one legendary theatre. Conceived and managed by Samuel "Roxy" Rothafel (who previously had been responsible for the famous Roxy Theatre on 50th Street), Radio City Music Hall opened December 27, 1932. The opulent 5,874-seat art deco theatre dazzled the Depression-weary nation and it immediately became a popular tourist destination. Rodgers and Hart decided its over-the-top grandeur needed a song. In 1938, they interpolated "At the Roxy Music Hall" into the staged version of the musical *I Married an Angel*. Even though the song was quite long and had little to do with the plot—which took place in Budapest!—it was too good not to be a hit. It began by exhorting listeners: *"You've got to come to New York. / It would be such a pity / For anyone to go through life / Without seeing Roxy City!"*

Hart then lists some of the high points "At the Roxy Music Hall":

Where an usher puts his heart into what he ushes, / Where a fountain changes color when it gushes, / Where the seats caress your carcass with their plushes, / At the Roxy Music Hall. / Hold my hand. / Don't be frightened when you hear the band: / They come up like Ali Baba from the cellar, / Through the courtesy of Mr. Rockefeller. / Then they play the overture from "William Tell"-er, / At the Roxy Music Hall.

Other treats in store for visitors include lights that change a million times a minute, a balcony so high that you get *"the fidgets,"* a Saint Bernard to find those who get lost going to balcony seats, a ladies' room bigger than a palace, free drinking cups, and a ballet so sweet with *"birds and roses"* that you *"break out in a rash before it closes, / At the Roxy Music Hall."*

During the 1940s and 1950s, 52nd Street, just north of Rockefeller Center, was home to such an extraordinary number of influential jazz clubs that it became known as Swing Street. Among the musical artifacts from this midtown neighborhood's brief tenure as a jazz capital are such well-known pieces as George Shearing's "Lullaby of Birdland" (1952)—named after Charlie Parker's famous jazz club, Birdland; and Thelonious Monk's "52nd Street Theme." (Years later, Billy Joel would evoke the memory of these years in his 1978 album *52nd Street*.) Cole Porter's song, "When Love Beckoned (In Fifty-Second Street)," from the 1939 musical *DuBarry Was a Lady*, describes how the heroine dreams of meeting her true love by a starlit stream and her surprise to discover him, instead, among the gin mills and jazz dives of 52nd Street.

The East and West Sides

Manhattan residents living north of 14th Street tend to divide themselves into two varieties: East Siders and West Siders. The two sides of Manhattan Island do, in fact, have a different ambiance; however, New Yorkers who insist that they are each inhabited by evolutionarily distinct species are perhaps guilty of exaggeration. Fortunately, both the Upper East and Upper West Side have inspired good songs, so it is not necessary to take sides. We begin with the East Side, which falls into two main sections, the Lower East Side, which runs from Corlear's Hook up to 14th Street, and the Upper East Side, which is located, roughly, between 57th and 96th Streets.

First settled by free black farmers in the seventeenth century, the Lower East Side began to be developed shortly after the Revolution as craftsmen, businessmen, and home owners flocked to the former farmlands just north of the expanding city. During New York's brief tenure as the nation's capital (1785–1790), President George Washington and his family lived in an elegant mansion on Cherry Street, which was only a short commute from the U.S. Capitol in the Old City Hall at Broad and Wall Streets.

Within a generation, industrial pollution, overcrowding, and the constant chaos created by the East River docks persuaded the more fashionable residents to move inland toward Broadway. As they left, the Lower East Side began its slide toward "slumdom." The city's first tenements were built near Corlear's Hook in 1833; and the intersection of Baxter, Worth, and Park Streets—later known as Five Points—became nationally infamous as a nest of urban vice and immorality. (Five Points attracted Victorian busybodies who liked nothing better than to go slumming and then write about how shocked they were by what they saw.)

During the nineteenth century, the Lower East Side was inundated by wave after wave of newly arrived immigrants—many of them literally just off the boats that docked at the edge of the neighborhood. Irish immigrants settled along "Cork Row" beginning in the 1820s, Germans established "Kleindeutschland" north of Houston Street in the 1840s, and from the 1880s to the 1920s, the neighborhood experienced an enormous influx of Italians, Eastern European Jews, Russians, Romanians, Hungarians, Ukrainians, Slovaks, Poles, and Greeks.

At one point the most densely populated place in North America, the Lower East Side was particularly noted for its enormous Jewish community. By 1920, four hundred thousand Eastern European Jews lived there.

"The Ghetto, New York" around Rivington Street, circa 1915.

5192 THE GHETTO, NEW YORK

Orchard Street, alive with pushcart vendors and poorly regulated sweatshops, served as the neighborhood's central commercial thoroughfare. Over on Second Avenue, dozens of Yiddish theatres flourished from the 1890s through the 1930s. An astounding number of American entertainers came from the Lower East Side, including such talents as Eddie Cantor, Ira and George Gershwin, Irving Berlin, Jimmy Durante, Al Jolson, and the Marx Brothers. Many of them came from Jewish backgrounds, but rather than heading for the Yiddish theatres on Second Avenue, they made their way to the vaudeville houses lining the nearby Bowery or headed west to the theatres springing up along Broadway. Lower East Side songs from this period include "Der Millionaire From Delancey Street" (1930), "I'm a Vamp From East Broadway" (1920), the German-language song "Pawn Broker von der East Side" (1894), and the parody "Down Where the East River Flows" (1930).

In recent years, Puerto Rican and Chinese immigrants and an increasing number of up-and-coming artists have settled on the Lower East Side. (The neighborhood's northern border acquired the nickname "Alphabet City" in the 1970s because it contains Avenues A, B, C, and D.) Although most immigrants left the Lower East Side for better neighborhoods, its dialect and attitudes, forged in poverty and immigrant pride, made an indelible mark on those who grew up there. In fact, much of what we today think of as stereotypical of New York was actually stereotypical of the Lower East Side. As Ed Gardenier and Gus Edwards explained in "Dear Old East Side" (1907):

Some people they view on Fifth Avenue / Its mansions big and grand, / Dudes and the belles and the swell hotels, / But I'll have you understand / They make no hit, gee!, I envy them nit! / I'll turn the whole bunch down. / Wherever I roam for my little home / On the East side of the town. // Chorus: Dear old East Side, dear old stand, / Hester, Chrystie, Houston, Grand and the Bowery; / Rachel, Rosie, Mamie, Josie. / They all live on the East Side, / That's the place for me.

A great Lower East Side song is Ira Gershwin's "I'm Something on Avenue A." Written to be sung by Bonnie, a tough neighborhood "goil" in the 1925 musical *Tell Me More*, the song was cut before the show's Broadway premiere, and unfortunately, George Gershwin's music has not survived. Nevertheless, Ira's brilliant lyrics, with their multicultural references, concerns

about crime and pregnancy, and deep-seated neighborhood loyalty, reflect a pride of place still found in many of New York's tougher neighborhoods:

There's a part of Manhattan / That's Jewish and Latin— / My neighborhood, Avenue A. / Where all Irish Roses have Abies,[3] / And our biggest product is babies. / Though gunmen may roam there— / I'm proud of my home there— / No matter what people may say. / If someone gets fresh from uptown, / This is how I call 'em down:

Refrain: I may be nothin' on Fift' Avenue, / But I'm somethin' on Avenue A. / Down there at least, I got my pals— / Way over East—where gals is gals. / There where a sweater's the fashion, / I am the queen of the May. / Though I'm not the berries / At Ciro's or Sherry's[4] / I'm somethin' on Avenue A.

A fashionably dressed East Side belle ready to go "spieling" in 1895.

RIGHT: Another song calling attention to New Yorkers' creative pronunciation of the name Myrtle.

BELOW: Theme song from 1939 film *East Side of Heaven.*

Some sections of Manhattan's East Side, especially those near Fifth Avenue, have always been fashionable, but before gentrification began in the 1950s and 1960s, much of the area between Third Avenue and the East River was fairly squalid. The area was primarily working class. Its residents, mostly recently arrived immigrants from Germany, Ireland, and Central Europe, were crowded into cheaply built walk-up tenements hastily constructed between the area's numerous factories, breweries, and slaughterhouses. Parts of the East Side were downright dangerous: the East 50s became infamous as "The Dead End" (because the streets "dead ended" on bluffs lining the East River). Sidney Kingsley's 1935 hit play about the area's street gangs, *Dead End,* inspired several popular Hollywood films starring the "Dead End Kids."

Songs written during the East Side's seedier past include several that emphasize the neighborhood's distinctive accent and irreverent attitude towards the outside world. Songwriters thought the pronunciation of "th" as "d" and the wholesale slaughtering of vowels were particularly amusing, so we have songs such as Ben Ryan's 1926 "Down on Thoity Thoid and Thoid":

Down on the East side, on the East side that's my home, sweet, home. / Some people think it's the home of black eyes. / Just because guys don't wear collars and ties. / That's all the bunk, they just say that in fun. / Real East side folks is the best what come. / They'd give you their shoit only they ain't got none / Down on Thoity Thoid and Thoid.

The very same corner received musical attention again in the 1946 novelty song, "Moitle From Toidy Toid and Toid" by Bobby Gregory—the same composer who was responsible for the memorably entitled "I've Been Out With the Glue Maker's Daughter":

I've got a goil on de East Side / Where goils are tough as can be. / She took a job as a bouncer. / And now she's bouncing me. / / Chorus: Who is de toughest goil in dis whole woild, / Moitle from Toidy Toid and Toid. / Who's got buck teeth that shine like a poil, / Moitle from Toidy Toid and Toid. / She wears a tight skoit right up to her knees, / Instead of poifume she wears Limboiger cheese. / Who leaves me limp when she gives me a squeeze? / Moitle from Toidy Toid and Toid.

Other songs painted a less raucous, if slightly romanticized, picture of life on the East Side. For example, there was the theme song from *East Side of Heaven,* a 1939 film staring Joan Blondell, Bing Crosby, and Baby Sandy:

*Chorus: I know an angel on the East Side of Heaven /
Who lives in a third story room. / We meet on a
rooftop and dream in the dark, / When the lights of
New York are in bloom. / All through the day-time,
it's the same old Manhattan, / But evening again sets
me free. / Then I turn off Broadway to the East Side
of Heaven / Where an angel waits for me.*

The distinctly local "Dear Old Yorkville
(You're for Us and We're for You)" with lyrics
by Steven L. Barmore and music by Hugh W.
Schubert was written in 1921 and *"Dedicated to
the Yorkville Chamber of Commerce."* It celebrates the
neighborhood around East 86th Street because,
as the lyrics explain, *"The Bowery has its ditty /
That you hear each place you go / But the strain of dear
old Yorkville is a song worthwhile to know."*

The Upper West Side

The Upper West Side is one of New York's most
beautiful neighborhoods. Situated between the
western boundary of Central Park and the
Hudson River, the neighborhood developed
rapidly in the 1910s and 1920s as new subway
lines made commuting to lower Manhattan
feasible. The most elegant apartments and
largest townhouses were built to the west of
Broadway, especially along Riverside Drive
and West End Avenue. These two north-south
avenues also inspired quite a few songs, such
as "On Riverside Drive" (1929) and "West End
Blues" (1936). Although Bernstein's musical
West Side Story was set on the Upper West Side
in slums near what is now Lincoln Center, its
lyrics contain few references to the surrounding
neighborhood. Two of the greatest songs about
the Upper West Side originated in musical
comedies. The first, "Way Out West (on West
End Avenue)" from Rodgers and Hart's 1937
show *Babes in Arms*, satirizes the widespread
popularity of cowboy songs during the 1930s:

*Git along, little taxi, you can keep the change. / I'm
riding home to my kitchen range / Way out west on
West End Avenue. / Oh, I love to listen to the wagon
wheels / That brings the milk that your neighbor
steals / Way out west on West End Avenue. / Keep
all your mountains / And your lone prairie so pretty, /
Give me the fountains / That go wrong at Rodeo
[sic] City. / I would trade your famous deer and
antelope / For one tall beer and a cantaloupe / Way
out west on West End Avenue / Yippee-aye-ay!*

*Git along, little elevator, climb once more / To my lone
shack on the fourteenth floor / Way out west on West
End Avenue. / When the sun's a-rising over Central
Park / I pull the blinds and it's nice and dark / Way
out west on West End Avenue. / [Indians] may battle /*

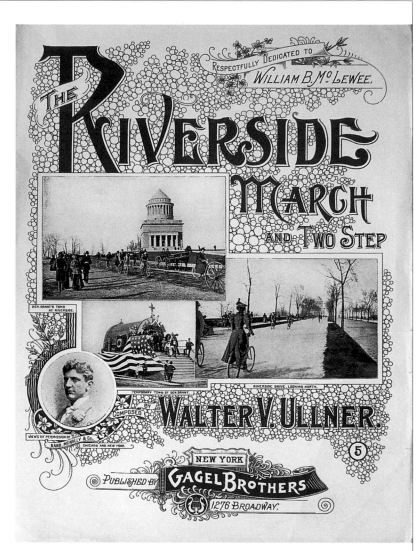

*With their tomahawks and axes. / I'll join the cattle /
In the big corral at Sak's. / Oh, the wild herd gathers
when the moon is full. / There's not much buffalo, but
lots of bull / Way out west on West End Avenue /
Yippee-aye-ay!*

And then there was "West End Avenue," from
Stephen Schwartz's 1974 musical *The Magic Show:*

*All of your life you woke up to the taxis and the
chimes, / To the bathroom with the roaches and the
breakfast with The Times. / And you subway to school
with kids whose folks all live in twenty blocks in a high-
rise rented carton or a co-op brownstone box. / With
double locks. / / Chorus: West End Avenue. / Babies
in carts and poodles barking, West End Avenue /
Planning a day around parking. / You tell yourself
"I will be free," / West End Avenue you won't get me.*

*All of your life you watch the shrinks and lawyers on
parade, / Watch the brokers in their worsted and the
ad men in their suede. / While upstairs a soprano tries
to sing the waltz from "La Bohème." / And you watch
them and you listen and you judge and you condemn. /
You're not like them.*

Cyclists, pedestrians,
and carriages on the
yet-to-be-developed
Riverside Drive and
visiting the newly
constructed Grant's
Tomb in 1897.

Chapter 4

BROADWAY RHYTHMS

hroughout the world, Broadway has become synonymous with one of New York's major industries, the theatre. New Yorkers have always loved the theatre. Perhaps because of their Dutch ancestry, New Yorkers never developed the moral reservations or enacted the legal restrictions that hampered the growth of the theatre elsewhere in America. During the 1750s, New York's first theatres were built around Beekman and John Streets. (Theatre Alley, between Beekman and Ann Streets leading to the once fashionable but long-forgotten Chapel or Beekman Street Theatre of 1761, still exists.) In the early 1830s, popular theatres catering to working-class audiences were built along Park Row and Chatham Square in present-day Chinatown. In addition to legitimate (dramatic) theatre, mid-nineteenth-century New Yorkers enjoyed minstrel shows, variety shows (a rough, ancestral version of vaudeville), saloon singers, concert halls, dime museums, panoramas, and circuses.

About the time of the Civil War, a row of minstrel halls sprang up along Broadway from Fellow's Opera House at 444 Broadway to the hall in Hope Chapel just south of Waverly Place. By the turn of the century, the area around Union Square had become the equivalent of today's Times Square. Scholars of the theatre consider *The Black Crook* to be the first real Broadway musical. It opened on September 12, 1866, in Niblo's Gardens at Broadway and Prince Street and ran an astounding 475 performances, earning its producers $1.1 million on an investment, some claim, of a mere $24,000. This fairly lame melodrama is best remembered for its then-shocking chorus line of voluptuous blonde beauties suggestively clad in flesh-colored tights, rather than for its convoluted plot or its mediocre music.[1]

As the city moved uptown, the Broadway theatre district followed. The two missing elements of the modern Broadway mystique were soon supplied: First, in 1880, as a demonstration of that new marvel, electricity, the city allowed the Brush Electric Light Company to illuminate Broadway between 14th and 34th Streets. Dazzled locals and tourists were soon referring to Broadway as "The Great White Way." Then, in 1904, when *The New York Times* moved into the Times Tower, its newly constructed uptown skyscraper on 42nd Street, its powerful owner, Adolph Ochs, insisted that the city change the name of the adjoining square from Long Acre to Times Square. And the rest, as they say, is history. . . .

There are many excellent studies of the art and artistry of Broadway musicals, but here we are interested in highlighting songs about the New York theatre—and particularly those songs about the actors and actresses who actually made Broadway run. There are literally hundreds of songs about the Broadway theatre. Most, but by no means all, come from Broadway shows, musical revues, or follies. For every glamorous, celebratory song about the Great White Way, there is another one about the loneliness, poverty, and disillusionment faced by theatre artists.

OPPOSITE: The cover of "Sing a Little Love Song" from *Carl Laemmle's Stupendous Talking and Singing Picture—Broadway* (1929) reflects a popular impression of the less-than-demure lives led by New York chorus girls.

Celebrating Broadway

As New York's theatrical party moved gradually uptown in the first decades of the twentieth century, songwriters were anxious to invite everyone to join them at Times Square. The title "All Aboard for Broadway," a George M. Cohan song from 1906, sums it up nicely. The theatre was an increasingly important part of the cityscape: after all, asked songwriters Mills, Sterling, and Costello in 1910, "What Would Become of New York Town If Broadway Wasn't There?":

> What would become of New York Town, if Broadway wasn't there? / Where would you go to spend your coin, / If somebody hid the Tenderloin? / Just turn out the lights over on the Great White Way / And the burgh is gone for fair. / You['d] all go to bed, New York town would be dead, / If old Broadway wasn't there.

Even worse, without the musicals, late-night revues, bright lights, and lobster palaces of Broadway, New York might resemble—excuse the expression—New Jersey. Or at least that was songwriters W.L. Beardsley and Ben Deely's contention in their slightly skewed 1915 recap of local history, "When the Sun Goes Down in Jersey Life Begins on Old Broadway":

> There's an island called Manhattan, sold to us by old Powhattan, / For four and twenty dollars, I am told; / History would never tell it, if the Indians didn't sell it, / 'Cause now the island's worth its weight in gold. / And the main street on this isle of wealth to-day / Is that lane of pleasure know as old Broadway—

> Chorus: When the Sun goes down in Jersey life begins on Old Broadway. / The lights are lit way up to Yonkers, turning night-time into day; / On the farm they chase the chickens,[2] they do the same on our White Way. / For when the Sun goes down in Jersey life begins on Old Broadway.

> Down among the high skyscrapers, where the wind cuts funny capers / The beginning of Broadway is to be found; / 'Twas a lane in eighteen-twenty, but old Gotham's grown a-plenty / Till now the street runs twenty miles up-town. / There's a Battery at one end, so they say, / Just to keep the lights a-burning on Broadway.

There is an endless list of songs with titles like "Bright Lights of Broadway" (1924), "Dear Old Broadway" (1907), "Meet Me in Times Square" (1940), and just plain "Broadway." There are "Broadway" entries from such songwriting teams as Herman Paley and Lew Brown (1913), G.E. Johnson and Hank Hawkins (1921), B.G. DeSylva and Ray Henderson (1927),

Longacre Square, New York City.

Con Conrad, Sidney Mitchell and Archie Gottler (1929), Woode, McRae, and Bird (1940), and Jule Styne and Stephen Sondheim (1959). In the wealth of celebratory songs, a few do stand out as classics. Some of the better-known ones were initially associated with films.

In 1929, Arthur Freed and Nacio Herb Brown had a major success—and won an Academy Award—with the score of *Broadway Melody*, a "Metro Goldwyn Mayer all talking picture with music." The title song, "Broadway Melody," was introduced by Charles King and later revived in the 1952 film musical *Singin' in the Rain*:

> Don't bring a frown to old Broadway. / You've got
> to clown on Broadway, / Your troubles there are out
> of style, / For Broadway always wears a smile, / A
> million lights they flicker there, / A million hearts beat
> quicker there. / No skies of grey on the great White
> Way, / That's the Broadway Melody.

"Lullaby of Broadway," by the successful Tin Pan Alley songwriting team of Al Dubin and Harry Warren, first appeared in the film, *Gold Diggers of 1935*, featuring Dick Powell and Gloria Stuart, and was later revived by the 1980 musical *42nd Street*. The lullaby's lyrics reflect a widespread stereotype about the loose morals and mercenary interests of chorus girls:

> Come on along and listen to the lullaby of
> Broadway. / The hip hooray and bally-hoo, the
> lullaby of Broadway. / The rumble of a subway
> train, the rattle of the taxis. / The daffydils who
> entertain at Angelo's and Maxie's. / When a
> Broadway baby says "Goodnight," it's early in
> the morning. / Manhattan babies don't sleep tight
> until the dawn. ~ ~ ~

> The band begins to go to town, and ev'ryone goes
> crazy. / You rock-a-bye your baby 'round 'til
> ev'rything gets hazy. / "Hush-a-bye, I'll buy you
> this and that," / You hear a daddy saying. / And
> baby goes home to her flat, to sleep all day. . . .

In addition to "Lullaby," Dubin and Warren wrote another classic New York song for the 1933 film *Forty-Second Street*, starring Dick Powell and Ruby Keeler. The spooky minor melody of "Forty-Second Street" is as distinctive as it is infectious; the lyrics give an overview of 1930s night life and invite listeners to:

> Come and meet those dancing feet, on the avenue I'm
> taking you to, Forty-Second Street. / Hear the beat
> of dancing feet—it's the song I love the melody of,
> Forty-Second Street.

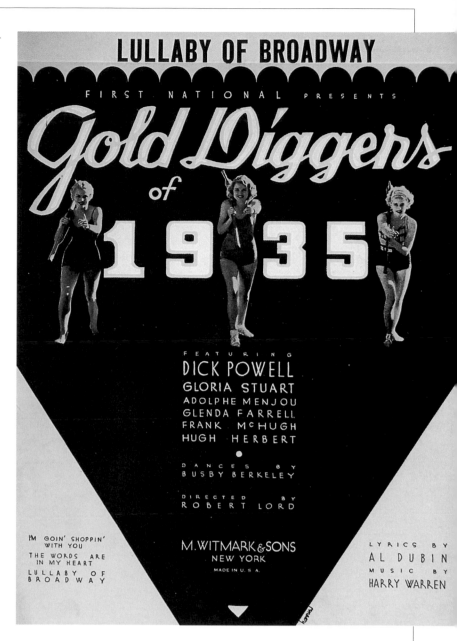

And, if you couldn't manage to "Hang Up Your Hat on Broadway" (1933) while you were alive, you would be comforted to know that "There's a Little Street in Heaven That They Call Broadway" (1903) and that "There's a Broadway up in Heaven" (1935).

There are more than a few nostalgic songs about Broadway, including "I Miss You Dear Old Broadway" (1917), "Broadway Gypsy" (1928), "Your Broadway and My Broadway" (1937), and "Broadway Reverie" from the 1931 *Ziegfeld Follies*, which *"regrets that grand old street is on the blink / It looks like Coney Island / It's not the place it used to be / For romance, life, and style."* Cole Porter expressed it best in "Please Don't Monkey with Broadway," which was introduced by Fred Astaire and George Murphy in the film, *Broadway Melody of 1940*. Father Knickerbocker's *"face is being lifted,"*

According to the cover illustration, these "Gold Diggers of 1935" came complete with pick axes!

wrote Porter, but before the City Fathers ruin Broadway, citizens must say *"Whoa!"* because, they can:

> *Glorify Sixth Avenue, / And put bathrooms in the zoo, / But please don't monkey with Broadway. / Put big floodlights in the Park, / And put Harlem in the dark, / But please don't monkey with Broadway. / Though it's tawdry and plain, / It's a lovely old lane, / Full of landmarks galore and memories gay, / So move Grant's tomb to Union Square / And put Brooklyn anywhere, / But please, please, / I beg on my knees, / Don't monkey with old Broadway.*

Life Upon the Wicked Stage

Generations of theatrically inclined young men and women have been attracted to the New York stage, but there is a disproportionate number of songs about the latter. Even before the days of *The Black Crook*, actresses had the reputation of being, well, more fun-loving than the girls back home. Their supposedly carefree and glamorous lifestyle was celebrated in songs such as "Broads of Broadway" (1926), "Broadway Baby Dolls" (1929), and "Milkmaids of Broadway" (1930). Ralph Freed and Burton Lane's "Babes on Broadway" (1941) spells out

The "Fine Art Edition" of "Broadway Rose" (1920).

the attractions of working on the Great White Way, even if only as a lowly chorus girl:

We're Babes on Broadway, / We're going places / When our new faces appear. / It's a wonderful street for babes like us to be on, / We're here because we want our names in neon. / We left Topeka, / We left Eureka, and came to seek a career. / Oh, we're milking applause instead of milking a cow,— / 'Cause we're Babes on Broadway now.

According to a widely held stereotype, appearing in a Broadway show offered young women an opportunity to meet and marry—or at least be supported by—wealthy, upper-class men. How often attractive young women were able to better their lot through a brief career on Broadway is debatable, but this idea did inspire a number of interesting songs. In 1920, for example, lyricist Ballard Macdonald (who also wrote "Rose of Washington Square") and composer Harry Carroll produced "I Was a Florodora Baby" for the Ziegfeld Follies:

Twenty years ago a musical show was a riot on Broadway. / Twenty years ago I joined that show and look at me today: / Six little happy show girls we, ev'ryone a Broadway pet. / Five of 'em married in society and I'm in the chorus yet.

Chorus: I was a Florodora Baby, with a chance to pick the best. / I had to fall in love with Abie, a dreamer with a fancy vest; / A girl's a fool to fool with millionaires, said he. / I should be his turtle dove; / All the other girls are living fancy. / My address is Seventeen Delancey; / Five darned fools got married for money / And I got married for love . . .

Chorus girls and leading ladies were often celebrated individually as well as en masse in songs such as "The Broadway Girl" (1904), "Broadway Belle" (1908), "Pearl of Broadway" (1927), "My Cherie of Broadway" (1930), "Broadway Lady" (1933), "The Lady From Broadway" (1935) —"She's got that look me over look," "Angel of the Great White Way" (1937), and "Dreamy Broadway Rose" (1948). When seen individually, these Broadway heroines have greater depth. For example, there was "Broadway Rose" (1920):

A pretty flower grows along old Broadway, / A-midst the throng, gay life and song / I found her drooping there, / My heart went out to her I met on Broadway / A faded little rose, / Beneath the white light's glare. // Chorus: Broadway Rose, there's a tear in your eye, / Broadway Rose, seems I oft' hear you sigh, / Though you wear fancy clothes and you show silken hose, / You're alone as they all pass you by. . . .

BLOSSOMS on BROADWAY
Words and Music by LEO ROBIN and RALPH RAINGER

EDWARD ARNOLD
Shirley Ross · John Trent
William Frawley · Rufe Davis
Joe Weber · Lew Fields

BLOSSOMS ON BROADWAY
A B.P. Schulberg Production

"BLOSSOMS ON BROADWAY"
"NO RING ON HER FINGER"
"YOU CAN'T TELL A MAN BY HIS HAT"

FAMOUS MUSIC CORPORATION, 1619 B'way, New York, N. Y.

Flowers (and true love) bloom amidst the neon in Times Square.

True, it was sometimes possible to find love on the Great White Way. According to the 1937 Robin and Rainger love song "Blossoms on Broadway": *"There are blossoms on Broadway when I'm walking with you, / Blossoms where trees never grew. / I forget the crowd and the loud rumble of cars / And all the bright lights turn into stars. . . ."*

But for most actresses, daily life was probably best summed up by songs like Lorenz Hart's "Chorus Girl Blues" (1921) or the "Broadway Baby" from Stephen Sondheim's 1971 masterpiece *Follies* who is waiting for her big chance:

Gee,/ I'd like to be /On some marquee, / All twinkling lights. / A spark / To pierce the dark / From Batt'ry Park / To Washington Heights. // Someday, maybe, / All my dreams will be repaid. / Heck, I'd even play the maid / To be in a show.

Broadway men were not as well-represented in song as were Broadway women, despite songs like "Broadway Caballero" (1941), "Mr. Hamlet of Broadway" (1908), or George M. Cohan's 1909 hit "The Man Who Owns Broadway":

The man who broke the bank at Monte Carlo is a joke . . . But cast your optics on a man who's all the money, all the honey, / Pride of the town, / Talk of New York, / You'd swear I'd won the championship or found the great North Pole, / The streets are all blockaded every time I take a stroll; / The staring crowds amass / And murmer as I pass / / Chorus: He is the man who owns Broadway, / That's what the daily papers say, / The girls are turned away / At ev'ry matinee / They go to see the player, not the play, they say; / Kings on their thrones may envious be, / He's got the popularity. / If there's anything in New York that you want just say, / Drop a line or wire to the sole proprietor / The man who owns Broadway / They say he is the man who owns Broadway.

Ambition on Broadway

Most young actors come to New York unencumbered by self-doubt. This often doesn't last beyond the first few months of cattle call castings, dining in cheap coffee shops, and working menial jobs to pay the rent. Still, it's great while it lasts. Ambition on Broadway has been immortalized by songs such as "I'd Rather Be on Old Broadway With You" (1909), "I Want to Be a Sheik on the Desert of Old Broadway" (1921), "The Call of Broadway" (1927), Rodgers and Hart's "Howdy to Broadway" (1926), Vernon Duke and Ogden Nash's "Turn Me Loose in Broadway" (1952), and Kurt Weill, Elmer Rice, and Langston Hughes's "Wouldn't You Like to Be on Broadway?" from the 1947 musical *Street Scene*. Jimmy Durante captured this attitude in his 1936 hit, "I Can Do Without Broadway (But Can Broadway Do Without Me?)":

I know darn well I can do without Broadway, can Broadway do without me? / Herald Square, Times Square, Columbus Circle, Ninety-Sixth Street / Where can I be? / I must have passed my station! / When they found out that I passed my destination ev'ry-body said, "Let's have a celebration 'cause it's JIMMY, that well dressed man." / That's why I know darn well I can do without Broadway, can Broadway do without me?

As early as 1905, a Sterling and Von Tilzer song entitled "I'm the Only Star That Twinkles on Broadway" celebrated the triumph of chutzpa—("I'm a public benefactress, I'm a lady, and an actress")—over talent:

When I was an amateur in Kankakee, / All my friends they just went crazy over me, / When they saw me act, they always used to say, / Maybe you ought to be down on Broadway . . .

Once when I was playing Juliet, I hope to die, / All the audience began to weep and sigh, / Someone shouted this is more than I can stand, / Then another yelled "strike up the band"; / Bernhardt can not act a part the way I do, / That's what ev'rybody says that sees me too, / Allan Dale remarked that if I got what I deserved, / I'd be canned—in other words, preserved.

Broken Hearts on Broadway

Not everyone became a star, of course. Despite Andy Warhol's contention, many never achieved even fifteen minutes of fame. Some of the most poignant songs about New York are about sad, lonely, and disillusioned people who are not making it on Broadway. Over the years, songwriters have frequently used Broadway as a metaphor for not making it in the big city. In George Whiting and Harry Von Tilzer's 1913 song, "I'm a Little Bit Afraid of You, Broadway," a newly arrived

Ambition meets chutzpa in this 1905 song.

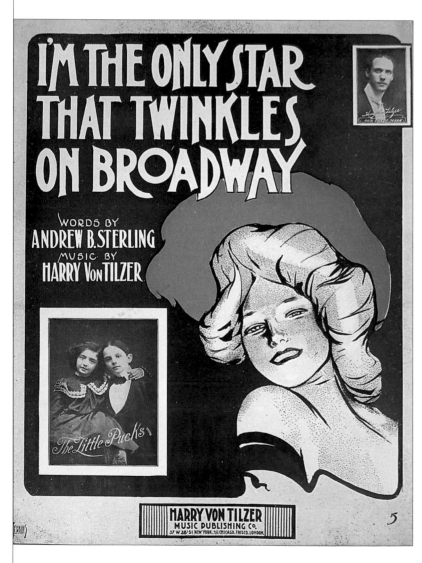

young innocent from the country expresses both her fear of the city and her fascination with Broadway and its latest decadent fad—daytime dancing at tango teas.

I haven't been in New York long, / Well, really not a year, / But I've learned an awful lot about you Broadway, / I didn't learn these things myself / Although I think them true, / For what I know is simply just from hearsay. . . / / Chorus: So I'm just a little bit afraid of you Broadway, / Your white lights are like goblins, when they gleam, / And your morning tango tea is too much for little me, / Though ev'rybody loves it so it seems. / How I long just once to turkey trot at Healey's, / Or, just a peek at Shanley's Cabaret, / But you're so big and I'm so small, / You'd swallow me right up, that's all, / So I'm just a little bit afraid of you, Broadway.

Like the previous example, Howard Johnson and Fred Fisher's 1915 song "There's a Broken Heart for Every Light on Broadway" uses Broadway as a metaphor for urban life in general:

There's a broken heart for ev'ry light on Broadway, / A million tears for every gleam, they say, / Those lights, above you—think nothing of you, / It's those who love you that have to pay. / There's a sorrow lurking in each gloomy shadow, / And sorrow comes to ev'ry-one some day, / 'Twill come to our brothers, But think of the mothers with broken hearts for every light on Broadway.

The most memorable thing about "There's No Room for a Dead One on the Great White Way," a 1905 effort by Joseph Herbert and Raymond Hubbell, is probably its title. When it was written, many of the theatres were still located near 23rd Street:

They sing of dear old Broadway as the only place to be. / Twenty-three, not for me; / They call it earthly paradise, a dream of ecstasy, / Can't agree, keep the key. / You mustn't think you own the town because you make a hit, / Today you are an idol and tomorrow you're a nit. / Fair weather friends will pass you by and give the icy mitt. / On that dear old street called Broadway.

Chorus: When your check comes back and it's marked N. G. [no good], / And you haven't got a nickel in your kick; / That's the time the tall grass whispers you'll come back to me. / For you can't do the Metropolis on tick. / When your friends have all deserted and you're up the spout, / And finances indicate a rainy day; / Just pack up your goods and chattels, make your mind up to get out. / For there's no room for a dead one on the Great White Way.

I'M A LITTLE BIT AFRAID OF YOU, BROADWAY

INTRODUCED BY Miss SADIE BURT OF WHITING AND BURT IN "The PASSING SHOW OF 1913" AT THE NEW YORK WINTER GARDEN

WORDS BY GEORGE WHITING MUSIC BY HARRY VON TILZER

HARRY VON TILZER MUSIC PUBLISHING Co.

It's hard to say if the heroine of this song is an actress or not, but the lyrics reflect the ambivalence of many who come to New York.

NOVELTY ON BROADWAY

Broadway has not been immune to novelty songs. Possibly under the misapprehension that songs about Broadway always did well, songwriters, in their rush to create the next major hit, have involved the street in such questionable musical efforts as "Broadway Caravan: An American Egyptian Fox Trot" (1923), "Broadway's Gone Hawaiian" (1937), "Broadway's Gone Hill-Billy" (1934), "There Wasn't Any Broadway on Robinson Crusoe's Isle" (1913), and "Broadway Bootlegger" (1929). Native Americans fared particularly poorly on Broadway given such songs as "Broadway Indians" (1923), "The Indians Along Broadway" (1905), and "Broadway Indian Chief" (1909). In the latter, an Indian chief tells off the Dutch with the deathless lines, *"You may be the great I am, but I don't give an Amsterdam / For I'm the greatest Indian chief that ever walked Broadway."*

AMERICAN SOCIETY OF COMPOSERS AND PUBLISHERS (ASCAP)

In 1914, Victor Herbert (1859–1924), the popular Irish-born composer and conductor, took his friend Giacomo Puccini to Shanley's, a lobster place in Times Square, for dinner. As they entered, the band was playing a song from Herbert's hit operetta *Sweethearts*. The Italian jokingly remarked that Herbert must be earning a fortune in royalties, and was astonished to learn that unlike Europe, American composers were not paid when their songs were performed by others. Herbert, apparently astonished to learn that bistros and restaurants throughout Europe *paid* an annual licensing fee, quickly organized a meeting of New York's leading composers and publishers. Nine of the thirty-five invited music industry bigwigs showed up for a planning meeting at Lüchow's and voted to found ASCAP. As a test case, it was decided that Herbert should sue Shanley's. The case dragged on for years, but in 1917, the Supreme Court finally decided it in Herbert's favor. Writing the unanimous decision, Justice Oliver Wendell Holmes noted that Shanley's "performances are not eleemosynary" but part of the ambience for which the public pays: "It is true that the music is not the whole subject, but neither is the food, which could probably be got cheaper elsewhere. The object is a repast in surroundings that to people having limited powers of conversation, or disliking the rival noise, give a luxurious pleasure not to be had from eating a silent meal."[3]

NAMING TIN PAN ALLEY

Several legends exist about how 28th Street acquired the name "Tin Pan Alley." Most revolve around a songwriter, gambler, and colorful man-about-town named Monroe Rosenfeld, whom even his publisher, the respected Edward B. Marks, once called a "melodic kleptomaniac." Rosenfeld, some say, coined the term himself when he remarked to fellow composer Harry Von Tilzer, who was playing a paper-muted piano: "That piano sounds like a tin pan. Matter of fact, this whole street sounds like a tin pan alley." Alternatively, others contend that Von Tilzer made the remark and Rosenfeld quoted him. The name stuck and years later, even after the music district followed the theatres north to Times Square, it was still called Tin Pan Alley. In 1931, many of the firms relocated to the newly opened Brill Building at 1619 Broadway at 49th Street. Before rock music irrevocably altered the dynamics of America's popular music industry in the 1950s, more than three hundred music publishers had offices in the Brill Building.

Perhaps the greatest disillusioned-with-Broadway song was the 1963 classic, "On Broadway." Written by Weil, Mann, Leiber, and Stoller, the song was a major hit for more than one artist. Despite the odds, and all the people who tell him that he won't make it, the narrator, an aspiring artist, remains hopeful:

> *They say the neon lights are bright on Broadway /*
> *They say there's always magic in the air. / But when*
> *you're walkin' down that street / And you ain't had*
> *enough to eat / The glitter rubs right off and you're*
> *nowhere. ~ ~ ~*
>
> *They say that I won't last too long on Broadway, /*
> *I'll catch a Greyhound bus for home, they all*
> *say. / But they're dead wrong, I know they are, /*
> *'Cause I can play this here guitar, / And I won't*
> *quit till I'm a star on Broadway . . .*

Tin Pan Alley

Intertwined with the rise of Broadway and the popularity of home music-making, was the birth of Tin Pan Alley. After the Civil War, music was being commodified in an entirely new way. New York's flourishing theatres, music publishers, and piano manufacturers were ravenous for fresh "product"—new tunes they could sell to a public hungry for novelty. Thousands of composers, lyricists, and performers flocked to the metropolis; by the 1890s, anyone wishing to succeed as a songwriter in America came to New York.

About 1900, many music-related firms began to rent office space on 28th Street between Fifth Avenue and Broadway, near what was then the heart of the theatre district. Partitioning off small, shabby offices in rows of once-dignified brownstones, abandoned as dwellings as the business district relentlessly crept northward, hundreds of composers, song pluggers, and small publishing firms labored to write, publish, or discover the next hit song. The financial rewards could be considerable, but on hot summer days, the noise coming from open windows along this row was deafening. To keep competitors from hearing (and appropriating) their next hit, some songwriters would place pieces of folded newspapers between the strings of their pianos to dampen the noise.

The heyday of Tin Pan Alley lasted from the late 1890s to the 1930s; its composers were responsible for an enormous number of classic

American songs. At its start, many of its composers and publishers were extremely young, most were from New York, and a high percentage of them came from recently arrived Eastern European Jewish families. At the turn of the century, hundreds of songwriters would go from one publishing firm to another trying to sell their latest sure-fire hit, or would gather at Everard's Café (24 West 28th Street) to discuss business deals over nickel beers. At night, to boost sheet music sales, publishers would personally take copies of their latest songs to cafes, vaudeville halls, music saloons, brothels, and other events (e.g., six-day bicycle races and balloon launches) trying to induce performers to introduce ("plug") them to the public. Publishers were not adverse to paying bribes, buying beers for entire pit orchestras, passing out chorus slips so the audience could sing along, or employing professional whistlers. Edward Marks, in his delightful memoir *They All Sang*, recounted how each night he and his partner, Joseph Stern, would visit more than a dozen establishments to promote their newest material, and how they would try just about anything to get a song before the public. For example, while Marks plugged his latest song to musicians and hall managers hoping to have it placed on the bill later that night, the professional whistler who accompanied him would circulate through the cafe's or saloon's audience distributing cheaply printed lyric sheets of the song to encourage sing-alongs.

While doing so, the whistler was trained to brush discreetly to the floor any plugs from competing music publishers that had the misfortune to arrive earlier in the evening.

The successful M. Witmark & Sons was typical of many firms in Tin Pan Alley. It was founded by five teenage brothers when the youngest, eleven-year-old Jay, won a toy printing press as a school prize the same day his fourteen-year-old brother got fired from a detested job. At first "Witmark Brothers, Printing" did odd printing jobs; but since Isidore, the oldest, liked to write songs, and Julius, the next oldest, was appearing around town as "The Wonderful Boy Soprano," they decided to concentrate on music. Their father, Marcus, agreed to sign the firm's incorporation papers, since the boys were not yet old enough to sign legal documents. Within a few years, M. Witmark & Sons' stable of composers included such front-runners as George M. Cohan, Gus Edwards, and Victor Herbert. Father Marcus took to appearing at theatres armed with a heavy cane, which he pounded noisily on the floor after the performance of a Witmark-published song. They soon leased an entire brownstone on 28th Street and inscribed the family motto, "Success Is Work," over the door. In the decades that followed, the five boys, who used to hold business conferences while shaving in the family bathroom, went on to become major players in the American entertainment industry.

IRVING BERLIN (1888–1989)

Irving Berlin was in many ways the quintessential Tin Pan Alley songwriter. The youngest of eight children, he was born Israel Baline to a Jewish family in Mohiler, Russia, in 1888. Fleeing a pogrom, the Balines immigrated to New York's Lower East Side in the 1893, but the family's poverty and his father's death in 1896 made the streets more attractive than his family's crowded tenement. Barely eleven, Berlin ran away from home and began his career in music by leading Blind Sol, a singing beggar, through the neighborhood. Before long, he found work as a singing waiter at Pelham's Café in Chinatown and then as a song plugger at Tony Pastor's Music Hall in Union Square. In 1907 his first song, "Marie From Sunny Italy," was published.

Beginning as a lyricist, Berlin was soon writing both the words and music to his songs. His first major hit, "Alexander's Ragtime Band," appeared in 1911. Berlin wrote over two thousand songs, including "White Christmas" and "God Bless America," numerous musicals, such as *Face the Music* (1932), *As Thousands Cheer* (1933), *Miss Liberty* (1949), and *Annie Get Your Gun* (1946), as well as scores for sixteen films. Berlin never learned to read or write music—he had a special piano built to help him sound out melodies in his favorite key, F-sharp—but as Jerome Kern once noted, "Berlin has no place in American music, he *is* American music." Berlin's fascination with the rhythms of urban life can be heard in the scores of songs he wrote about New York throughout the course of his long career.

Chapter 5

"HARLEM ON MY MIND"

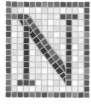ew York has always had a large black population. By the 1740s, twenty percent of the city's eleven thousand residents were black. Most early black New Yorkers had to endure the degradation of slavery, and although under Dutch laws enslaved Africans had more opportunities

OPPOSITE: Celebrating urban night life "Underneath the Harlem Moon" (1932).

than they had after the British took over, early New York blacks lived in a much more restricted world than their white neighbors. At the time of the Revolution, Kings County (Brooklyn), then mostly farmland, had the fifth largest slave population in the United States, and New York was second only to Charleston as a center of urban slavery. Although not officially a slave state, the New York State legislature did not get around to abolishing slavery until 1827, and non-residents were permitted to bring black slaves into New York as late as 1841. Despite legal inequities and periodic anti-black riots (most notably in 1712, 1741, and the notorious Draft Riots of 1863), New York's black community opened businesses, founded newspapers, organized churches, operated mutual aid societies, and generally joined other New Yorkers in building their city.

Manhattan's first black neighborhood developed in the 1640s, not far from present-day Astor Place, and as the city moved northward, so did its African Americans: to the Sixth Ward near Five Points in the 1820s, to Greenwich Village and the Tenderloin in the mid-nineteenth century, to South Fifth Avenue in the 1870s, and to San Juan Hill (just south of present-day Lincoln Center), about 1900. Significant black communities also flourished in areas such as Brooklyn's

Weeksville and Sandy Ground on Staten Island. Following the Civil War, New York experienced a large influx of black migrants from the South, as well as a smaller but influential influx of black immigrants from the Caribbean and Latin America.

Even before the Harlem Renaissance, New York's black neighborhoods had made their way into songs. Unfortunately, many of these were of the "coon song" variety, which made heavy use of dialect and unflattering racial stereotypes. Some, such as J.W. Wheeler's "The Colored Four Hundred" (1890), made fun of the idea of a social elite among blacks. The Harrigan & Hart shows of the 1870s and 1880s featured "The Skidmore Guard," a black militia company, as the long-suffering rivals of the Irish-American "Mulligan Guard." Despite reiterating many of his era's racial prejudices, Edward Harrigan's lyrics often reflected a fascination and fondness for New York's black community. For example, in "South Fifth Avenue" from the 1881 show *Mulligan's Silver Wedding,* he highlighted upper-class black society:

> *We are de leaders of the fashion, prime colored quality. / We're recognized where'er we go as elite society; / At all de grand receptions, it's come along, oh do / And ornament the mansions on South Fifth Avenue . . .*

In "The Sunny Side of Thompson Street," from the 1893 musical *The Woolen Stocking*, Harrigan's lyrics provide an interesting snapshot of who actually lived in the Village's black neighborhood:

> *If you want to find de people of de colored population, / Indigo, de Japanese, de black and de brown, / De greatest place in all de State, oh yes, in all de nation, / [Is] de sunny side of Thompson Street away down town.*

About 1900, Manhattan's northern expansion finally ran out of steam. Developers had built thousands of new apartments in the northern hamlet of Harlem, betting that the new subway lines and the spacious luxury apartments would attract middle- and upper-class residents. Then, in 1904–1905, the real estate market collapsed. Harlem landlords reduced rents, but middle-class white New Yorkers were still reluctant to move so far uptown. Anxious to fill their empty buildings, the landlords began to rent to blacks. Desperate for better housing, black New Yorkers flocked to Harlem rental agencies, despite the fact that they were often offered leases only at vastly inflated rates. By 1914, fifty thousand black New Yorkers lived in Harlem and black churches and businesses from downtown began to relocate to the neighborhood. In the 1920s, a critical mass of artists, writers, philosophers, and musicians had settled in the uptown neighborhood, and their presence generated enough artistic and intellectual heat to ignite the Harlem Renaissance. Langston Hughes, Countee Cullen, Zora Neale Hurston, Romare Bearden, Louis Armstrong, Duke Ellington, Coleman Hawkins, Bessie Smith, Bill "Bojangles" Robinson, and Ethel Waters were just a few of the major talents involved.

As the black neighborhood developed in Harlem, so too did an active entertainment industry. The opening of clubs such as the Cotton Club, Connie's Inn, the Savoy Ballroom, Small's Paradise, and the Apollo Theatre coincided with the blossoming of ragtime, blues, and jazz (and their accompanying dances) as major American art forms. White New Yorkers, suddenly aware of the richness of black culture, began to visit Harlem clubs in large numbers. True, many whites visited Harlem on slumming expeditions; and, it should be noted, although Harlem nightclubs featured black talent, some of them did not permit black patrons. Nevertheless, Harlem offered a place where New Yorkers, both white and black, could hear a talented array of artists. And, as always, the changing cultural landscape inspired numerous songs.

Favorite subjects for songs about Harlem included both African exoticism and the compelling new syncopated ("ragged" or "ragtime") rhythm. "Drop Me Off in Harlem" asked Nick Kenny and Duke Ellington in their 1933 hit, and many songwriters seconded their request. To get there, according to Billy Strayhorn, all you had to do was "Take the 'A' Train":

> *If you want to go to Harlem, 'way up to Sugar Hill, / Where those dancing feet you read of are never, never, still, Then / / Chorus: You must Take the "A" Train / To go to Sugar Hill 'way up in Harlem. / If you miss the "A" train, / You'll find you've missed the quickest way to Harlem. . . .*

The lyrics of many Harlem songs reflect the changing social and political landscape of the 1930s. On the one hand, there was nostalgia for the Old South and the migrant's longing for home; on the other, the rejection of those values and a celebration of urban opportunities. Mack Gordon and Harry Revel's 1932 hit "Underneath the Harlem Moon" is a good example of a song with a mixed message: like earlier "coon" songs, it makes patronizing references to Southern cooking, mammy, and cotton picking, but the lyrics also acknowledge that *"up on Lenox Avenue"* Harlemites lived in penthouses rather than cabins.

Songwriters, both black and white, rushed to compose celebratory songs about Harlem: Cole Porter's "Happy Heaven of Harlem" (1929), "Harlem Lullaby" (1932), Jerome Kern and Oscar Hammerstein's "High Up in Harlem" (1939), "I'm Slapping Seventh Avenue With the Soles of My Shoes" (1938), "I Dreamt I Dwelt in Harlem" (1941), Hoagy Carmichael's "Old Man Harlem" (1933), Earle Hagen's lovely "Harlem Nocturne" (1940), and the interesting, socially conscious lament "Home to Harlem" written by the well-known songwriting team of Ray Henderson and Lew Brown for the 1933 musical *Strike Me Pink*. In the revue, the song is sung by a black prisoner on a Southern chain gang who complains of his powerlessness and dreams of fleeing to Harlem where he will have more rights.

Among the hundreds of songs about Harlem written in the 1930s and 1940s, one of the best-remembered is Irving Berlin's "Harlem on My Mind." Written for the 1933 revue *As Thousands Cheer*, a topical show made up of

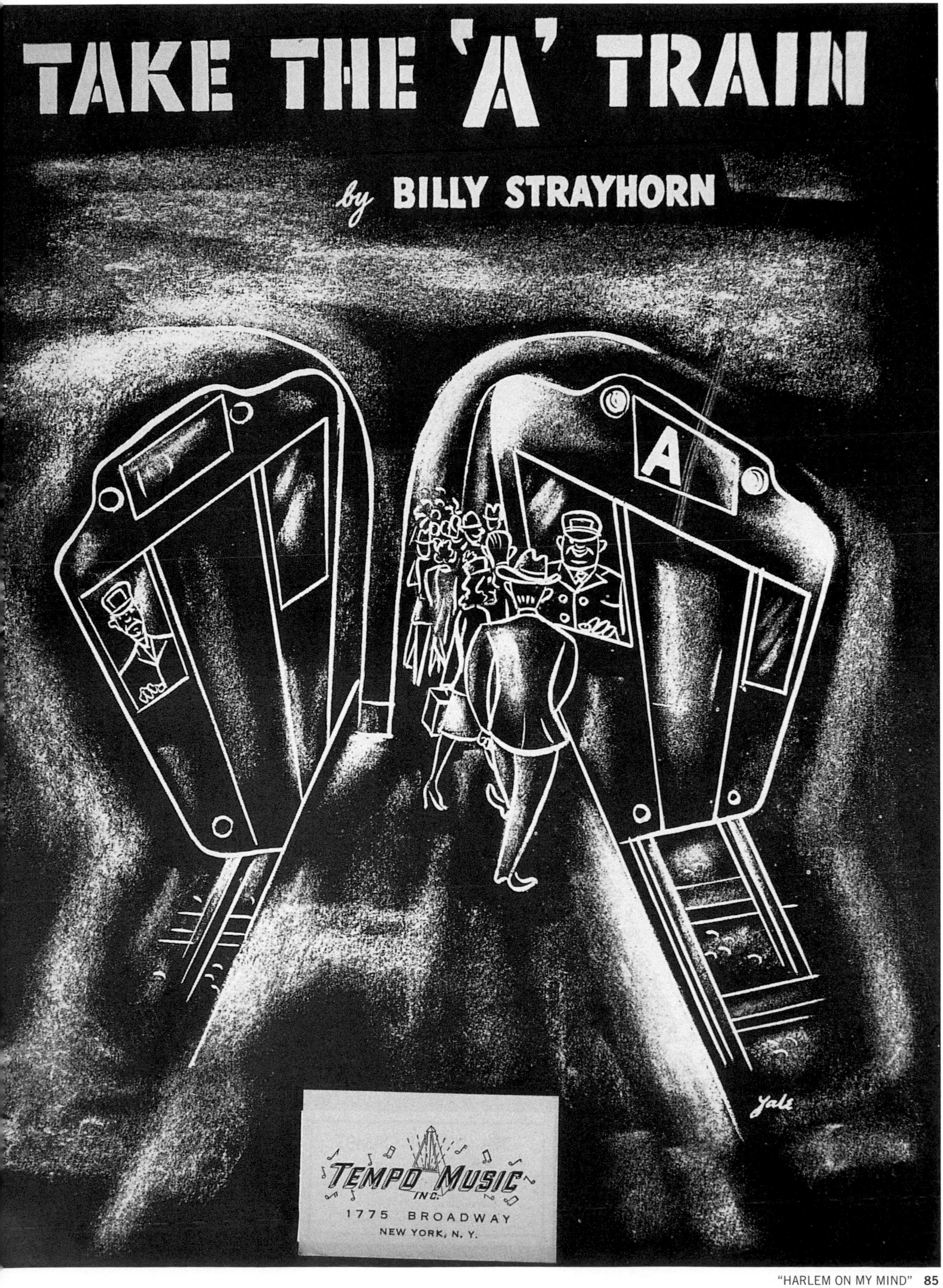
TAKE THE 'A' TRAIN
by BILLY STRAYHORN
A
Yale
TEMPO MUSIC INC.
1775 BROADWAY
NEW YORK, N. Y.

OPPOSITE: Moonlight illuminates Manhattan in Earle Hagen's 1940 "Harlem Nocturne."

short scenes satirizing famous people and events of the day, the song poked gentle fun at Josephine Baker, the American jazz singer who had been dazzling French audiences at the Folies Bergère and the Casino de Paris since 1925. Sung and recorded by the legendary Ethel Waters, "Harlem on My Mind" tells a tale of a black American living in France who is blue despite,

> Em'ralds in my bracelets and diamonds in my rings, / A Riviera chateau and a lot of other things . . . Lots of ready money in seven diff'rent banks / I counted up this morning, it's about a million francs . . .

And the reason for her blues?:

> I've got Harlem on my mind / I've a longing to be lowdown / And my "parlez-vous" will not ring true / With Harlem on my mind. ~ ~ ~

DUKE ELLINGTON (1899–1974)

Edward Kennedy Ellington came to New York from Washington, D.C., to study art at the Pratt Institute, but his interest in jazz soon lured him into the local musical scene. In 1918 he organized his own jazz band, and during the 1920s he appeared regularly at such Harlem hot spots as the Hollywood, the Kentucky Club, and, for five years, the famous Cotton Club (1927–1932). His influence as a pianist and composer was enormous, and his compositions were often inspired by Harlem and its people. Among his New York–related works are the "Harlem Flat Blues" (1929), "Harlem Speaks" (1933), "Uptown Downbeat" (1936), "Echoes of Harlem" (1936), "Harmony in Harlem" (1938), "Boys From Harlem" (1939), "Harlem Airshaft" (1940), "Blue Bells of Harlem" (1945), and "Harlem (A Tone Poem Parallel to Harlem)" (1952).

Duke Ellington at the keyboard.

The Depression hit Harlem particularly hard. Some residents held rent parties at which visitors, often whites from outside the neighborhood, would pay an entrance fee to dance to hot neighborhood combos and drink questionably obtained beverages. Other Harlemites tried to change their luck by rubbing "The Wishing Tree" on the corner of 132nd Street and Seventh Avenue. Although now largely forgotten, it was well enough known in its day for Ira Gershwin and Vernon Duke to write a song about it for the 1936 Ziegfeld Follies. "The Wishing Tree of Harlem" did not make it into the finished show and, unfortunately, the music has not survived, but the lyrics speak to the desperation of the time:

> They tell me that with a touch / My luck is bound to change. / I really ain't askin' much; / Any old job that you can arrange.

For pure lyricism, it would be hard to surpass Andy Razaf, Russell Wooding, and Paul Denniker's 1935 ballad "What Harlem Is to Me":

> Poet and sage turn out page after page about Harlem; / Views about Harlem, true and untrue, / I'm neither poet or sage, and I know it, / However, I may be clever, so here is my point of view:

> Chorus: It's a symphony of many moods and shades, / It's a tapestry of all designs and grades, / It's a hand behind the bars, / Ever reaching for the stars, / That's what Harlem is to me. ~ ~ ~

> There is no place you will ever see, / Like this dusky town within a town; / It's a showcase full of novelty, / Sophistication done up brown; / That's what Harlem is to me. ~ ~ ~

"Uptown Saturday Night": Harlem Dances and Nightclubs

The earliest music celebrating black Harlem tended to be ragtime instrumentals and blues songs. Tom Turpin and Joseph W. Stern published the "Harlem Rag" as early as 1899. This was followed in the 1920s by the "Upper Madison Avenue Blues," the "Uptown Blues," Duke Ellington's "Harlem Flat Blues," and W.C. Handy's 1922 classic, "Harlem Blues."

Despite its title, Handy's hit was really not blues at all, but rather a sophisticated lyrical melody, the core of which was based upon the American folk song, "I've Laid Around and Stayed

STOMPIN' AT THE SAVOY
A Modern Piano Solo
by BENNY GOODMAN • CHICK WEBB • EDGAR SAMPSON
PRICE
40¢ net
EXCEPT CANADA & FOREIGN
ROBBINS MUSIC CORPORATION
799 SEVENTH AVENUE – NEW YORK

Around This Old Town Too Long." Handy (1873–1958), a minister's son from Florence, Alabama, was trained in classical music, but was also steeped in Southern black folk music. Often called the "Father of the Blues," Handy's talents allowed him to bridge the two musical worlds. His hit, "The Memphis Blues" (1909), was the first blues song ever published; his next, "St. Louis Blues" (1914), was an international sensation. A few years later, he moved to New York, where he wrote several blues songs about New York, including the "Harlem Blues":

> You can never tell what's in a woman's mind / And if she's from Harlem, there's no use o' tryin' / Just like the tide, her mind comes and goes, / Like March weather, when will she change, / Nobody knows. . . . ~ ~ ~
>
> Now you can have your Broadway, give me Lenox Avenue, / Angels from the skies stroll Seventh Avenue and for that thanks are due, / To Madam Walker's Beauty Shop and Poro system too,[1] that made them angels without any doubt. ~ ~ ~
>
> Refrain: Ah, there's one sweet spot in Harlem, / It's known as Striver's Row, / Dicty [high-class] folks some call 'em live there and you should know, / That I have a friend who lives there / I know he won't refuse to put some music to my troubles, and call 'em Harlem Blues.

In addition to blues and rags, there were any number of syncopated dance pieces celebrating black life in Harlem: There was the "Harlem Drag" (1928), the "Harlem Fuss" (1925), "Harlem Mania" (1932), the "Harlem River Quiver" (1927), the "Harlem Twist" (1928), "Harlem Congo" (1934), "Harlem Bolero" (1937), and Rodgers and Hart's "Harlemania" (1930). Then there were the scores of songs without Harlem in their titles that celebrated the latest neighborhood dances. These included Duke Ellington's "Bumpty Bump" (1930)—"Grab somebody just your height," Mack Gordon and Harry Revel's "Doin' the Uptown Lowdown" (1933), and Eubie Blake's "Truckin' on Down"—a 1935 piece distinguished primarily by its early use of the word "truckin'." Several songs commemorate black dance halls, including Count Basie's "Jumpin' at the Woodside" (1938) and, of course, the 1936 Benny Goodman, Chick Webb, Andy Razaf, and Edgar Sampson classic "Stompin' at the Savoy."

As more and more New Yorkers made their way to Harlem's nightclubs and cabarets, a whole host of self-referential Harlem "show-biz" songs appeared. In "Harlem Serenade," a George and Ira Gershwin and Gus Kahn song from the 1929 musical Show Girl, stage star Ruby Keeler, ably assisted by members of the chorus, even gave downtown audiences directions to Harlem:

> Take a taxi and go there; / You'll meet people you know there; / Where the trumpeters blow their / Harlem Serenade. . . . Oh, stop! Look! Listen to that / Uptown jungle wail! / Book your passage to that / Harlem Congo Trail . . .

Songs, revues, and dance numbers with titles such as "Blackberries" (1932)—"Up in Harlem, life's a bowl of blackberries," "Frosted Chocolate" (1934), and "Formal Night in Harlem" (1936) celebrated Harlem night life. Jerome Kern and Dorothy Fields wrote a song tribute to the renowned black tap dancer "Bojangles of Harlem" (1936) for the Fred Astaire and Ginger Rogers' film Swing Time. For the 1938 film Fools for Scandal, Rodgers and Hart wrote one of the few period songs that clearly acknowledged white songwriters' indebtedness to black musical culture. "There's a Boy in Harlem" is an elegy to "a new dark music by a new dark man who writes his symphonies in black and tan" whom "all the writers copy." He writes "all the songs" and:

> Manhattan belongs to him. / Oh, he won't leave Harlem, / But his tunes get about. / He pounds them out / When the lights are dim. . . . / Oh, he lives for pleasure, / He's in no one's employ. / And Harlem lives off its Harlem boy!

WILMOTH HOUDINI AND CALYPSO HARLEM

In addition to jazz, during the 1920s and 1930s Harlem was also the center of an active calypso music scene. As early as 1912, George ("Lovely") Bailey brought a band from Trinidad to New York to make recordings, which were sold primarily in the Caribbean. In the late 1920s, the influential Trinidadian performer and composer Wilmoth Fredericks ("Houdini") arrived and quickly established himself as "the Calypso King of New York." In 1940 Houdini and His Royal Calypsonians made an important crossover recording for the Decca record company entitled, "Harlem Seen Through Calypso Eyes." The first concept album in calypso music, it included such Houdini songs as "Harlem Alley Cat," "The Million Dollar Pair of Feet," (a song about the Harlem-based dancer Bill "Bojangles" Robinson), "Good Old Harlem Town," "Harlem Popcorn Man," "Harlem Night Life," and "Married Life in Harlem."

OPPOSITE: When the Savoy Ballroom (Lenox Avenue and 140th Street) opened in 1926 it claimed to be "the world's most beautiful ballroom." For two decades, it featured the biggest of the big bands and the hottest dancing in town. (The Lindy hop was just one of several dance crazes said to have originated there.) The hall could accommodate up to five thousand people, and both black and white patrons were welcomed.

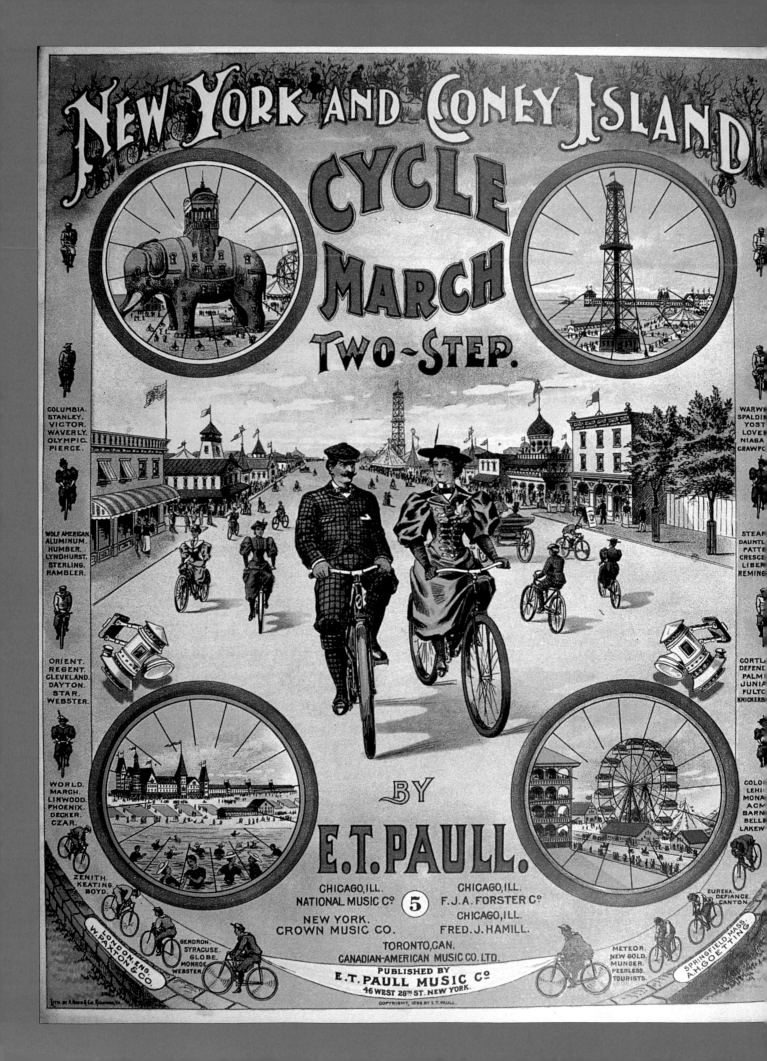

Chapter 6

A MUSICAL TOUR OF THE BOROUGHS

Brooklyn: From Rural Oasis to America's Fourth Largest City

The most populous of the five boroughs, Brooklyn, with a population of almost 2,500,000, is among the largest cities in the United States. Brooklyn's eighty-one square miles contain more than two dozen distinct neighborhoods and more ethnic diversity than just about anywhere else on earth. Brooklyn is also strikingly beautiful. Although its nineteenth-century mills, lofts, and warehouse districts do have a certain charm, neighborhoods such as Park Slope, Brooklyn Heights, and Cobble Hill with their tree-lined streets and historic row houses remind us of how civilized urban living can be.

Founded in 1636, just a few years after Manhattan, Brooklyn soon developed an identity all its own. Always competitive with the rapidly expanding metropolis just across the East River, Brooklyn, led by the League of Loyal Citizens of Brooklyn, came close to voting against joining Greater New York in 1898. Even today, Brooklynites often refer to consolidation as "The Mistake of '98," and the celebration of its centennial in 1998 was pointedly ignored and/or lamented by quite a few highly placed Brooklynites.

Nineteenth-century Brooklyn called itself "The City of Homes and Churches." It was primarily middle class and, like today, many of its residents commuted into Manhattan for work. The building of the Brooklyn Bridge (1883), the Williamsburg Bridge (1903), and the Manhattan Bridge (1905), and the extension of trolley and subway lines throughout the borough were followed by a real estate boom. New, modestly priced housing encouraged many recently arrived immigrants to flee older, overcrowded Manhattan slums and settle in Brooklyn.

By the early years of the twentieth century a stereotypical "Brooklyn" character had developed. In addition to a distinctive accent, Americans came to think of Brooklynites as streetwise, cocky, sarcastic, tough (but with hearts of gold), and fiercely loyal to their hometown. The stereotype was not without some basis in reality, and although many outsiders found the accent and the attitude amusing, Brooklynites remained extremely proud of their heritage. (A "Society for the Prevention of Disparaging Remarks about Brooklyn"[1] was active in the 1940s; and over the years, ex-Brooklynites living in outposts like Boston and Los Angeles have formed clubs for mutual support in the hinterlands.) Not surprisingly, an enormous number of songs have celebrated Brooklyn.

Celebrating Brooklyn

Located on the bluffs overlooking lower Manhattan, the Brooklyn Heights neighborhood is one of the most beautiful in all of New York. It was just beginning to be developed in the 1850s when William Mitchison wrote a lovely ode that began: *I love the Heights of Brooklyn with its green and shady bowers.*

During the War of 1812, a British fleet appeared off the East Coast and a rumor spread that they were heading for Brooklyn. In anticipation of the attack, volunteers worked

OPPOSITE: One of the most spectacular of New York sheet music covers, this elaborately illustrated 1898 lithograph celebrates the attractions of early Coney Island, including the Ferris Wheel and the Elephant Hotel (1882). Bicyclists and the names of bicycle makers adorn the edges of the cover.

furiously to build breastworks along Brooklyn Heights. In 1813, Samuel Woodward (who later gained fame as the composer of "The Old Oaken Bucket" and "Hunters of Kentucky") wrote "The Patriotic Diggers" to commemorate the citizens who turned out to build the defenses. The song gives us an interesting glimpse of who lived and worked in early Brooklyn:

> *See on yonder Heights our patriotic diggers. / Men of every age, color, and profession / Ardently engaged, labor in succession. . . . Scholars leave their schools with their patriotic Teachers, / Farmers seize their tools, headed by their Preachers. / How they break the soil; Brewers, Butchers, Bakers; / Here the Doctors toil, there the Undertakers. . . .*

> *Plumbers, Founders, Dyers, Tinmen, Turners, Shavers, / Sweepers, Clerks, and Criers, Jewelers, and Engravers, / Clothiers, Drapers, Players, Cartmen, Hatters, Tailors, / Gaugers, Sealers, Weighers, Carpenters, and Sailors. / / Chorus: Better not invade; recollect the spirit / Which our dads displayed and their sons inherit. / If you invade, friendly caution slighting, / You may get by chance a bellyful of fighting.*[2]

Even after the consolidation of Greater New York in 1898, Brooklynites were still competitive with Manhattan and determined to retain their own identity. This resulted in songs such as "Brooklyn Mighty Brooklyn" (Anthony Gale: 1924); "Brooklyn, My Brooklyn" (Dr. D.B. DeWaltoff: 1928); "Hail, Brooklyn" (Edwin Franko Goldman: 1944); and the Brooklyn Boosters Club's 1911 anthem "Boost Brooklyn" written by the well-known Tin Pan Alley team of William Jerome and Jean Schwartz to *"wake up old Manhattan town, wake it from its dream"*:

> *Join the Brooklyn Boosters Club, come on Brooklynites, / Get a button for your coat, stand up for your rights; / Help the good old cause along, we want men of steel, / Get on the job and put your shoulder right against the wheel, / Get right upon the roost, and boost, and boost, and boost.*

> *Chorus: Boost Brooklyn, keep on boosting till you die / Boost Brooklyn, boost it, boost it to the sky; / Mention Brooklyn, Greater Brooklyn, ev'ry time you talk / Tell the world that Brooklyn is the best part of New York.*

Almost since its founding, Brooklyn has had a love-hate relationship with Manhattan. In Manhattan, Brooklynites are thought to lack some of the sophistication and polish of those living in "The City." So for every song that claims, "It's a Privilege to Live in Brooklyn" (1951),

there is another one that asks, "Why Do They All Pick on Brooklyn?" (1945). In 1944, several songwriters, ignoring a plethora of evidence to the contrary, got together to ask the musical question "(Why Doesn't Someone Write a Song About) Brooklyn?":

> *Why doesn't someone write a song about good old Brooklyn / I heard a man who lives in Flatbush say. / Why doesn't someone write a song about good old Brooklyn / Instead of Timbuctoo or Mandalay? / They write about those Pennsylvania Polkas, Rave about Georgia's charms, / But they're just as nice in Brooklyn when you're holding 'em in your arms. / (Oh!) Why doesn't someone write a song about good old Brooklyn / And do right by the town where I belong. . . .*

Someone once said that more people come from Brooklyn than anywhere else because more people have left. This may not be true, but there are certainly a great many nostalgic songs about life in Brooklyn such as Jason Matthews and Terry Shand's 1946 hit "Give Me the Moon Over Brooklyn." Its lyrics touched a responsive chord with thousands of ex-servicemen returning from World War II:

> *I used to read the travel literature and longed for distant places / Now I have seen the wonders of the world, I'll take old familiar places.*

> *Just give me THE MOON OVER BROOKLYN when the long, long day is through. / I'll be walking with Maizie on Flatbush Avenue. / Just give me THE MOON OVER BROOKLYN when the old, old world is right, / I'll be dancing with Maizie at Coney Island ev'ry night.*

Another nostalgic tune, "Just Over the Brooklyn Bridge," was written by Alan and Marilyn Bergman and Marvin Hamlisch for a short-lived 1991 television series and sung by Queens native Art Garfunkel:

> *A world of its own, the streets where we played, the friends on ev'ry corner were the best we ever made. / The backyards and the schoolyards and the trees that watched us grow, the days when love and dinner time was all you had to know. / / Chorus: Whenever I think of yesterday, I close my eyes and see that place just over the Brooklyn Bridge that will always be home to me.*

> *No locks on the doors, no room of your own, no chance of being lonely, you were never alone. / With mama in the kitchen and good neighbors down the hall, might look like we had nothing but we really had it all . . .*

Let's You and I Just Say Goodbye
George M. Cohan's Comedians in the New American Song and Dance Show
The Rise of Rosie O'Reilly
Book - Lyrics and Music by
GEORGE M. COHAN
A Ring to the Name of Rosie . 60
Born and Bred in Brooklyn . 60
(Over the Bridge)
I Never Met a Girl Like You . 60
In the Slums 60
Keep A-Countin' Eight . . 60
Love Dreams 60
Let's You and I Just Say Goodbye 60
Poor Old World . . . 60
The Marathon Step . . 60
When June Comes Along With a Song 60
Selection 1.00
Theatrical and Music Hall Rights of these Songs are fully protected by Copyrights and MUST NOT be used for public performances without permission.
OPERATIC EDITION
M. WITMARK & SONS
NEW YORK
PRINTED IN U.S.A.

Many songwriters attempted to write Brooklyn songs. For example, in 1923 George M. Cohan's musical, *The Rise of Rosie O'Reilly*, featured the song, "Born and Bred in Brooklyn," which introduced Rosie O'Reilly, a young woman who was:

Born and bred in Brooklyn, / Proud of it too, tells it to you / Should she ever decide to fly / Over the Bridge, oh, the town would die . . . "

In "Brooklyn, U.S.A." (1947), comedian and songwriter Abe Burrows, who once referred to Brooklyn as the "Left Bank of New York," expressed his longing to return:

I wanna go back, hey / To my home there / In Brooklyn U.S.A. there / Back to the whence I first came from / I wanna see once more my little old home next to the subway station / I wanna see once more that little school, where they learned me my education . . .

And more lyrically, Neil Diamond wrote about his childhood in his 1968 hit "Brooklyn Roads" in which he recalls his apartment, *"Two floors above the butcher, first door to the right,"* and muses:

Does some other young boy come home to my room? / Does he dream what I did as he stands by my window and looks out on those Brooklyn Roads?

In 1951, a musical version of Betty Smith's 1943 classic tale *A Tree Grows in Brooklyn* opened on Broadway. Written by Arthur Schwartz and Dorothy Fields, it told the tale of the Irish-American Nolan family in Williamsburg (a section of Brooklyn), but it was not well-received by the critics. Few of the play's songs were specific to the borough, although its theme song did join several other songs about Brooklyn's foliage, most notably, "I'm Gonna Hang My Hat (On a Tree in Brooklyn)" (1944) and Irving Berlin's 1948 tongue-in-cheek, "A Beautiful Day in Brooklyn," in which he contends that a beautiful day in Brooklyn was more beautiful than a beautiful day anywhere else because, among other things, the sun comes up over Flatbush Avenue. Furthermore, he assures us, if that famous tree that grows in Brooklyn could speak, it would agree. For the record, the tree that grew in Brooklyn was an ailanthus, better known to locals as the "stink or weed tree."

As in Manhattan, specific Brooklyn neighborhoods made their way into song and dance titles. There was "The Midwood March & Two Step" composed for the 1895 Midwood Club Lawn Fete; the "Salute to Williamsburg" march (1906); the "Brighton Beach March" (1904); as well as "The Brighton Beach Rag" (1895)—from the musical *The Girl From Brighton Beach*; the "Brighton Beach Galop" (1878)—*"As played at the Beach by Conterno's 23rd Regt Band;"* a song entitled "(Come Take a Trip Down to) Old Sheepshead Bay" (1919); and the "Fort Hamilton Polka Redowa" (1852).

FORT·HAMILTON POLKA REDOWA.

New York, Published by Jaques & Brother, 385 Broadway.

LEFT: Lovely sheet music illustration of Fort Hamilton and Fort Diamond. The latter, renamed Fort Lafayette, was used for ammunition storage and survived until the 1960s, when it was replaced by an anchorage for the Verrazano Narrows Bridge.

OPPOSITE: George M. Cohan's 1923 musical *The Rise of Rosie O'Reilly* featured New York viewed from the Brooklyn shore.

Humorist Abe Burrows once remarked that Brooklyn was New York's "clown town," a vaudeville expression meaning a place that performers could mention to get a cheap laugh. Sometimes, the urge to be funny even overpowered geography, as in the 1936 novelty song "In a Little 'Jernt' in Greenpernt (By the Gowanus Canal)." As any Brooklynite will immediately notice, the neighborhood of Greenpoint is miles away from the Gowanus Canal—a fact that did little to faze the songwriters in their attempt to capture accents and attitudes in a neighborhood bar:

> *In a Little "Jernt" in Greenpernt, By the Gowanas Canal, In a Little "Jernt" in Greenpernt / That's where a pal is a pal. / If you gets busted, you don't have ta go, / They'll hold your coat if you ain't got the dough, / In a Little "Jernt" in Greenpernt, By the Gowanas Canal.*

> *Somebody floited, with somebody's wife, / Did he get hoited, we ruined him for life. . . . We calls the bartender Al / They never closes, the boss knows his stuff, / He's got the cops eating there on the cuff . . .*

Of course to Brooklynites, Brooklyn was the center of the universe. At least that's what songwriters Lee Pockriss and Paul Vance averred in "The Rich People of Brooklyn" (1956) which tells the tale of

> *"A sultan who lives in Mogador / Who has a harem of twenty wives or more. / And yet he's always complaining 'Life's a bore' / 'I'd rather be in Brook-a-lyn!'"*

BROOKLYN COWBOYS

"Ride, Tenderfoot, Ride" from the 1938 film *Cowboy From Brooklyn*. Lyrics by Johnny Mercer and music by Richard A. Whiting.

By the mid-twentieth century, Brooklyn became the quintessential stereotype for urban America. And if no place was more urban than Brooklyn, nothing was less urban than the wilderness of the Old West. Perhaps this explains a mysterious outbreak of humorous songs, plays, and films about tenderfoot cowboys from Brooklyn. During the late 1930s and 1940s, there appeared such near classics as "Brooklyn Buckaroos," "The Brooklyn Cowboy," "Texas, Brooklyn and Heaven" from a film of the same title, "Ride, Tenderfoot, Ride," from the film *Cowboy From Brooklyn*, and "Texas, Brooklyn and Love," from the 1946 musical *Sweet Bye and Bye*. The latter, which was written by that distinctly urban songwriting team of Ogden Nash and Vernon Duke and based on a book by fellow city slickers S.J. Perelman and Al Hirschfeld, included such lines as:

> *I'm a tin-pan alley cowboy, with a living solar plexus, / So when you yield at Ebbets field, / They can hear me yell in Texas . . . You've got ev'rything, My dream girl, my ev'rything, / You're Texas, you're Brooklyn, you're love . . . Your form is kosher with Durocher / To me, my darling, you're the Bums . . .*

Coney Island

Brooklyn has sixty-five miles of shoreline, but by far the best-known section is a five-mile stretch called Coney Island. A popular seaside spot since the 1870s, the neighborhood was transformed at the turn of the twentieth century when three giant amusement parks, George C. Tilyou's Steeplechase Park (1897), Luna Park (1903), and Dreamland (1904), opened along Surf Avenue. Before the area began to decline in the 1960s, the parks, the wide sandy beach, and the Boardwalk, built in 1923, would attract more than a million New Yorkers on a hot summer's day. Coney Island was the playground for the generations of working-class New Yorkers who could not afford to travel beyond the city's boundaries. Expeditions to Coney Island were the highlight of many urban childhoods. In 1902, songwriter Warren R. Walker wrote about what to expect "At the Steeplechase." Since the piece was "Published expressly for George C. Tilyou," it is likely that Walker was commissioned to write it as an advertisement for the amusement park:

I went to Coney Island, the funny sights to see. . . . I paid a dime admission, And saw the funny stairs / I walked up to the top and / It almost turned my hairs . . . / / Chorus: At the Steeplechase, at the Steeplechase; / It costs but a dime, But you'll have a good time.

The narrator then goes on to enjoy the Steeplechase ride, a water fountain that gives him an electric shock, and such attractions as the Windy Cave, the Electric Cave, the Aerial Slide, the Midget Railway, the Airship Luna, the Upside Down House, the Maze, and the Barrel of Love.

Luna Park was one of the wonders of its day. Featuring a stage spectacle about a journey to the moon, at night the park's spires and minarets were illuminated by more than a million light bulbs. In the summer of 1904, it attracted over ninety thousand visitors per day, and before it burned in 1944, it sparked the imagination of a generation of songwriters, including the noted bandmaster and composer John Philip Sousa, who celebrated Luna Park in his 1907 song "I've Made My Plans for the Summer."

ABOVE LEFT: "In a Little 'Jernt' in Greenpernt (By the Gowanus Canal)"

ABOVE RIGHT: Cover art celebrates the highlights of Brooklyn life in 1943.

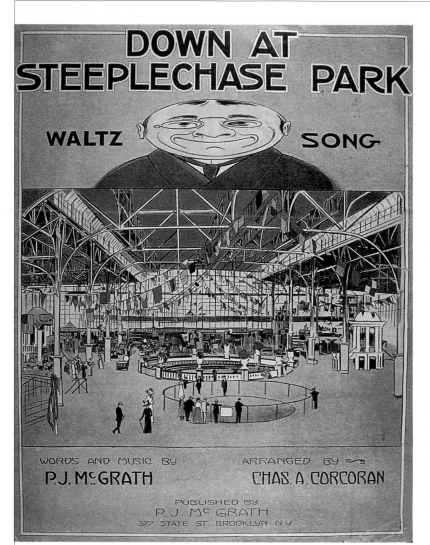

ABOVE: The interior of Steeplechase Park in 1911.

OPPOSITE: The "Official Luna Park Song." Because of the illuminations, nighttime views of the park were extremely popular.

The course of a Coney Island romance was neatly charted in the 1946 John Redmond and Marty Fryberg song "The Tune of Luna Park":

Romance by chance began at Coney Isle. / She looked, he looked, it started with a smile, / She tried, he tried to win a baby doll, he got lucky, life had begun / When he gave her a babydoll he won. // Chorus: They danced to a tune down in Luna . . . the noise from the Penny Arcade, sounded like a serenade / The barker, they thought, was a crooner, so they fell in love so much sooner . . .

Of course, Coney Island and its attractions were not to everyone's taste. According to "Coney Island," a song from Rodgers and Hart's 1930 show *Simple Simon*:

Ev'ry Sunday all Manhattan, / Gallic, African and Latin, / Spends its sal'ry with a smile, / Scrambling to the Isle of Coney. . . . Till the atmosphere is vile. / All the democratic horde walk / Upon the boardwalk / In triple file. . . . Good old phony Coney Isle.

Despite the occasional sour note, most Coney Island songs were both celebratory and formulaic; meeting members of the opposite sex was almost always mentioned. Examples include such tunes as "Coney Boy" (1912), "Take Me Down to Coney Island" (1897), "Coney Island for Mine" (1910), "By the Beautiful Sea" (1914), "My Coney Island Girl" (1900), "My Little Coney Isle" (1903), "Just a Peep at Coney Island" (circa 1900), "Coney Island Boardwalk" (1936), and years later, Lou Reed's "Coney Island Baby" (1975). There are Coney Island songs in languages as diverse as Yiddish and Greek, and according to the composers of "Dear Old Coney Island (That's the Only Place for Me)" (1912), it even compares favorably with Ireland, for *"There's a little spot in my land, / And they call it Coney Island, / There is not a place to beat it, / In that land beyond the sea . . ."* And leaving was always difficult, according to Les Applegate's 1948 hit "Goodbye, My Coney Island Baby."

The Bronx, Queens, and Staten Island, Too

The majority of New York's population lives in the boroughs of the Bronx, Queens, and Staten Island, but for obscure reasons, there have been far fewer attempts to describe these three boroughs in song. Nevertheless, there have been a few classic songs written about "the outer boroughs." Our musical tour next visits the only part of New York City on the North American mainland, the Bronx.

Early on, songwriters realized that Coney Island was popular not only because of the beach and the amusements but also because it was one of the few places where people from different neighborhoods and backgrounds could meet each other in a relaxed, democratic atmosphere. As songwriter Charley Fremont explained in 1895 in "Down at Coney Isle":

There's the Bow'ry boys with Nellie, and the East Side girls in style, / The girls from up in Harlem, too, and Johnny with his smile; / The merry-go-round and coasters are crowded all the while, / With future wives and husbands, down at Coney Isle.

In an 1897 song, also entitled "Down at Coney Isle," songwriters M.K. Aherns and Theodore Mertz list other Coney Island attractions:

You can watch frisky bathers as you stroll along the sand, / You can eat a Frankfort sausage while you listen to the band. / You can shoot the dizzy chutes or ride the giddy carousel, / If you have lots of money you can play the heavy swell.

The Bronx

The Bronx has had its ups and downs. Given all the bad press that parts of the borough received a few years back, some people are surprised to learn that the Bronx is actually composed of many lovely and liveable neighborhoods; or that almost a quarter of the Bronx's forty-two square miles is parkland. The first European settler was Jonas Bronck, a Scandinavian sea captain from the Netherlands who in 1639 built a farmstead at what is now 132nd Street and Lincoln Avenue. Local folklore relates how Jonas and his family loved to entertain and that people in New Amsterdam would talk enthusiastically about going up to visit "The Bronxes." Whatever the truth, today it is impossible for native New Yorkers to talk about the borough without putting "the," or at least "da," before "Bronx."

In 1919, one of the developing middle-class neighborhoods in the Bronx was portrayed as a quasi-suburban paradise, a refuge from the ills of city life, in the Victor Jacobi and Fritz Kreisler song "On the Banks of the Bronx" from the musical *Apple Blossoms*. The Bronx River, by the way, is about fifteen miles long and flows south through the New York Botanical Garden into the East River near Hunt's Point:

I know a place where we can dwell / Way up beyond the noisy "El" / There are no wealthy social leaders there. / A taxi siren never honks / Where we will settle in the Bronx. / The ladies do not smoke or drink or swear. / There when we want a special lark / There's lots of benches in the park / Where we can sit and almost see the moon. / The neighbors all live simple lives . . .

Chorus: There's a little flat a-waiting / On the Bronx's banks for you / Where the janitor is honest and the ice man's word is true. / Where the neighbors all are moral and the cops don't need to roam. / Where a room and bath and kitchenette are home, sweet, home.

The Bronx developed slowly until about 1910 when better transportation and newly built blocks of middle-class apartment houses began to attract large numbers of recently arrived, increasingly prosperous immigrant families. Hopping on a "Bronx Express" (1922), immigrant families could reach places such as the "Two Lots in the Bronx" that Adolf Philipp wrote about in his 1913 German-American musical *Was Kostet Amerika?*

BELOW LEFT: The Jerome Park Racetrack was built by entrepreneur, sportsman, and developer Leonard Walter Jerome in 1866. Some years later, his beautiful daughter Jenny took British society by storm, married an English nobleman named Churchill, and later had a son named Winston. The Belmont Stakes were inaugurated at Jerome Park in 1887 and held there annually until 1889, when the track was torn down to make room for the Jerome Park Reservoir.

BELOW RIGHT: According to the 1913 sheet music cover, the two lots were situated near Haight and Van Nest Avenue in the Morris Park section.

Queens

Queens is New York's largest borough, in fact, it is almost as large as Manhattan, the Bronx, and Staten Island combined. It is home to many of the city's most recently arrived ethnic groups; more than a third of its population is foreign-born. Historically, Queens was a series of separate towns, and perhaps because of this, Queens residents are more likely to speak about their neighborhood (i.e., Flushing, Astoria, or St. Albans) than their borough as a whole. Songwriters have also followed this pattern. Setting aside for a moment the many songs about Queen's two World's Fairs, which took place at Flushing Meadow Park in 1939 and 1964, the balance of Queens songs have been about the borough's other great resource—miles and miles of beaches. One of the earliest of these songs was Henry Russell's "Rockaway, or On Long-Island's Sea-Girt Shores" (1840):

> On old Long Island's sea-girt shores many an hour
> I've whiled away, / In listening to the breakers' roar
> that washed the beach at Rockaway . . .

Over the years, other Queens-related music has included the 1955 dance "The Rockaway" and "Rockaway Beach" by the Ramones (1977).

Staten Island

The sixty square miles of Staten Island are home to only about five percent of the city's residents. The least urban of the five boroughs, Richmond (Staten Island) is separated from Manhattan by five miles of water. Only the Verrazano Narrows Bridge (1964) and the celebrated Staten Island Ferry connect this borough with the rest of the city. Although many island residents commute daily to jobs in Manhattan and Brooklyn, they understandably feel somewhat removed and neglected by the other four boroughs. In fact, in 1990, after years of grumbling, Staten Islanders overwhelmingly approved a referendum to explore seceding from New York City. To date, the matter remains unresolved.

Introduced by the George William Curtis quote, "GOD might have made a more beautiful Island than Staten Island, but He never did," and "Dedicated to Hon. Joseph A. Palma, President of the Borough of Richmond," "Staten Island, The Gem of New York Bay" (1935) was songwriters Charles Edwin Lyman and George S. Dare's attempt to write an anthem for Staten Island. It begins:

> A sentinel to guard the bay, / Our Staten Island stands; /
> Firm and erect she points the way / That storm-toss'd
> vessels may convey / The wealth of many lands. . . .

LEFT: Rockaway in Queens had the perfect name for composers of early rock-and-roll.

BELOW: Looking out across New York Harbor from Staten Island in 1854.

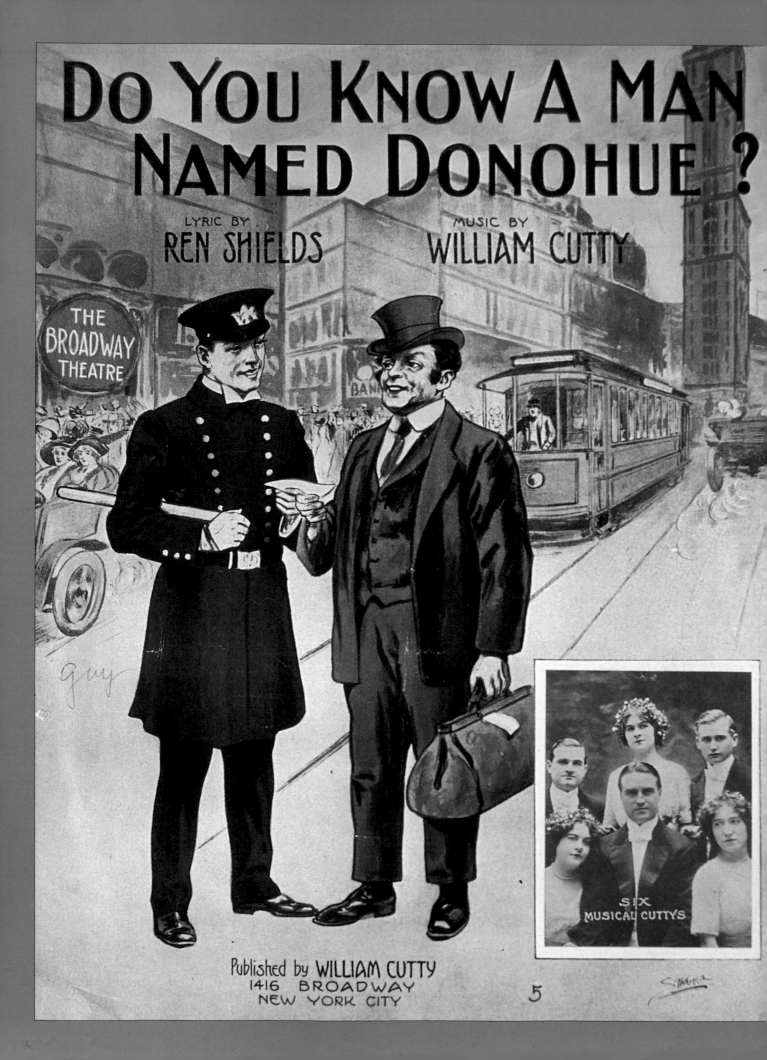

Chapter 7

ETHNIC NEW YORKERS

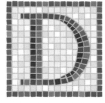 iversity is New York City's greatest strength. Nowhere else in the world do more people from more varied backgrounds live together in relative peace. A significant percentage of American families has an ancestor who entered the United States through the Port of New York.

OPPOSITE: In the midst of Times Square, one of "New York's Finest" tries to help one of New York's newest.

Many New York families never made it west of the Hudson River; in fact, some of them never made it west of the East River. Then, too, many nineteenth- and early-twentieth-century immigrants came directly from the countryside and faced the double challenge of adjusting to urban life as well as to American life in general. Although many stayed just long enough to clear customs and find a train, some stayed for a few years, and others remained permanently.

The number of immigrant songs that mention New York City is staggering, and this book cannot begin to do justice to the hundreds of songs in scores of languages that talk about coming to New York; however, there are some common themes. Although ninety-eight percent of all prospective immigrants who entered through Ellis Island were admitted—and eighty percent spent less than eight hours on the Island—it was a terrifying ordeal for sea-weary travelers. As the 1914 Yiddish song "Elis ayland" explained:

> O Ellis Island, you border of Freeland / How big and how terrible you are. / Only demons can commit such outrages / You harass the harassed for nothing. / Having come with troubles, having barely crossed the sea / Having seen the Statue of Liberty / There's Ellis Island, on the border of Freeland / Saying: "Stop, you can go no further."[1]

Just off the Boat: Coming to the Big City

Finding one's way around New York was the first challenge faced by the newly arrived. Even if you spoke English, urban customs were confusing. There are a number of great "lost in New York" songs, including Nora Bayes's 1910 hit "Has Anybody Here Seen Kelly?," Lopez Anguita's "Un Jíbero en el Subway" (circa 1952), and "Do You Know a Man Named Donohue?," a 1912 tale about a possibly illiterate newly arrived Irishman named Daniel J. O'Connor with no knowledge of Manhattan street names:

> Who landed in New York the other day. / In his mouth a dudeen [pipe] and on his face a smile, / A laugh to every one upon Broadway. / He held a slip of paper tightly in his hand, / Looked queerly then and slowly scratched his head. / And like a cunning rogue, / In his rich old Irish brogue, / To a big policemen then he said, "Say! / Do you know a man named Donohue? . . . Lives somewhere about here on the avenue". . .

> Daniel J. O'Connor then got on a subway train, / And Danny wasn't riding very far. / Noticed when Conductors they would call out a name, / That someone would get up and leave the car. / At one stop the Conductor came and yelled out "Jones," / And Jones got off right away. / Conductor next yelled "Pearl," / And right then off jumped a girl, / O'Connor says "conductor listen, say, Now! Do you know a man named Donohue?". . .

Another great "lost in New York" song was written by the famous calypsonian, Lord Invader (Rupert Grant), who migrated to New York in the early 1940s. In his 1946 song "New York Subways," he complains not only about getting lost, but also the reluctance of New York cab drivers to pick up black customers— "I had money yet I had to roam, / and still I couldn't get a cab to drop me back home"—a situation that sadly continues today:

> I met a cop and I told him I'm a stranger, / Lord Invader a calypso singer. / I live in Harlem and came here yesterday. / But now I want to go home I can't find my way. / He told me, "Walk back three blocks" and further explain, / "Go to the subway and take the uptown train." / I got confused, I was in a heat, / I couldn't find my way to One-Twenty-Fifth Street.
>
> I came out of the subway and didn't know what to do, / Looking for someone to help me through. / You talk about people as bad as crab, / Is the driver who driving the taxicab. / Some passing you empty and yet they wouldn't stop, / Some will say they have no gas or they can't make the drop. . . .[2]

The Immigrant's Dilemma: Torn Between Two Lands

According to American mythology, life in the United States is so obviously superior to life anywhere else that no immigrants even thought about returning. In recent years, historians have begun to rethink this conceit, and now believe a significant number of nineteenth- and early-twentieth-century immigrants returned to the lands of their birth. Of course, these percentages varied widely between groups: a far higher percentage of Greeks and Italians returned than did Eastern European Jews or Armenians. Today, the advent of cheap airplane tickets and significant immigration from countries only a few hours away—such as Trinidad, Jamaica, and Mexico—are changing the very concept of immigration.

One of the best recent songs about immigrating to New York is Liam Reilly's "The Streets of New York" (circa 1981). Well-known and widely sung by Irish Americans, it traces the events that shape a young immigrant's life and his mixed feelings as he watches his own American-born children. His first trip to America at the age of eighteen is a lark:

> At the time, Uncle Benjy was a policeman in Brooklyn, / And my father, the youngest, looked after the farm. / 'Till a phone call from America said "Send the lad over." / And the old fella said,"Sure, t'wouldn't do any harm". . .
>
> So, I landed in Kennedy, and a big yellow taxi / Carried me and my bags through the streets and the rain. / Well, my poor heart was thumping around with excitement, / And I hardly even heard what the driver was saying. / / We came in the Shore Parkway through the flatlands of Brooklyn, / To my uncle's apartment on East 53rd. / I was feeling so happy, I was humming a song, / And I sang "You're as free as a bird."

Just as the young narrator is arriving, his policeman uncle is killed "in an uptown foray," leaving him to confront New York alone. Suddenly, the narrator's life becomes more serious. He turns to the Irish immigrant community in the Bronx for help:

> So, I went up to Nellie's beside Fordham Road, / And I started to learn about lifting my load. / But the heaviest thing that I carried that year / Was the bittersweet thoughts of my homeland so dear. / / I went home that December cause my old fella died. / I had to borrow the money from a fella on the side. / And all the bright flowers and brass couldn't hide / The poor, wasted face of my father.

Caught between two cultures, and faced with a future of poverty in his homeland, he decides for New York, and like millions before him, trades the prosperity of America for his beloved homeland:

> I sold off the old farm yard for what it was worth, / And into my bag stuck a handful of earth. / Then I boarded a train and I caught me a plane, / And I found myself back in the U.S. again. / / It's been twenty-two years since I set foot in Dublin. / My kids know to use the correct knife and fork. / But I'll never forget the green grass and the rivers, / As I keep law and order in the streets of New York.

Compromising and learning to adapt were the keys to making it in the city. As Puerto Rican composer Ismael Santiago explains in his 1967 plena (a type of Puerto Rican narrative song) "La Metrópolis," immigrants may criticize life in the city, but if they leave, they come back right away. The narrator goes on to proclaim his pride in being Puerto Rican, but he refuses to criticize the place where he earns his living. And, he adds, his New York "barrio" (neighborhood) has become his "segunda islita" (second little island) where he can eat island delicacies as cuchifritos, avocados, and oranges and live next door to other Puerto Ricans.[3]

Hardships and Complaints

Not that life was easy for immigrants: In the classic Yiddish-language tear jerker "Di nyu-yorker trern" ("New York Tears") published by H. Altman in 1910 (but possibly older), the litany of urban horrors is strangely reminiscent of today's headlines:

> New York bubbles like a pot / There's constant tumult and hubbub. . . . A man leaves home healthy / He runs to look for work to seek his fortune. / A car comes and cuts him up quickly / / They bring him home dead. . . . / / Who hasn't heard of the murder / That took place not long ago on Montgomery Street? / They found three people stabbed / A man, a wife, and a mother-in-law in a pool of blood. / And there you hear a boy shot his friend. / Two children were playing with a pistol. / A boy of 14, what has he seen of life? / The second boy, still younger, aimed at him. / When he felt the shot / He screams "mama" loudly / And, running from the third floor / He lies dead in the hall.[4]

More recent immigrant groups have also complained about the violence of urban America in song. Since the 1970s, Dominican merengue groups have been composing songs addressing issues of crime, drugs, and loneliness in New York. La Patrulla 15, in the song "Nueva York Es Así" ("That's How New York Is"), warns potential immigrants that life in the big city will be much harder than they anticipate. More recent Dominican songs about hardships in New York have included Wilfrido Vargas' "El Gringo y el Cibaeño," which recounts a debate between an enthusiastic New Yorker and a homesick Dominican, and Los Hermanos Rosario's recording, "Un Día en Nueva York" ("A Day in New York"), which complains about living in an apartment in the middle of the Bronx surrounded by gunfire, sirens, gangs, and hold-ups.[5]

Immigrants also had to confront the prejudice and ignorance of their fellow New Yorkers. Although written by a non-Italian, and probably meant to be a humorous novelty song when it was published in 1908, James Brockman's "Wop, Wop, Wop" conveys some of the frustration and anger about being derogatively labeled:

> When first I come to dees-a countiree all people call me Dago man. / And you can bet dot was no fun to me . . . / Den dey change and call me Guinie, twice as bad-a name dey gimme, / I say please make-a drop, I beg-a dem to stop, now dey call me Wop! / / Chorus: Wop! Wop! Wop! I wish a cop would make-a dem stop. / First dey change and call me Dago, den Guinie, Guinie, Guinie, / Now it's Wop! Wop! Wop!

For some immigrants, even the weather was a shock. As the singer for the Puerto Rican group El Jíbarito de Adjuntas explained in their classic 1951 recording, "Yo Vuelvo a Mi Bohío" ("I'm Going Back to My Shack"), if things were bad back home, they are worse here: sometimes it's hot, other times it's terribly cold, and when it freezes you often feel like a bundle sliding around on the snow.[6]

On top of everything else, many immigrants had to deal with severe cases of homesickness. Nostalgia for the old land produced some interesting songs, however. Usually the old homeland looked much better in retrospect, but sometimes, with a little imagination, the

YIDDISH THEATRE IN NEW YORK

From the 1890s to the 1950s, Yiddish theatre flourished in more than a dozen Lower East Side theatres along Second Avenue and the Bowery. At its height from 1910 to 1920, more than a dozen Yiddish companies presented serious dramas, musicals, and comedies reflecting important issues in the New York Jewish community such as immigration and acculturation. Music was important in the Yiddish theatre and composers such as Alexander Olshanetsky, Joseph Rumshinsky, and Sholem Secunda provided Yiddish songs about New York and the experience of immigration. In the 1920s, many Yiddish theatre stars made a successful transition into mainstream theatre and films; however, some of its greatest stars—including such legendary performers as Boris Thomashefsky and Moyshe Oysher—remain unknown outside of the Jewish community.

new homeland could take on aspects of the old—at least according to the 1916 song "Twas Only an Irishman's Dream":

> Sure the shamrocks were growing on Broadway, / Ev'ry girl was an Irish colleen. / And the town of New York was the county of Cork, / All the buildings were painted green, / Sure the Hudson looked just like the Shannon, / Oh, how good and how real it did seem, / I could hear mother singin', / The sweet Shannon bells ringin', / 'Twas only an Irishman's dream.

Americanization

Before today's more sophisticated, multicultural approach to American life, it was thought that to become fully American, you, and certainly your children, had to leave behind your ethnic customs and preferences. In many cases, moving beyond the ethnic neighborhood was more complex than merely taking advantage of economic success; you had to change your identity. The 1916 novelty song "My Yiddish Matinee Girl" pokes fun at a young, upwardly mobile Jewish woman confronting this dilemma:

> When Rosie lived in Essex Street, She liked the Yiddish plays, / She had artistic temper, all the actors she would praise, / But since she moved up to the Bronx, she has got high tone, / She gave up Thomashefsky [a major Yiddish theatre star] and she took to Georgie Cohan. / She's now got lots of whims, since father's business pays, / From moving picture films, She changed to Broadway plays. . . .

In the 1978 song "Un Jíbero en Nueva York," Puerto Rican singer Sonora Ponceña complains about those fellow islanders who pretend they have forgotten how to speak Spanish. In particular, the singer ridicules Mariano, a "jíbaro from Jagüey," who she sees on the subway. When she asks, in Spanish, how he is doing, he tells her, in English, "I don' know wha you say."[7] Even those who arrive speaking English often confront culture shock in New York. You can hear it in Sting's song "Englishman in New York" (1987) when he proclaims his preference for such British fare as tea and bread toasted on only one side, sports a walking cane, revels in his accent and good manners, and acknowledges that he, too, is an alien, albeit a legal one.

Sometimes, New Yorkers purposely use music to bridge cultural boundaries, as in the amusing novelty tune "Abie Sings an Irish Song." Written by Irving Berlin in 1913, it tells of a Jewish storekeeper named Abie who uses music to increase his sales:

> In an Irish neighborhood / Abie kept a clothing store / But business wasn't good. / No one came into the store and Abe wondered why / But soon winked his eye / Then bought up ev'ry Irish song he could buy. / In an hour and a half / Someone taught him how to sing the Irish songs somehow. / He learned them all with ease, / Them Irish melodies, / He knows them all by heart and now // Chorus: When an Irishman looks in the window / Abie sings an Irish song . . .

Harrigan and Hart and Braham

The prize for writing nostalgic songs about ethnic New Yorkers goes to the enormously influential team of Edward Harrigan and Tony Hart. Actually, Harrigan & Hart were the performers who electrified New York from 1870 to 1885 with a series of musical plays based on local urban life. The songs were really written by just one of the partners, Edward Harrigan (1844–1911), and set to music by his father-in-law, David Braham (1838–1905). It would be hard to overstate their impact on the American theatre. Like their British contemporaries, Gilbert and Sullivan, Harrigan and Braham managed to capture the essence of their society in a series of musical comedies about inner-city life. Most of their rather thin plots revolved around the misadventures of the Irish-American Mulligan family, the voluntary militia company led by Dan Mulligan called "The Mulligan Guard," and the Guard's archrivals, an African-American militia group called "The Skidmore Guard." In all, the team presented over forty plays and numerous sketches from the 1870s through the 1890s. Hart (1855–1891), who specialized in "wench roles" (female impersonations), dissolved the partnership in 1885 and retired soon thereafter, but Harrigan and his large ensemble company of comedians struggled on until the early 1900s.

At their height, a Harrigan & Hart premiere could literally stop the city: however, time has not been kind to their legacy. Today, the plays, with their convoluted plots and unflattering racial and ethnic stereotypes, strike modern audiences as unpalatable. Yet, many who actually saw the company live considered it one of the high points of their lives. Perhaps it was Harrigan's ability to poke gentle fun at cultural differences and playfully address racial and ethnic tensions in an era of vast social change that made him such a favorite with the audiences of his day. But Harrigan and Hart's comedies were more than mere safety valves for urban tensions. At his best, Harrigan's lyrics present a deep love and respect for New York, and explain why a sense of belonging—either to a neighborhood, an ethnic group, or a voluntary organization—was so important. As such, Harrigan's songs remain unparalleled descriptions of nineteenth-century New York life.

"The Old Neighborhood" (1891) appeared in *The Last of the Hogans*, one of Harrigan's last plays. It describes the multi-ethnic Cherry Hill neighborhood of Harrigan's youth during the 1840s:

It's close to an alley that leads to the rear / Of a shanty so old and so worn; / Oh, down in the Fourth Ward that I love so dear— / The place where the babies are born. / An old-fashioned lamp stands close to the door / To light up the stoop made of wood; / There mothers and dads, sweet lassies and lads / All meet in the old neighborhood.

Chorus: And they call it Cherry Hill, my boys / Where the girls are beautiful and good / And I'm not too proud to mingle with the crowd / Down in the old neighborhood.

In 1890 Harrigan built his own theatre on West 35th Street off Sixth Avenue. Financial circumstances forced him to sell it in 1895. Renamed the Garrick Theatre, it was used until 1932.

*There stands the Dutch groc'ry just over the way, /
With its awning to keep off the rain; / It's there on the
coal box the neighbors each day, / Talk politics over
again. / Old Horseshoer Mike, right out of his shop. /
With brogue that we all understood, / Would tell you
the name of the Gov'ner next fall— / Wise man of
the old neighborhood.*

Another Harrigan and Braham salute to the
many ethnic groups that lived together in the
urban landscape was "Our Front Stoop" (1878).
On stage, it is introduced by *"the father of the
family"* complaining about his children and

their friends: *"It's every summer evening when the
heat would make you droop, / Friends they meet from
every street, to gossip on our front stoop . . . Then their
conversation for a mile or two you'll hear . . ."* Even
a century later, their conversation sounds
familiar to every New Yorker who has ever
sat on a front stoop:

*They talk about the Murphys, and say they put
on the style. / And how their daughter Mary went
down to Coney Isle / With a German music teacher,
who filled her with clam soup. / Then they say,
don't give it away, what you hear on our front stoop.*

You'd have to run the gauntlet if ye were walking by, / They'd have your family history in the twinkling of your eye; / They'd turn it over gently, while they sit there in a group, / They'd give to you sweet ballyhoo while passing our front stoop.

Just hanging out was also the theme of Harrigan and Braham's two biggest hits. The first, "Paddy Duffy's Cart," from the 1881 play *Squatter Sovereignty*, is a nostalgic look back at a group of boys in an immigrant neighborhood who would congregate on a lamp-lit corner on summer nights to sing, chat, and flirt with passing girls:

The many happy evenings I spent when but a lad / On Paddy Duffy's lumber cart, quite safe away from dad; / It stood down on the corner, near the old lamp-light. / You should see the congregation there on ev'ry summer night . . .

We'd gather in the evening, all honest working boys, / And get on Paddy Duffy's cart for no one marr'd our joys; / All seated in the moonlight, laughing 'mid its rays, / Oh, I love to talk of old New York, and of my boyish days . . .

THE IRISH IN NEW YORK

New York's Irish community has had a significant impact on music in New York. Although many Irish and Irish-American composers had little trouble entering the mainstream music business, some chose to stay solidly within the large Irish-American community. Today, in addition to a vibrant folk music scene of traditional *ceili* dancing, sessions, and *fleadhs*, there are also a number of "Green Card Rock" bands that combine elements of Irish traditional music with the drive and syncopation of late-twentieth-century rock. Led by bands such as Black 47, these groups specialize in songs that address issues faced by contemporary immigrants. Black 47, for example, performs songs like "Mammy Dear, We're All Mad Over Here," "Up on Fordham Road," and "Our Lady of the Bronx," in which an immigrant tries to convince his partner Mary that New York is tearing them apart and that they need to return home to Ireland. Even as he pleads, he realizes that she won't return, preferring to stay and *"pray for redemption"* in the Bronx.

One of the most interesting contemporary Irish-American songs is Terence Winch's instant classic, "When New York Was Irish" (1987), which nostalgically recalls the heyday of Irish immigration, *"When people from Galway and the County Mayo / And all over Ireland came over to stay / And take up a new life in Americay"*:

We worked on the subways, we ran the saloons / We built all the bridges, we played all the tunes / We put out the fires and controlled City Hall / We started with nothing and wound up with it all.

They were ever so happy, they were ever so sad / To grow old in a new world through good times and bad. / All the parties and weddings, the ceilis and wakes / When New York was Irish, full of joys and heartbreaks.

You could travel from Kingsbridge to Queens or mid-town / From Highbridge to Bay Ridge, from up town to down / From the East Side to the seaside's sweet summer scenes— / We made New York City our island of dreams. ~ ~ ~

Most of Harrigan's plays had some connection with the New York Irish community. Although not Irish himself, Harrigan was strongly identified with the Irish and Irish Americans. In his 1879 song "The Babies on Our Block," he gave an indelible portrait of what summer was like in his neighborhood for newly arrived immigrants:

If you want for information, Or are in need of merriment, / Come over with me socially, To Murphy's Tenement. / He owns a row of houses, In the First Ward, near the dock, / Where Ireland's represented, By the Babies on our Block . . .

On a warm day in the summer, When the breeze blows off the sea / A hundred thousand children, Lay on the Battery; / They come from Murphy's building, Oh! their noise would stop a clock! / Oh there's no perambulatory, With the Babies on our Block . . .

Although slightly saccharine for modern tastes, Harrigan and Braham's song "Maggie Murphy's Home" from *Reilly & The 400* (1890) was also a major success, and continued to be sung long after the play was forgotten. Even now, it gives us a sense of the fun and community that existed in modest working-class tenements:

Behind a grammar school-house / In a double tenement, / I live with my old mother / And always pay the rent. / A bedroom and a parlor / Is all we call our own, / And you're welcome ev'ry evening / At Maggie Murphy's home. // Chorus: On Sunday night, 'tis my delight / And pleasure don't you see, / Meeting all the girls and all the boys, / That work downtown with me, / There's an organ in the parlor / To give the house a tone, / And you're welcome ev'ry evening / At Maggie Murphy's home.

Such dancing in the parlor, / There's a waltz for you and I, / Such mashing in the corner, / And kisses on the sly. / O bless the leisure hours, / That working people know, / And they're welcome every evening, / At Maggie Murphy's Home. . . .

LATIN NEW YORK

There are many Latin music scenes in New York—from Puerto Rican bomba y plena and salsa, to Dominican merengues, to Columbian huaynos, to Brazilian sambas—and songs about the city and the experience of immigration have appeared in all genres. As early as 1929, Puerto Rican immigrants were composing songs such as "En la 116" ("On 116th Street"), a plena about going to the movies, learning English, and having a Puerto Rican girlfriend next door in Spanish Harlem. During the late 1930s and 1940s, the popularity of Latin music led to a number of "faux" Latin hits (e.g., "She's a Latin From Manhattan"), but the real thing also flourished in New York's Latin communities.

New York mambo bands led by such greats as Machito and Antonio Arcaño recorded hits like "Conozca a New York" ("Get to Know New York"), plena masters like Canario sang songs like "Qué Vivo!" ("What a Way of Life!"), and Rene Touzet wrote rumbas like "Yo Vengo de Nueva York" ("I Come From New York"). More recently, in the 1990s, songs such as "Nueva York No Duerme" ("New York Doesn't Sleep") by Dominican composer Ramon Orlando, "Salsa en Nueva York" and "La Batalla de los Barrios" by the charanga group Típica Novel, and "Nueva York" by Willie Colon reflect the importance and excitement of the urban landscape in contemporary Latin music.

The narrator of this 1946 Guaracha-Rumba comes to New York because it is the place, they say, where the music really swings.

Chapter 8

URBAN LIFE IN THE BIG APPLE

Slice of Urban Life

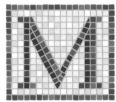any New York composers were adept at writing slice-of-life ballads that painted realistic portraits of the city. In fact, some of these "supreme ballads of songdom," as they were touted in a 1916 ad, were rather generous slices of daily urban life. James Thornton's

OPPOSITE: Except for their period clothing, these early straphangers from 1907 could easily pass for modern commuters.

1891 ballad "Scenes in New York" falls into this category. The English-born Thornton (1861–1938), who is best-remembered today as the composer of "When You Were Sweet Sixteen" and "My Sweetheart's the Man in the Moon," toured the vaudeville circuit for many years with partner Charles B. Lawlor—himself the composer of that inimitable anthem "Sidewalks of New York." In "Scenes," Thornton frames his observations through the device of giving an out-of-town friend a tour of several colorful neighborhoods. On Baxter Street, in what is today Chinatown, Thornton poetically describes some character types who can still be observed in the modern urban landscape:

Crossing sweepers, door-step sleepers, / Tramps who take the sidewalk for a bed; / Doubtful girls in paint and powder, talk quite loud, dress much louder / Men who have their noses colored red; / Organ grinders, cigar-stump finders, / Chinese joints, where [opium] smokers like to meet; / Salvation Army out parading, beating drums and serenading, / That is what he thought of Baxter Street.

The mixture of different classes has always held a fascination for New York's songwriters. As songwriters Jean Havez and W.B. Gottlieb put it in their 1901 song "Broadway Promenade": *"Impecunious people walking where millionaires have trod; / Rich and poor are all alike upon the Broadway promenade."*

One of the best lyrical overviews of daily city life is the 1940 musical setting of Arthur Guiterman's 1919 poem "New York" by the impressively named classical composer Mario Castelnuovo-Tedesco:

The city is cutting away, / The gasmen are hunting a leak; / They're putting down asphalt today, / To change it for stone in a week. / The builders are raising a wall, / The wreckers are tearing one down, / Enacting a drama of all our changeable, turbulent town.

For here is an edifice meant / To stand for an eon or more; / And there's a gospeler's tent, / And there is a furniture-store. / Our suburbs are under the plow, / Our scaffolds are raw in the sun; / We're drunk and disorderly now, / But—'Twill be a great place when it's done.

Living in New York is many things, but it is rarely easy. Some composers like to complain about specific problems, others have written songs to complain about the city in general. Noise is an ongoing complaint of all urban dwellers. This fact was recognized musically by songwriters Arnold Horwitt and Richard Lewine in the song "Noises in the Street" from the 1947 revue *Make Mine Manhattan*. It was sung by a chorus consisting of a taxi driver, a street digger, a newsboy, and a milkman:

Songs about night life in New York fall into two distinct categories: good and evil. Many, such as Leo Robing and Ralph Rainger's "Night in Manhattan" from *The Big Broadcast of 1937*, advise listeners to *"come and have a wonderful time . . ."* The attitude of New York's night owls was amusingly summed up in 1908 by the songwriting team of Harry B. Smith and Maurice Levi, who wrote a wonderfully wacky song for the Ziegfeld musical *The Soul Kiss* entitled "I'm the Human Night Key of New York" about a self-appointed "human night key" who personally closes up New York each evening:

They tell me there are people who go home and go to bed / Before the midnight hour, that's queer to me; / I don't know what they see in life, you might as well be dead. / The fun don't really start till two or three. / The pikers and the quitters then remark they must skidoo, / But I'm just beginning to feel bright; / At four the few remaining wrecks sneak off and leave their unpaid checks / Leaving me to close the town up for the night.

Chorus: Oh, I'm the man who shuts New York at night. / Some fellow has to do it, I'm the one; / One day by a mistake at five P.M. I chanced to wake, / First time in many years I've seen the sun. / My quarts of wine, if they were placed in a line, / Would build a Trans-Atlantic bridge of cork; / My heart will always stay light, While I keep away from daylight, / For I'm the human night key of New York.

From eight o'clock till twelve I'm always loafing 'round the club . . . / Then I stroll into Brown's or Rector's or some place. / The others soon for home begin to steer; / Then the waiters pull their freight with a scowling look of hate. / And there's no one left but me and the cashier.

Chorus: Oh! I'm the man who closes up the town. / The milkman has one friend, and I'm the one; / Evening ends when I let the baker in, / He brings the rolls, yours truly brings the buns. / When pikers quit I do not care a bit. / If I have any pull it's with a cork; / I still sit at the throttle, taking one last lonely bottle, / For I'm the human night key of New York.

Not all New Yorkers are out partying at night; many are working. For example, in the Gene DePaul and Don Raye hit "Milkman, Keep Those Bottles Quiet," sung by Nancy Walker in the 1944 film *Broadway Rhythm*, a night worker returning at dawn from her plant job demands:

Milkman, stop that Grade A riot! / Cut it out if you can't lullaby it! / Oh, Milkman, Keep Those Bottles Quiet! . . . I want-a give my all if I'm going to give it / But I gotta get my shut-eye if I'm gonna rivet, / So bail-out Bud with that milk barrage, / 'Cause it's unpatriotic, it's sabotage.

There is also Frank Loesser's lyrical elegy to late night/early dawn from the 1950 musical *Guys and Dolls*, in which the gambler Sky Masterson tries to explain to the Salvation Army heroine why early morning is "My Time of Day":

When the street belongs to the cop and the janitor with the mop, and the grocery clerks are all gone. / When the smell of the rain-washed pavement comes up clean and fresh and cold, / And the street-lamp light fills the gutter with gold, / That's my time of day.

For every song that celebrated beauty and excitement in the New York night, there was another one that cautioned of its evils. As early as 1916, "While the City Sleeps," a song by William Downs and Jack Denny, warned of the hop (opium) dens of Chinatown, in which *"dreamers now turn into schemers / heartless, godless, cruel . . ."* And, in written instructions, the composers recommend: *"A splendid effect . . . may be obtained by stopping singing [at the end of Verse 1] and reciting the following Poem, accompanied by slow chords p.p. [softly] on the Piano."* Though not great literature, the poem was enough to make anyone think twice about living in New York:

ABOVE: Three verses dealing with seduction, childbirth, suicide, and a criminal awaiting execution at dawn are confusedly intertwined in this 1900 ballad by W.T. Bryant. The chorus asks: *"When New York sleeps, / How many ever dream / Of all the hungry homeless ones, / Whose hearts with anguish team? / To more than one faint heart / How oft the tempter creeps! / Some lover sighs, some mother cries, / When New York sleeps!"*

OPPOSITE: Tommy Dorsey and Nancy Walker's hit from the 1944 film *Broadway Rhythm*.

Stand in your window and scan the sights, / On Broadway with its bright white lights, / Its dashing cabs, and its cabarets. / Its painted women and its fast cafes. / That's when you really see New York. / Vulgar of manner, overfed, / Over dressed and underbred. / Heartless, Godless, Hell's delight; / Rude by day and lewd by night. / Bedwarfed the man, enlarged the brute / Ruled by crook and rum to boot, / Purple robed and pauper clad, / Raving, rioting, money mad. / A squirming herd in Mammon's mesh; / A wilderness of human flesh . . .

Perhaps because nighttime was so important to the city's culture, New York composers excel at songs about moonlight. Moonlight titles include: "Moon About Town" (1933), "Manhattan Moonlight" (1930), "Broadway Moon" (1933), "Harlem Moon" (1931), "Moon Over Mulberry Street" (1935), and "A Latin Tune, A Manhattan Moon, and You" (1940). If Mother Nature disappointed, songwriters were perfectly willing to turn to artificial moonlight: "It's Moonlight All the Time on Broadway" songwriters Percy Wenrich and Ren Shields wrote in 1908. "Dr. Edison," asked songwriters Sigmund Romberg and Irving Caesar in *Marjorie* (1924), "Turn on That 42ND STREET MOON."

Mass Transit in Song

Living in New York is only part of the challenge. Getting around town is what really separates the tourists from the natives. Car ownership is still rare in New York. In a city where the costs of owning and parking a car can be prohibitive, most of today's New Yorkers, like their ancestors before them, still rely on an intricate system of subways, buses, ferries, and taxis.

New York's early mass transit was horse-powered, and carriages, coaches, and horse-drawn trolleys or "railroads," were musically celebrated in such songs as "Waiting for a Broadway Stage" (circa 1870), the "Franklin Avenue Rail Road Gallop" (1883), and the "Seventy-Six Polka," which was composed circa 1852 for "Johnson & Hudson, Stage Proprietors" and features a six-horse coach with the city's skyline in the background on its cover. Trolley-related music includes "Gliding on the Rail: A Descriptive Rail Roadway Gallop" (1881) with an illustrated cover featuring a cut-away of a spacious Manhattan Beach Railway car, "On a Good Old Trolley Ride" (1904), and "The Girl I Met on the Car!" (circa 1870), which was *"Composed for and Dedicated to the Nostrand Avenue Railroad"* in Brooklyn.

New York ferries have received less musical attention, although as early as 1836 composer W. H. Parker did write "The Brooklyn Ferryman." In 1847, Samuel Owne Dyer, who claimed to be "The Ferry Turner," published "The Ferry Quick Step," which he somewhat mysteriously "composed and respectfully dedicated to Dr. W. H. Chadwick (The Ferry Confectioner)." More recent ferryboat compositions include Emerson Whitmore's "On the Ferry" (1922) and Harold Adamson and Eldo di Lazzaro's "Ferry-Boat Serenade" (1939).

In the 1870s and 1880s, before the first underground subways opened, several elevated railroads ("els") were built. Powered by small steam engines, they were dirty, noisy, sometimes dangerous, and popular. Major lines ran along Second, Third, and Sixth Avenues. (Elevated tracks still exist, especially in the outer boroughs, but most have either been torn down or rebuilt.) Several songs were written about the els, including vaudeville banjoist Sam Devere's risqué, double-entendred description of his journey down the Bowery "Riding on the Elevated Railroad" (1890) and "Third Avenue El" (Michael Brown: 1956).

Subways

With 258 miles of tracks and 469 stations, New York City's subway is the most extensive in the world. Traffic has always been a problem on Manhattan's narrow island and New York began to think about building a subway soon after London opened a successful system in 1863. An experimental 312-foot pneumatic subway was built (illegally) under Broadway near City Hall in 1870, and New York's first real subway, the Interborough Rapid Transit Company (IRT), opened in 1904. Two other lines, the Brooklyn-Manhattan Transit Corporation (BMT) and the Independent Subway System (IND), opened in the following decades. In 1953, the New York City Transit Authority, a public agency, took over the management of all the city's subway and bus lines. Since that time, mass transit in New York has seen its ups and downs, but is still used by more than five million travelers every weekday. Running from one end of the city to the other, and operating twenty-four hours every day of the year, the subway is one of the few unifying factors in an otherwise disparate city. Among early attempts at subway songs were "Take a Ride Underground" (1904)—interpolated into the long-running musical "A Trip to Chinatown," "The New-York Subway or Rapid Transit Intermezzo" (1907), and "The Subway Glide" (circa 1907).

Supplement to the Brooklyn Daily Eagle, Tuesday, January 29, 1907

Commuting to the New Jersey suburbs was portrayed as less than idyllic in the 1914 song "On the 5:15." Despite his best efforts, Dashing Dan misses his train, has a few drinks with other commuters while waiting for the 7:38, looses track of time, and finally arrives home after midnight to find he has been locked out by his infuriated wife:

Talk about your subway, / Talk about your "L" / Talk about your street-car lines as well; / But when you're living out where the fields are green / You got to go home on the five fifteen. / You leave the office at five o'clock, / You stop in the butcher's for a steak or chop / You get the ev'ning paper and a magazine / And you run like the dickens for the five fifteen . . .

Taxis

With the introduction of internal combustion engines, horse-drawn cabs became motorized almost overnight. At the turn-of-the-century, the novelty of a motorcar, a meter, and the privacy of the back seat led to a whole rash of taxicab songs, including Edgar Selden and Melville Gideon's 1908 "Take Me 'Round in a Taxi Cab":

There's a new-fangled cab that's designed to keep tab, / To show you how far you may go; / But if you're discreet it is easy to beat. / As any wise person may know. / A register's there to keep track of your fare, / While you watch the girl at your side; / Now what could be fairer than that as a squarer. / So come, take me out for a ride.

Chorus: Take me 'round in a taxicab, a taxicab for two. / Start a pace the machine can't trace, be game and I'll stick with you; / Toot, toot, toot goes the tooter, / tick, tick the meter can't blab. / If you want to know if I'm speedy or slow, / Take me 'round in a taxi cab. . . .

Over the years, New York cab drivers gained a reputation for being fonts of urban wisdom. New York cabbies have been celebrated in films, Broadway musicals (e.g., Bernstein's *On the Town*, which features a female cabby named Hildy), and the television series *Taxi*, which revolves around a central character named Alex. Hailing a cab even inspired the 1919 song "Taxi":

One evening while dining, Where Broadway lights are shining, / A bellboy stood waiting, A twinkle in his eye; / On tiptoes a-perching, For someone he was searching, / I pondered and wondered / Till he began to cry, // Chorus: Taxi! (whistle) None anywhere, / Taxi! (whistle) I've got a fare, / And he tells me he wants a double seater, / He's all dolled up like he was goin' to meet'er. / Taxi! (whistle) Drive anywhere, / Taxi! (whistle) They'll never care, / He's thinking of little turtle dove, / They only take a taxi, When they love, love, love.

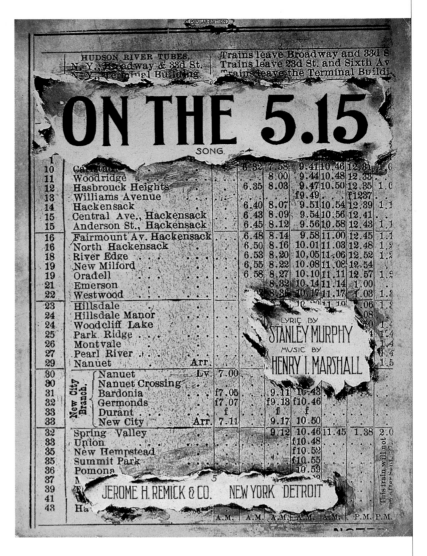

ABOVE: Commuting to *"where the fields are green"* "On the 5:15."

LEFT: Hailing a "Taxi" in 1919.

OPPOSITE: Flatbush commuters meet mass transit on the cover of William Slafer's "Brooklyn Daily Eagle Bridge Crush March, Descriptive."

OPPOSITE: A classy art deco cover illustration promoted this classy piece of music.

Crime and Punishment

Since its founding, one recurring quality-of-life issue confronting New Yorkers has been crime. As one recent scholar has elegantly phrased it, "the city's vast array of people has long made it a place of divergent moral codes."[1] Like all other large urban areas, New York has always attracted criminals; and as the city's population and wealth increased, so, too, did its attractiveness to various forms of lowlifes. Although many other American cities experienced proportionally more crimes per capita, an upsurge in drug-related street crimes in the 1980s made New York a national symbol of urban disorder and lawlessness. New Yorkers like to think of themselves as tough, and few musical forms come off as tougher than the ultra-urban hip-hop genres known as rap, and particularly "gangsta rap," which has been heavily criticized in recent years for celebrating crime and violence. However, three hundred years before gangsta rap, New Yorkers were singing about the exploits of another controversial citizen, Captain William Kidd:

My name is Captain Kidd, as I sailed, as I sailed. / My name is Captain Kidd, as I sailed. / My name is Captain Kidd, God's laws I did forbid. / So wickedly I did, as I sailed. / / I murdered William Moore, as I sailed, as I sailed, / I murdered William Moore, as I sailed, / I murdered William Moore, and left him in his gore, / Not many leagues from shore, as I sailed . . .

The Scottish-born captain and privateer William Kidd moved to New York in 1691 and married a wealthy local widow named Sarah Oort. They lived at 119–121 Pearl Street, and local legend says his treasure is still buried near Wall Street. In the late 1690s, with the blessings of the British government, he went out hunting Spanish and French ships on the Spanish Main, but the political winds shifted while he was away and he was ultimately arrested for piracy in Boston and shipped to London, where he was tried and hanged in 1701.

Crimes of passion, con games, prostitution, and street violence have provided material for the majority of New York's crime songs. (Insider stock trading and white collar crimes have yet to receive the musical attention they deserve from city songwriters.) In the early years, broadside ballads giving the gory details of notorious New York crimes were enormously popular. The ballads were usually marketed as being composed by the criminal just before he (or she) was executed. Long before the appearance of modern tabloids, these cheaply printed song texts were set to popular tunes of the day. For a penny or two, New Yorkers could sing Henry Bachus's (a.k.a. "The Saugerties Bard") song about "The Thirtieth Street Murder" (1858); or enjoy the broadside ballad "Hicks the Pirate" (March 1860), about a New York thief who stowed away on an oyster barge and murdered the crew. Hicks, like all broadside subjects, was ultimately captured, and:

By a true and faithful jury / He was found guilty of the crime. / Some raved and cursed like fury, / But he had met his fate in time. / 'Twixt heaven and earth suspended, / On Bedloe's Island Hicks was hung. / Some thousand there attended / To see the horrid murderer swung.

As early as the 1830s, the folk song "Oh, You New York Girls, Can't You Dance the Polka?" warned sailors about local ladies of the evening. More than one warning was clearly needed, and in the 1860s, a localized version of the English song "The Dark Girl Dressed in Blue" appeared:

From a village up the Hudson, / To New York here I came, / To see the park call'd Central, / All places of great fame. / But what I suffer'd since I came I now will tell to you, / How I lost my heart and senses too, / Thr' a dark girl dressed in blue . . .

As the song continues, the handsome con woman picks up the out-of-town narrator on a Broadway stagecoach and convinces him to pass her bogus $10 bill and give her the change: *"She thanked me, and said, 'I must away, Farewell, till next we meet, / For on urgent business I must go, / To the store in Hudson Street.'"* After she flees, he is arrested by the police and forced to make restitution.

Other songs to address crime in New York have ranged from Harrigan and Braham's "Callahan's Gang" (1873), the "Broadway Bootlegger" (1929), to Barry Manilow's story of murder and loss at the "Copacabana" (1978). Broadway shows have contributed such commentaries on local lawlessness as Frank Loesser's "Oldest Established Permanent Floating Crap Game in New York" from the Damon Runyon–inspired musical *Guys and Dolls* (1950), and Richard Rodgers' 1936 entr'acte "Slaughter on Tenth Avenue," a ground-breaking dance sequence set in a West Side dive and choreographed by George Balanchine for the musical *On Your Toes.*

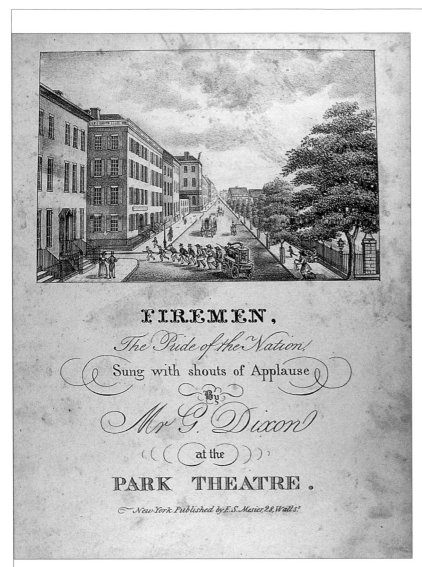

FIREMEN,
The Pride of the Nation!
Sung with shouts of Applause
By
Mr G. Dixon
at the
PARK THEATRE.

New-York Published by E.S.Mesier,28,Wall s.

Firemen

New York has had a professional fire department since 1865. Before that, volunteer fire companies took care of conflagrations. New York suffered major fires in 1776, 1811, 1835, and 1845 and numerous fire-related tragedies, including the Brooklyn Theatre Fire (1876), the fire on the cruise ship General Slocum (1904), and the Triangle Shirtwaist Factory Fire (1911). Music celebrating New York firemen includes "The New York Fireman" (circa 1836), "The Diligent Hose Company Quick Step. As Performed by Dodworth's Cornet Band of New York" (1849), "The Fireman's Polka" (1851), the "Friendship Quick Step"—"*Composed for Phoenix Hook & Ladder Co. No. 3 of New York*" (1850), and George M. Cohan's "The Boys Who Fight the Flames" (1908).

Military

Although New York was originally founded as a trading post, it was not long before its military importance became obvious. One of the first Revolutionary engagements, the Battle of Long Island, was fought in Brooklyn's Prospect Park, and New York then became the center of British military operations for North America. The British handed over a ring of forts in New York Harbor when they evacuated in 1783, and for the next two centuries the American military, especially the Navy, remained a presence in the city.

Semi-private militia companies were popular in early America. Usually underwritten by a wealthy community leader who appointed himself commander, and expensively dressed in dashing uniforms, the companies would assemble regularly to practice target shooting, drilling, and parading. Militia companies would also organize balls and dinners, and belonging to a militia was quite fashionable. Of course, the militia also inspired a great deal of music, especially marches and quick steps, many of them dedicated to the company leaders and illustrated with elaborate color covers. Examples celebrating New York militia companies include the "Brooklyn City Guard Quick Step" (1843), the "Brooklyn Lafayette Guards Grand March" (1855), "City Guard's Quickstep" (1842), "Eighth Company National Guard Quick Step" (1841), "The New York Light Guards Quick Step" (1839), and "Hewitt's Quick Step" (1840)—"*As performed by the Jefferson Guards Band.*"

After the carnage of the Civil War, private militias lost some of their appeal to upper-class New York men. Private militias were increasingly

ABOVE: Members of a volunteer fire company race past City Hall Park and up Broadway on their way to a blaze in the 1830s.

OPPOSITE: One of the great illustrated sheet music covers, this piece documents the 1858 burning of the Crystal Palace in what is now Bryant Park. The French-born composer and conductor Louis-Antoine Jullien was a major figure in New York musical circles during the mid-nineteenth century.

A passing policeman found a little child, / She walked beside him, dried her tears and smiled. / Said he to her kindly, "Now you must not cry, / I will find your mama, for you bye-and-bye." / At the station when he asked her for her name, / And she answered "Jennie," it made him exclaim: / "At last of your mother I have now a trace; / Your little features bring back her sweet face."

Finally, it must be noted that New York police have not been immune to musical ridicule. Examples range from "Gee, Officer Krupke," a colorful exchange between a beat cop and local wiseguys in Stephen Sondheim and Leonard Bernstein's *West Side Story* (1957), to the 1961 television theme song written by Nat Hiken and John Strauss for a series about two incompetent local cops called "Car 54 Where Are You!":

There's a holdup in the Bronx, / Brooklyn's broken out in fights / There's a traffic jam in Harlem / That's backed up to Jackson Heights. / There's a scout troop short a child, / Khruschev's due at Idlewild, / Car 54, where are you!

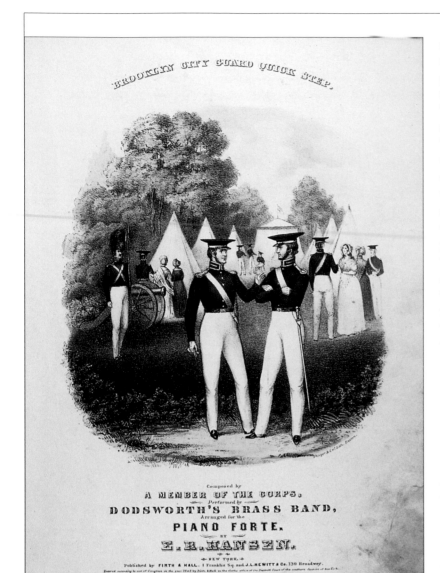

ABOVE: Well-dressed militiamen pose on the cover of E.R. Hansen's "Brooklyn City Guard Quick Step" (1843).

RIGHT: A bedraggled Edward Harrigan (right) and Tony Hart in formation—or as close as they got—with the Mulligan Guard's shooting target in the background.

OPPOSITE: Bridging the Atlantic divide during World War I.

made up of working class members, many of them recently arrived Irish immigrants. They provided a tempting target for the comedy team Harrigan & Hart to take aim at. In 1873 "The Merry Partners" introduced a theatrical sketch about a fictional militia troop named "The Mulligan Guard." Led by Dan Mulligan, the Guards, and their African-American counterparts, "The Skidmore Guard," romped through a dozen or so plays with titles like *The Mulligan Guard's Picnic* and *The Mulligan Guard's Christmas*, poking fun at the local militias, politicians, and anything else that got in their way. The plays were wildly successful with New York audiences. The song "The Mulligan Guard," which launched the series, was an international smash: Kipling recorded British troops singing it during maneuvers on the plains of India. It began:

> We shoulder'd guns and march'd, and march'd away, / From Baxter street, we march'd to Avenue A, / With drums and fife, how sweetly they did play, / As we march'd, march'd, march'd in the Mulligan Guard.

Occasionally, inspired by the local militias, a New Yorker would get excited enough about military life to join the U.S. Army—an entirely different animal. According to Harrigan and Braham's 1874 song "The Regular Army O!," this course of action was not recommended, even if strongly advised as an alternative to jail:

> Three years ago this very day, We went to Governor's Isle; / For to stand fornist [against] the corner, / In true military style. / Seventeen American dollars, Each month we surely get; / For to carry a gun, and bayonet, with a regimental step. / / We had our choice of going to the army, or to the jail; / Or it's up the Hudson River, with a "copper" take a sail! / Oh, we puckered up our courage, Wid bravery we did go, / And we curse the day we went away / Wid the Regular Army O!

During World War I, Americans experienced an avalanche of patriotic music. Perhaps no piece had a greater New York connection than the hit song "Good-bye Broadway, Hello France" from the *Passing Show of 1917* at the Winter Garden:

> Good-bye Broadway, Hello France, / We're ten million strong, / Good-bye sweethearts, wives, and mothers, It wouldn't take us long, / Don't you worry while we're there, / It's for you we're fighting too, / So Good-bye Broadway, Hello France, / We're going to square our debt to you.

Disasters, Riots, Civil Unrest, and General Mayhem

Fate has not always been kind to New York. Major fires in 1776, 1811, and 1835 destroyed large portions of the city. Riots, such as the Astor Place Riot (1849), the Civil War Draft Riots (1863), the Harlem Riots (1935, 1964), and the Crown Heights Riot (1991) have intermittently threatened urban stability. And unfortunately, New York's history has also been darkened by numerous tragedies. Many of these events were duly recorded by urban songwriters.

In 1871, the Staten Island ferryboat *Westfield* blew up at its South Ferry dock, killing forty and injuring more than two hundred. The broadside ballad "Terrible Disaster—Boiler Explosion on Board a Staten Island Ferry Boat With Dreadful Loss of Life" by A.W. Harmon (1871) appeared shortly thereafter giving details and, in the best of broadside tradition, asking listeners to reflect on their own mortality:

> Full three hundred pleasure seekers, / On July, the eleventh day, / Went on board the steamer Westfield / For excursion down the bay. ~ ~ ~ When a crash like awful thunder / In a moment rent the air, / Changed the happy scene of pleasure / To death, sorrow, and despair.

> Women, men and little children / Where blown up into the air. / Some fell on the shattered steamer, / Others watery graves did share. ~ ~ ~ Yes, the cause of all this suffering / And the loss of life so dear / Was for the want of a safe boiler / And a careful engineer. / Oh, our lives they are uncertain, / Death is on our track today. / It may take us unexpected. / God, prepare us all, I pray.

During a performance of *The Two Orphans* on December 5, 1876, a backstage fire broke out in the elegant Brooklyn Theatre at 313 Washington Street. Although the leading actress, Kate Claxton, took the stage and bravely tried to calm the crowd, panic broke out among the 1,200 theatre patrons, and in the stampede that followed, some three hundred people died. (The bodies were so badly burned that the exact number of fatalities was never established.) Many of the victims were buried in a mass grave in Greenwood Cemetery; Reverend Henry Ward Beecher delivered their funeral oration.

A broadside ballad about the event quickly entered the American folk tradition. Variants of the ballad, commonly known as "The Two Orphans," have been collected throughout the country. (The author was once introduced to a janitor at an Ohio museum who, upon learning she came from Brooklyn, said, "I know a song about your hometown," and launched into "The Two Orphans.") As often happens with folk songs, the actual events have become somewhat garbled over the years, and many singers believe that the fire was *set* by two mysterious orphans. As a version collected some years ago in Texas relates:

> We ne'er can forget those "Two Orphans," / Bad luck seems to dwell in their wake. / It seems they were brought to our city, / The lives of our dear friends to take.

> It's hark, don't you hear the cry "fire"? / How dismal those bells they do sound. / It's Brooklyn Theatre that's burning, / Alas, burning down to the ground. ~ ~ ~ It's away to the cemetery of Greenwood / Where the winds of the cold winter blow / It's there where the funeral is going / The dead and unknown for to lie.

In addition to the activity on and off stage, note the specter of death holding out a brand that ignites even the song's title.

'MID FLAME AND SMOKE

A DESCRIPTIVE SONG OF THE BURNING OF THE BROOKLYN THEATRE

WORDS & MUSIC BY J. W. TURNER

BOSTON.
Published by OLIVER DITSON & CO. 451 Washington St.

NEW YORK
C.H.DITSON & CO.
711 BROADWAY.

CHICAGO.
LYON&HEALY.

BOSTON
J.C.HAYNES & CO.

PHILA.
J.E.DITSON & CO.
SUCCESSORS TO LEE &WALKER.

Another major New York tragedy resulted from a fire. On March 25, 1911, a blaze broke out in a tenth-floor sweatshop owned by the Triangle Shirtwaist Company. Before it was brought under control, 146 workers had died—most of them young Jewish and Italian girls from the surrounding neighborhoods, who, due to the lack of fire escapes and illegally locked doors, were forced to leap to their deaths to escape the flames. As the building burned, their horrified families and friends, who gathered in the streets below, could do nothing but watch. The city was deeply shaken; tens of thousands—perhaps as many as one hundred thousand—from all walks of life marched in the funeral procession. The tragedy became a rallying point for the American labor movement. It led to major reforms in workplace safety regulations throughout the nation, but it also seared itself into local history and legend. (Each March 25th, roses are still placed in front of the building, which stands on the northwest corner of Washington Place and Greene Street and is now owned by New York University.) Two generations later, songwriter and Yiddish music scholar Ruth Rubin was still haunted by the tragedy. Following the broadside ballad tradition, she set the story to music in "The Ballad of the Triangle Fire" (1968):

> In the heart of New York City near Washington Square, / In nineteen-eleven, / March winds were cold and bare. / A fire broke out in a building ten stories high, / And a hundred and forty-six girls in those flames did die. ~ ~ ~ A hundred thousand mourners, they followed those sad biers, / The streets were filled with people, weeping bitter tears. / Poets, writers everywhere, described that awful pyre— / When those young girls were trapped to die in the Triangle Fire.

Few songs have been written about rioting, although Gordon Lightfoot's powerful "Black Day in July" about the 1967 Detroit Riots is a notable exception. Strikes are only slightly more popular as topics for popular songs. New York's first strike took place in 1677 when a dozen local cartmen walked off the job and were quickly convicted of contempt of court. During the famous Brooklyn Motormen's Strike of 1895, 5,500 transit workers on the Brooklyn Surface Railroad went on strike for a twenty-five cents per day pay raise. To break the strike, management imported scabs, and when this tactic failed, Brooklyn's mayor, Charles A. Scheiren, called in the militia. In the rioting that followed, several people were killed and many more injured; extensive damage was

done to the city's trolley lines. Soon thereafter, song publisher William Delaney, under his pen name, "William Wildwave,"[5] wrote a song about "The Brooklyn Strike":

> As I strolled through Brooklyn City not many days ago. / The workingmen were idle, for out they had to go. . . . The soldiers and policemen were called to take a hand / To terrorize the motormen in this our own free land. / The mayor who called for troops should ever bear in mind / That capital is never right when it attempts to grind.
>
> Chorus: Remember we are workingmen and honestly we toil; / And, gentlemen, remember, we were born on Brooklyn soil. / Nor can the pampered millionaires the spirit in us break. / The fame of our fair city is clearly now at stake.

"Solid Men to the Front": Songs About Politics and Politicians

New York's urban life has been led, or at least closely followed by politicians. Over the years, New York has had more than its fair share of colorful politicians. From Peter Stuyvesant, to Boss Tweed and Tammany Hall, "Gentleman" Jimmy Walker, Fiorello La Guardia, and Ed Koch, composers have sung to praise, or more often to ridicule, New York's political leaders. It's a tough town.

In the 1870s and 1880s, Harrigan and Braham's musicals were filled with tuneful swipes at the graft and corruption of New York politics. It was the era when political bosses such as Tammany Hall's William Tweed controlled every aspect of city government from the mayor's office to the street sweepers. Years later, ward heeler[6] and political hack George Washington Plunkitt in "A Series of Very Plain Talks on Very Practical Politics"[7] heroically tried to differentiate between honest and dishonest graft: "I might sum up the whole thing," he told a reporter, "by sayin': I seen my opportunities and I took 'em." A similar philosophy was shared by members of "The Aldermanic Board" in the 1885 Harrigan and Braham musical The Grip:

> Behold these statesmen bold, who never yet were sold, / We handle from one million up to ten; / The makers of your laws, each section and each clause. / The people's choice, the Board of Aldermen. / / Chorus: As rulers of New York we have a right to talk, / Supreme in district, precinct or in ward; / From the captain to a cop, we bring them to a stop, / This ornamental Aldermanic Board.

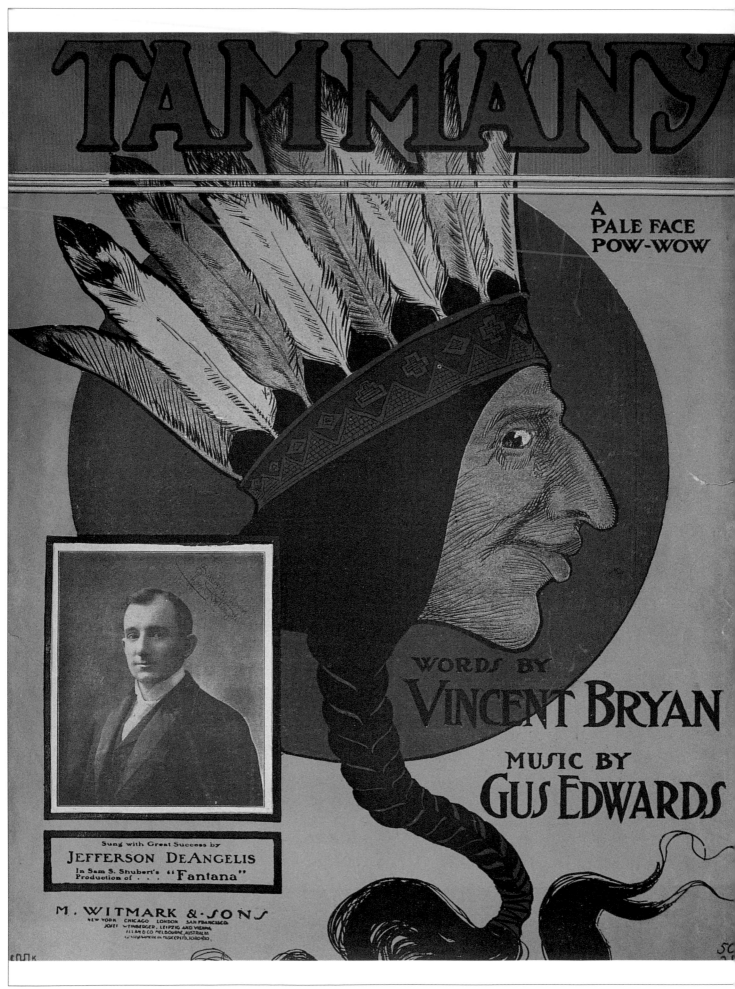

*We look out for your votes, your lamp-posts and
your goats, / In ev'ry district and in ev'ry ward; /
Put up your apple stands, engage your German
bands, / By order of your Aldermanic Board. //
To stop all future strife just put us in for life, / Upon
that point we members all accord; / We'll save the
city cash when banks they go to smash, / This
intellectual Aldermanic Board.*

Harrigan and Braham were also responsible
for the song "Oh, He Promises" from the 1880
musical *The Mulligan Guard Nominee*, in which Dan
Mulligan, running for alderman of his ward,
vows to create jobs for his cronies:

*I promise you employment, / But you must keep it
dark; / I'll have you count the sparrows, boys, /
Flying in Central Park . . .*

Other featherbedding jobs mentioned
include inspecting lampposts and keeping
goats from grazing along the old reservoir.
Of course, some immigrants were eminently
qualified for their public jobs. After President
Chester A. Arthur signed the Civil Service Act
in 1883, which reformed government hiring
practices, the great Irish-American comedian
Harry Cornell introduced a song entitled
"Encyclopedia McFlynn: The Irish Applicant
for Civil Service Honors" (1885):

*I have found Darwin's link so long missing / In
Brooklyn's dark city of sin. / Where Beecher gives
lessons in kissing / Says Encyclopedia McFlynn . . .
Public Office a great public trust is, / Without merit
promotion's a sin, / For every man, white and black,
Justice, / Says Encyclopedia McFlynn.*

The greatest of all Harrigan and Braham
political songs was undoubtedly "Muldoon, The
Solid Man," which was introduced in the 1874
Harrigan & Hart sketch *Who Owns the Clothes
Line?* The "Tombs" mentioned in the final verse
refers to the city jail on Foley Square; the *Daniel
Webster* was an Atlantic sailing packet built in
the 1850s for the White Diamond Line; and the
"Island" alludes to the city prison on Blackwell's
(now Roosevelt) Island in the East River:

*I am a man of great influence / And educated to a
high degree / I came here when small from Donegal /
In the Daniel Webster across the sea. / In the Fourteenth
Ward I situated / In a tenement house with my brother
Dan. / By perseverance I elevated / And went to the
front like a solid man.*

*Chorus: Go with me and I'll treat you decent / I'll set
you down and I'll fill your can / As I walk the street
each friend I meet / Says: "There goes Muldoon, he's
a solid man." ~ ~ ~*

SONG
FOR
MAYOR WOOD

MUSIC COMPOSED & DEDICATED TO
FERNANDO WOOD ESQ.

BY
The Hutchinson Family.
as sung at their concerts with the greatest success

NEW YORK.
PUBLISHED BY HORACE WATERS, 333, BROADWAY.

*I control the Tombs, I control the Island / My
constituents, they all go there / To enjoy the
summer's recreation / And the refreshing East River
air. / I'm known in Harlem, I'm known in Jarsey
[Jersey] / I'm welcomed hearty on every hand /
Wid my regalay [regalia] on Patrick's Day / I
march away like a solid man.*[8]

Tammany Hall was founded in 1788 as
a political club. Named after a legendary
Delaware Indian chief, the club gradually
grew into a disciplined political machine with
ties to the Democratic Party and New York's
immigrant communities, particularly the Irish.
In the first half of the nineteenth century, the
club's "sachems" occupied a series of increasingly
larger "wigwams," and in 1868, its ornate hall
on East 14th Street hosted the Democratic
National Convention. Tammany reached its
zenith about 1928 when club members Al
Smith reigned as governor of New York State
and James J. Walker served as the city's mayor.
By the late 1940s, reform movements and
scandal investigations brought about its demise.
Tammany inspired many songs, including
"Tammany: A Pale Face Pow-Wow" (1905),
by the songwriting team of Vincent Bryan
and Gus Edwards (who had just written "In
My Merry Oldsmobile"):

ABOVE: Fernando
Wood was a two-
time mayor of New
York (1855–1857
and 1859–1861).
A thoroughly corrupt
individual, Wood
advocated Southern
slavery and was a
leading Copperhead
(Confederate
sympathizer) during
the Civil War. The
Hutchinson Family
Singers, on the other
hand, were nationally
recognized liberals
who opposed
everything Wood
represented.

OPPOSITE: Throughout
its history, Tammany
Hall used Native
American images and
terminology in a futile
attempt to make the
political club seem
more respectable.

The SIDEWALKS of NEW YORK

(EAST SIDE WEST SIDE)

Words and Music by
Chas. B. Lawlor
and
James W. Blake

Published for
BAND
and
ORCHESTRA

WITH UKELELE
AND SAXOPHONE
ARRANGEMENTS

Hon. "AL" SMITH'S
Official Campaign Song

PUBLISHED BY PAULL-PIONEER MUSIC CO. 119 FIFTH AVE
NEW YORK

ABOVE: Tin Pan Alley lyricist Al Dubin wrote *Special Campaign Choruses* to "The Sidewalks of New York" when it was used as the Honorable "Al" Smith's Official Campaign Song in 1928.

OPPOSITE: La Guardia's squat figure is immediately recognizable on the sheet music cover of *Fiorello!*

Hiawatha was an Indian, so was Navajo, / Paleface organ grinders killed them many moons ago. / But there is a band of Indians, that will never die, / When they're at the Indian club, this is their battle cry:

Chorus: Tammany, Tammany, / Big Chief sits in his tepee, cheering braves to victory. / Tammany, Tammany, / Swamp 'em, Swamp 'em, get the "wam-pum," Tammany.

Tammany, Tammany, Stick together at the poll, you'll have long green wam-pum rolls. / Tammany, Tammany, / Politicians get positions, Tammany. ~ ~ ~

Other Tammany-inspired songs include the novelty song "Since I Joined Tammany Hall" (1893) and "Solid Men to the Front," an 1870 Quickstep *"Composed and Dedicated to Hon. William M. Tweed"* by C.S. Grafulla just before the political boss's fall from power.

A son of the Lower East Side, reformer Alfred E. Smith (1873–1944) rose through the ranks of Tammany Hall and the Democratic Party to become first a state assemblyman and later governor (1918). In 1928, Smith became the first Catholic to be selected as a presidential candidate by a national party. Although he lost,

he did prove himself a winner in his choice of a campaign song when he chose a revised version of "Sidewalks of New York" as his theme:

East Side, West Side / Three more cheers for Al / America was his cradle / Uncle Sammy is his pal. / When he is elected / How the grafters will squawk / He learned just how to fight them / on the Sidewalks of New York.

East Side West Side / Homes for those in need / Short working hours for women / Widows' pensions, yes, indeed. / Legal education / For these blessings he fought / Al learned just what was needed on the Sidewalks of New York.

German, Frenchman / Irishman or Swede / Italian, Hebrew or Scotchman, / Makes no diff'rence race or creed / Englishman or Russian / Al is all for you / 'Long as you will be loyal / To the Red, White, and the Blue.

There have probably been as many musicals written about New York's mayors as about any other category of American elected official. Take La Guardia, for example: Fiorello La Guardia (1882–1947), one of New York City's most popular mayors, was elected as a fusion candidate in 1933. La Guardia, a reformer, did much to modernize city government and was well liked by city voters. In 1959, Sheldon Harnick and Jerry Bock wrote *Fiorello!* a hit musical that included such tunes as "Politics and Poker," "Gentleman Jimmy," "The Name's La Guardia," "The Bum Won," and the "Little Tin Box," in which a judge questions a political hack about how he was able to amass a fortune on a modest public salary:

[Judge] Mister "X" may we ask you a question? / It's amazing, is it not? / That the city pays you slightly less than fifty bucks a week, / Yet you've purchased a private yacht. / / [Witness] I am positive your Honor must be joking, / Any working man can do what I have done / For a month or two I simply gave up smoking / And I put my extra pennies one by one / / Chorus: Into a little tin box, a little tin box / that a little tin key unlocks. / There is nothing unorthodox about a little tin box . . .

Fiorello! won a Pulitzer Prize, and composer Jerry Bock and lyricist Sheldon Harnick went on to write *Tenderloin* (1960), another musical comedy set in New York which revolved around a minister's misguided crusade to close down Manhattan's notorious red-light district in the 1890s, inspired by the exploits of real-life minister Charles Parkhurst. Several years later, the songwriting team had an even bigger hit with *Fiddler on the Roof*, a musical about a group of Eastern European Jews—some of whom undoubtedly became New Yorkers.

In 1934, soon after La Guardia assumed office, the eminent songwriting team of Harold Arlen, Ira Gershwin, and Yip Harburg wrote "Life Begins at City Hall," burlesquing "The Little Flower"'s ("*fiorello*" in Italian) attempt to improve urban life. Introduced in the revue *Life Begins at 8:40*, it also lampooned Grover Whalen, a politician who served as the city's official greeter and headed the mayor's reception committee from 1919 to 1953:

We're here, we're here, assembled here today / To help the Great La Guardia beautify the bay. / He's beautified Manhattan / And the Bronx and Queens and Staten, / And tonight this mighty Latin / Wants to beautify the bay.

The Grover Whalens: He gave the city class, oh! / There's dancing on the Mall. / He introduced Picasso / To the boys at City Hall. / Delancey Street has flowers / The Bow'ry has no bums; / With chromium-plated showers, / He has beautified the slums. ~ ~ ~

La Guardia was preceded in office by the debonair James J. Walker. "Gentleman Jimmy," as he was known, had a multifaceted career that included a short stint as a songwriter, during which he wrote the lyrics for the hit, "Will You Love Me in December as You Do in May?" Ernest Ball, composer of "When Irish Eyes Are Smiling," wrote the music. The 1969 musical *Jimmy* by Bill Jacob and Patti Jacob recorded Walker's difficult tenure as mayor and included songs such as "The Charming Son-of-a-Bitch," "Darlin' of New York," "Riverside Drive," and "They Never Proved a Thing." Walker's own reign as mayor ended abruptly in 1932 when, surrounded by suspicion of corruption, he unexpectedly resigned and left for Europe with his mistress, the actress Betty Compton. It was, to put it mildly, the scandal of the decade, and Walker's reputation never recovered.

One of the greatest New York mayor shows was Charles Strouse's 1985 revue *Mayor*, based on the autobiography of Edward I. Koch. Strouse, a student of Aaron Copland and Nadia Boulanger, wrote both words and music for *Mayor*. He had earlier made his mark on Broadway with such classics as *Applause*, *Bye, Bye, Birdie*, and *Annie*, as well as the theme song "Those Were the Days" for the television series *All in the Family*. *Mayor's* opening title song sums up Koch's delight with his job:

What a lovely feelin' / waking ev'ry morning / looking in the mirror / knowing I'm the mayor. / Someone brings me tea, someone reads to me, someone laughs at what I say. / Someone brings the Post, they love me the most . . .

Not that the job is not without its drawbacks:

Sure the job gets manic, one day Blacks berate me. / But I never panic, next day cops all hate me. / Ev'ry cabby here, ev'ry waiter there, there is nothing they don't know. . . .

Mayor also contained a song simply entitled "Ballad," that asks many of the questions that every native New Yorker has occasionally pondered: e.g., who bought all those Grumman buses, whose bright idea is it to close major bridges during rush hours, and who is, or was, the Major Deegan, who lent his name to the expressway?

Newspapers: Sing All About It

Civic pride, patriotism, and political intrigue all cried out for publicity, which was duly provided by generations of newspaper reporters—driven men and women who sometimes were as much local heroes and characters as the people they wrote about. The press has always been an important part of New York life and there are a surprising number of songs and marches about New York newspapers. One of the earliest of these songs comes from John Peter Zenger's 1734 libel trial and had the "dubious distinction of being the only song ever burned at the stake."[9] In 1733 Zenger's *Weekly Journal* had some less than complimentary things to say about New York's British governor William Cosby. The governor was furious. On November 5th, a broadside ballad entitled the "Magistrate's Song" appeared, which was immediately declared libelous by a now irate Cosby. His handpicked jury met on October 19, 1734, but was unable to discover the broadside's composer or publisher. Rather than let the matter drop, they ordered that the song be publicly burnt! Zenger was later imprisoned for libel and defended at his trial by the famous Philadelphia lawyer Andrew Hamilton—who some believe might have written the infamous song. In the landmark case, Zenger was acquitted and the precedent of free speech was firmly established in America. The song itself included such lines as:

To you, good lads, that dare oppose / All lawless power and might, / You are the theme that we have chose / And to your praise we write. / You dared to show your faces brave / In spite of every abject slave. . . . Your votes you gave for those brave men / Who feasting did despise / And never prostituted pen / To certify the lies / That were drawn up to put in chains / As well our nymphs as happy swains. . . .

In the nineteenth century, marches and two-steps were particularly popular with newspaper publishers. Although none of the New York pieces achieved the lasting fame of John Philip Sousa's "Washington Post March," local examples included the "Evening World Gallop" (1888), which was *Respectfully Dedicated to the Hon. Joseph Pulitzer*"; "The New York Herald March & 2-Step Dance" (1893)— "*As Performed in All the Prominent Dancing Academies*" and "*Respectfully Inscribed to a Universally Popular Man and a True Journalist, James Gordon Bennett, Esq.*"; the "New York Press Patrol" (1894)— "*Dedicated to the Journalists of New York City*"; "The Sun March & Two-Step"(1894)—"*The Latest Dance and Instrumental Success*"; and "The Brooklyn Times March & Two-Step" (1897).

Even before the yellow journalism of the 1890s, New York newspapers could be downright nasty. In 1856, Erastus Brooks was the editor of a violently pro-South, anti-Catholic "rag" called *The Express*. When he decided to run for governor, this broadside ballad appeared on the streets of New York:

> *Erastus Brooks of "The Express" / Is really nominated / For Governor of New York State / Oh! Isn't he elated? / He'll swell and strut and strut and swell, / And cut up many a caper, / And lots of dirty lyin' stuff / He'll publish in his paper. . . .*

Reading New York papers could also be educational. In 1902, songwriters Paul West and John W. Bratton published a novelty song about a young Connecticut woman who acquired "street smarts" because "She Reads the New York Papers Ev'ry Day":

> *Once there lived a farmer's daughter down in old Connecticut, / Where they get the New York papers ev'ry day. / She was shy, and oh, so tender, unsophisticated, but / She read the New York papers ev'ry day. / She had never dined on lobsters or had tasted of champagne, / She'd never smoked a cigarette nor ridden on a train, / But those who tried to fool her found their labors all in vain, / For she read the New York papers ev'ry day.*

As the song progresses, the papers teach the heroine how to ensnare a wealthy summer boarder from New York, and, when he turns out to be *"a rounder,"* how to sue him for divorce. She then flew *"off to Europe"* where:

> *She captivated dukes and earls and even princes, too, / But she didn't let them marry her, too much for that she knew, / For she read the New York papers ev'ry day. / She soon came back very famous . . . [and] is now a prima-donna on the comic opera stage. / Her jewels look like headlights, and her gowns are all the rage. / And if you want to know her name, just look on any page / Of most any New York paper any day.*

Manhattan's City Hall and Newspaper Row, circa 1900.

The personal ads in the James Gordon Bennetts' (father and son) *New York Herald* were legendary. They appeared until 1906 when rival publisher William Randolph Hearst charged that "immoral assignations" were being made through the *Herald* and brought the matter before a federal grand jury. Convicted of publishing information about prostitutes, Bennett was fined $25,000, but the case did little to discourage future publications from featuring personals. In the 1870s, an anonymous wit even wrote a song about "The Herald Personals":

> *Of course now you all read the Herald, / For the topics and news of the day. / And other affairs interesting / Some are sad and some are gay. / But the subject I wish now to mention, / Perhaps you have noticed before, / As you read down the columns each morning, / And smiled at the things you saw. / / Chorus: The Personals in the Herald, / Herald! Herald! / The Personals in the Herald, / The Herald Personals!*

The song goes on to list a few examples:

> *Oh, my husband's gone out of the city, / And father will be at the store. / I'm lonely, so lonely without you, / Oh, say, can you meet me at three? / There's boned turkey, champagne and oysters, / Your answer send quickly to me.*[10]

Before the advent of child labor laws, newsboys or "newsies" were a constant presence on New York streets. They came from families that desperately needed the small income they earned; many of them were homeless and lived in alleyways and basements when not working long hours peddling papers. Most were under the age of twelve. Their circumstances inspired a number of songs, not to mention a recent Disney film, *Newsies*. One of the most famous period songs was A. Baldwin Slone's 1900 vaudeville hit "Jimmy, De Pride of Newspaper Row":

> *Jimmy Jones is me name; / Selling papes is me game / I'm the toughest kid ever on earth, / If you ask where's me home, / From a box to de dome of de World Building [on Park Row] does for me berth . . .*

Being a newsie seems to have been a character-building experience. Anyway, poverty always looks better in retrospect, as we hear in the 1895 song "Broadway and Union Square," when a wealthy grandfather reminisces to his grandchild:

> *Johnny Jones and I were comrades, ev'ry night you'd find us there / Selling papers on the corner of Broadway and Union Square; / We were only two of many who had to face the bitter fight, / But I'd gladly give this fortune just to be back there tonight.*

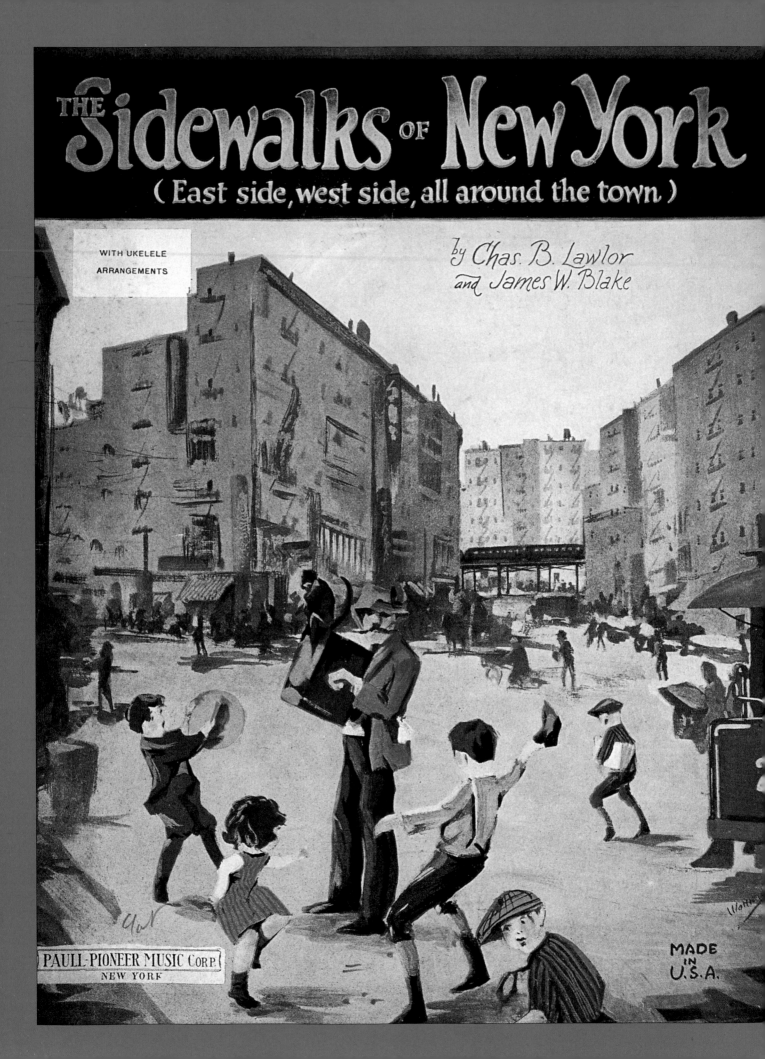

Chapter 9

LEISURE TIME IN GOTHAM

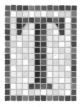ourists vacationing in New York often accomplish a phenomenal amount of sightseeing, dining out, museum visiting, and theatre going in an amazingly short time. Although the natives are loath to admit it, most of them don't actually live like that. Part of the secret to long-term survival

OPPOSITE: The 1932 edition of Lawlor and Blake's classic "The Sidewalks of New York."

in New York is the ability to pace oneself, and sometimes, even the most urban of New Yorkers sneak back to their apartments and just relax. Chilling out, urban style, can take a number of forms—hanging out at home, on the stoop, or up on the roof, strolling through a park, going for a bike ride, or enjoying a weekend, holiday, or parade. Watching sports, dining, and dancing have also been popular with generations of New Yorkers. Over the years, hardworking city songwriters have spent a lot of time and effort writing about New Yorkers at play.

The Old Neighborhood

More than anything else, it is the people of New York who make their neighborhoods special. Hanging out is a highly developed New York art form. Traditionally, New Yorkers hung out on their "stoops"—a steep flight of six to ten steps leading up to the front door of most houses and apartment buildings. (Stoops, by the way, are a legacy of the Dutch, who originally raised the first floors of their houses several feet above street level to prevent flooding, a constant concern in their flat, canal-endowed homeland.) Stoop-sitting is still practiced in many neighborhoods, especially on hot summer evenings.

In the late nineteenth century, in part because of the prevailing fashion for sentimental songs, and in part because the city was changing so rapidly, a whole host of nostalgic songs about the joys of neighborhood life in little old New York began to appear. Undoubtedly the most famous of these is "East Side, West Side," or as it is also known, "The Sidewalks of New York."

In 1894, James W. Blake was a young salesman at John Golding's East Side hat shop with a talent for writing song lyrics. One day, Charles B. Lawlor, composer, actor, and partner of James Thornton in the small-time vaudevillian team Lawlor and Thornton, entered the shop humming a catchy tune he had just composed. The two men struck up a conversation about songs and songwriting and Blake agreed to try writing lyrics for Lawlor's tune. Some say it was Lawlor who suggested that "something about New York might be nice," but whatever the case, over the next few days, between hat sales, Blake wrote three verses and a chorus to the most famous of all New York songs. Even today, almost every New Yorker can sing you the chorus, although the verses have been largely forgotten. Here, then, for the record, are the complete lyrics as they appeared in the first 1894 edition published by Howley, Haviland & Co.:

Down in front of Casey's / Old brown wooden stoop, / On a summer's evening, / We formed a merry group; / Boys and girls together, / We would sing and waltz, / While the "Ginnie" played the organ / On the sidewalks of New York—

Chorus: East side, West side, / All around the town, / The tots sang "ring a rosie," "London Bridge is falling down"; / Boys and girls together, / Me and Mamie Rorke [sic], / Tripped the light fantastic, / On the sidewalks of New York.

That's where Johnny Casey, / And little Jimmy Crowe, / With Jackey Krause the baker, / Who always had the dough, / Pretty Nellie Shannon, / With a dude as light as cork, / First picked up the waltz step / On the sidewalks of New York.

Things have changed since those times, / Some are up in "G," / Others they are wand'rers. / But they all feel just like me, / They would part with all they've got / Could they but once more walk, / With their best girl and have a twirl, / On the sidewalks of New York.

The characters in the song are based on real people, neighbors of Blake who lived near the row house at 312 East 18th Street where his family had lived since the 1820s. The Blakes bought bread from the local baker, Jakey Krause, and a real Mamie O'Rourke had taught Blake to waltz. The real Nellie had a well-dressed beau, or, in the slang of the 1890s, "dude," who was probably named James C. Shannon. Shannon was a "gallery-stooge" (paid claque member) for the vaudeville star Lottie Gilson, and he eventually became Nellie's husband. At the time, the derogatory term "Ginnie" or "Guinie" was used for Italians, and most of the street organ or "hurdy-gurdy" players were Italian immigrants. The "G" in verse 3 probably refers to "Glory," (Heaven). The old brown wooden stoop mentioned in the song actually led to a house owned by a Mr. Higgins, but apparently Blake thought "Casey" sounded better. The song was "Dedicated to Little Dollie Golding," who was undoubtedly related to John Golding, Blake's boss at the hat shop.

Perhaps because James Shannon was her gallery-stooge, Lawlor and Blake were able to persuade vaudeville star Lottie Gilson, called "the Little Magnet" because of her box office draw, to introduce "Sidewalks" at the Bowery's Old London Theatre. It was an instant hit. (Writer and music critic Gilbert Douglas, in his amusing book, *Lost Chords*, claimed that Gilson was such an effective performer that she "could wring sex from a dissertation on integral calculus.") The publisher Pat Howley immediately bought the song outright from the composers for $5,000 and issued it within the year. Since that time, it has remained one of the most popular and best known of all New York songs.

Always a local favorite, "East Side, West Side" gained national attention in 1924 when New York Governor and Democratic presidential candidate Alfred E. Smith selected it as his campaign song. Blake eventually returned to his job as a salesman and Lawlor continued his career in vaudeville, and neither he nor Blake ever managed to write a hit again. Nothing further was heard from Blake until January 14, 1933, when the seventy-year-old former salesman and lyricist, destitute, homeless, and the sole support of a blind brother and elderly sister, appealed to the New York *Herald Tribune* for help. The family, he explained, had recently been dispossessed from their Bronx apartment. From an article written at that time, it appears that Blake had continued his career as a velour and velvet salesman until the Depression ended the demand for such luxury goods. The *Herald Tribune* notified the Emergency Unemployment Relief Committee of Blake's plight and also created a special fund (which was personally endorsed by Al Smith) that supported Blake and his family until his death two years later.[1]

"Sidewalks of New York" was so popular that it almost immediately sparked parodies. In 1895, when the original was barely a year old, Andrew Sterling wrote a parody about local newsboys which included the chorus: *"Uptown, downtown, all around the street, / The boys shoot craps for pennies while the cop is off his beat; / Large and small together, hear 'em shout and cry / How they love to gamble on the Sidewalks of New York."* About the same time, vaudevillian Charles McIntosh was singing a parody which began:

Down in front of Casey's good old liquor store, / On a summer's evening they'd gather by the score; / Bums they were together, some would sing and talk, / While the gin ran down their throats on the Sidewalks of New York. /

Chorus: East side West side, all around the town / All the noses are red now, from putting whiskey down; / Hunting the free lunch together, for baked beans and pork, / Everyday they're loaded on the Sidewalks of New York.

Music in the Streets

While on the topic of street life, it might be appropriate to mention street music. Today, New York's streets and subway stations are full of street musicians, or "buskers." In addition to ubiquitous guitar-strumming singer/songwriters, there are Chinese dulcimer players, South American accordionists, and even very loud Scottish bagpipers. Several forms of street music, however, are now extinct. The first are street organs. Until the 1930s, street organs—also called barrel organs or "hurdy-gurdys"—were usually played by recently arrived Italian immigrants, who rented their instruments from contractors at exorbitant rates. Frequently accompanied by pet monkeys that were taught to beg for pennies, organ grinders provided a musical backdrop for turn-of-the-century New Yorkers. Mayor La Guardia banned organ grinders in an early "quality-of-life" dispute. (Most people thought he banned them because he was embarrassed to see fellow Italian Americans begging.)[2] Before they disappeared, they had a significant impact on the musical landscape. In 1893, for example, W.S. Mullaly wrote a song entitled "The Italian Organ Grinder" in what was supposed to be an Italian accent:

I landa here in Castle Garden, playa de org' all 'round de street, / Me poor Italian, a padrone, playa de music vera sweet. . . . Wand'ring up an' down all day, for de rich, de poor I play . . . And de monk take de nic' and de centa / While de org' I grind away . . . I gota license ina mya pocket, I dressa de monk up in fasha . . .

Also vanished from New York's musical landscape are the once-popular German brass bands and alley or courtyard singers—wandering minstrels who sang in tenement courtyards while housewives hung out their wash on clotheslines. When they finished, listeners would wrap pennies in bits of newspaper and drop them from the window. Yiddish writer Morris Rosenfeld, in his essay "A Cantor Without an Altar," wrote of hearing such a singer in a Jewish neighborhood sometime before 1912:

We were all sitting comfortably at the table eating lunch when . . . a weeping High Holiday tune could be heard from the window that leads to the courtyard . . . An old man, with white hair like milk, with a respectable snow-white beard, tall and slender, stood leaning on a staff. Holding his quick eyes aloft, he was rapt in recitatives, which a small pale boy supported with resonant accompaniment. . . . When he began to recite "Unsane toykef" they began to throw coins from all sides . . . Older women shook their heads and wiped away the tears, but the younger folk, who came from the factories and shops to gulp their lunch, had no interest . . . they ran to the windows but soon disappeared.[3]

ABOVE: This 1936 hit focuses on *"good old organ grinder Pete"* and all the stereotypes.

LEFT: The lyrics, in German dialect, begin: *"In the neighborhood I liff ev'ry day at twelff / Comes around a certain band and I enchoy myself . . ."*

Apartment Life

Almost all New Yorkers live in apartments—be it a six-story walk-up tenement on the Lower East Side with a bathtub in the kitchen, a partitioned brownstone in Harlem, an anonymous thirty-storied white-brick 1960s high-rise on Second Avenue, or a luxurious twenty-room duplex on Park Avenue. If you live in a New York apartment you probably have upstairs neighbors, downstairs neighbors, share a common wall with at least one other family, and split a front door with dozens, if not hundreds, of neighbors. In many parts of America, this would be considered strange; but it comes as second nature to New Yorkers, who after generations of apartment life have fully adapted to their vertical lifestyle. Occasionally, they even sing about it.

Life in New York's early tenements could be rough. At the beginning of the nineteenth century, old mansions, churches, warehouses, and breweries began to be subdivided into low-rent multiple family dwellings called "rookeries."

Rosie must have lived in a tough neighborhood—the welcome mat is chained to the wall!

Dedicated to Mrs Maurice Coughlin

DOWN AT ROSIE RILEY'S FLAT

Maude Nugent.

WORDS & MUSIC BY MAUDE NUGENT THE GIRL WHO WROTE "SWEET ROSIE O'GRADY"

SHAPIRO BERNSTEIN VON TILZER

WELCOME

These, in turn, inspired the earliest tenement houses: cheaply built multi-storied apartment buildings intended to serve as housing for New York's working class. The first tenements were built near Corlear's Hook on the Lower East Side in the 1830s. In an effort to be fashionable, early apartments were often referred to as "French flats" or "flats." In 1882, Edward Harrigan and David Braham wrote "McNally's Row of Flats" for their musical *McSorley's Inflation*. One of the earliest songs about a New York apartment house, it tells the story of a politician/slumlord (McNally), who owns a tenement with a *"great conglomeration of men of every nation"* and more variety than *"a Babylonian tower"*:

*It's down in Bottle Alley lives Timothy McNally /
A wealthy politician and a gentleman at that. /
The joy of all the ladies, the gossoons [lads], and
the babies / Who occupy the building call'd
McNally's Row of Flats.*

*Chorus: It's Ireland and Italy, Jerusalem and
Germany, / Oh, Chinamen and [blacks], and a
paradise for cats, / All jumbled up togayther, in
the snow or rainy weather, / They represent the
tenants in McNally's Row of Flats.*

For many, the modest housing provided by the tenements was fine. As songwriter Edgar Seldin put it in his 1894 song, "Bob, The Bowery Boy":

*Oh, I'm not a Wall street broker, with a white
necktie and choker, / An East Side Bow'ry boy
just tops 'em all. / And my girl's a beauty bright,
we go spieling [dancing] ev'ry night / Down at
Guggenheimer's Hall. ~ ~ ~*

*When we're respliced [married] I'll be contented,
two neat rooms will then be rented / I'll go house
keeping with my bonnie bride. / With an oil stove
and a cot, who could ask a better lot? / Then we'll
own the whole East Side.*

In 1902, songwriter Maude Nugent, "The Girl Who Wrote 'Sweet Rosie O'Grady,'" composed the popular song "Down at Rosie Riley's Flat." Probably inspired by Harrigan and Braham's earlier hit "Maggie Murphy's Home" (1890), it celebrates urban hospitality, even in humble surroundings: *"No home on Fifth Avenue has faces half so bright as down at Rosie Riley's flat."*

*Down to Rosie Riley's flat, After work at night, /
I go to have a social chat, after work at night. /
Boys and Girls around the block with faces shining
bright, / They gather there at eight o'clock, after
work at night.*

Chorus: Down at Rosie Riley's flat, There's welcome printed on the mat, / Ev'ry-one happy and free from care, / Nothing but pleasure is reigning there. / If you're passing make a call, / Touch the bell that's in the hall, / They'll be glad to meet you, with kindness they'll treat you, / Down at Rosie Riley's flat.

New York did have its share of luxury apartment buildings, but except for penthouses (see Chapter Two), basic, three-bedroom apartments in elevator buildings in the Bronx or Queens rarely inspired songs. "Kitchenettes" were another matter. Like many other types of New York housing (e.g., single-room "studios" and "maisonettes"), "kitchenettes" (one-room apartments with kitchens) arose when New York real estate agents—a particularly rapacious type of land shark—needed a new term for small, vastly over priced tenement rentals. But in the 1920s, "kitchenette" must have sounded both modern and cute—just the thing for newly married couples. Soon there were songs, such as Irving Berlin's "In a Cozy Kitchenette Apartment" (1921) from *Music Box Revue*, and the 1929 Al Dubin and Joe Burke song, "In a Kitchenette," from *The Gold Diggers of Broadway*. Although the same film gave the world "Tip-Toe Through the Tulips," the "fella" looking for his Cinderella "In a Kitchenette" primarily serves to remind us why the women's rights movement was needed:

Wanna girl who looks good / In a kitchenette, / Wanna girl who cooks good, / And one who can pet, / Wanna a girl who takes well / To a coffee pot, / Wanna girl who shakes well / To music that's hot. / I want a somebody, who can drive / My little flivver, / Somebody who can stew / My chicken liver; / Wanna girl to keep me, / Keep me out of debt, / Wanna girl who looks good / In a kitchenette.

In verse two, this sport goes on to ask for *"some somebody to mix a toddy when I feel shoddy and nervous, / To give me the service I like to get."* Other paeans to New York's middle-class housing include the 1937 "Our Penthouse on Third Avenue"—at the time, Third Avenue was noted for its noisy and dirty elevated train, not for its fine housing—and a P.G. Wodehouse and Jerome Kern song about "Nesting Time in Flatbush" from the 1917 musical *Oh, Boy!*

One of the major housing and neighborhood-related issues of the last few decades has been gentrification—the moving of upscale people into downscale neighborhoods. Although the infusion of more affluent people often leads to the revitalization of an area, it also frequently

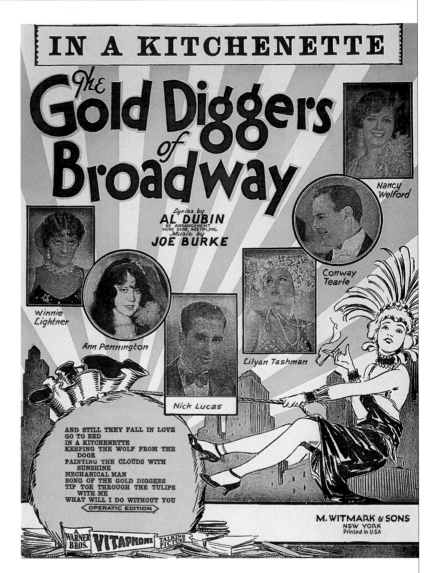

forces up rents, which, in turn, drives out long-term residents and older, less trendy businesses. Composer Charles Strouse, in his 1985 musical *Mayor*, wrote an amusing song on this subject entitled "March of the Yuppies," in which young professionals who *"eat nouvelle cuisine, support Channel Thirteen"* announce their intention of coming to *your* neighborhood to make it more charming and hip:

You probably shop at Key Food. / You probably ate Cantonese. / You buckled the belt on your trench coat. / Well, my friends, we're putting an end to these transgressions! / / Look at Tribeca and Amsterdam Avenue. / The local hardware store sold out to Rive Gauche. / The tuna on rye is now "en brioche." / The neighborhood bookies are now David's cookies. . . .

And, they ominously warn:

We won't rest until your block is quaint. / With sweaters round our necks, we run to eat Tex-Mex / And none of you suspects his neighborhood is next in line. . . .

Note the cigarette-smoking flapper trying to haul off a bag of gold.

Up on the Roof

If you live in a New York apartment and are very lucky, you may have access to the roof of your building. Some fancier apartment buildings have roof gardens, complete with swimming pools, picnic benches, flower beds, and fully grown trees. Most rooftops, however, are barren patchs of asphalt that the locals optimistically refer to as "tar beaches." Nevertheless, in the summer, the roof is usually cooler at night and a better spot for sunbathing during the day than the tenement dweller's other access to the great outdoors: the fire escape. And the view of the skyline from many New York roofs is spectacular. Here, between the water towers, chimneys, and pigeon coops, one can also catch up with neighbors, make out with a date, get a tan, or just ponder life.

There have been a number of classic New York roof songs. One of the earliest was Harrigan and Braham's song "Mulberry Springs" from the 1886 play *The O'Reagans*, which told of the *"neighborly people from Cork and Kerry"* living in one of the notorious tenements near Spring and Mulberry Streets, who, on hot summer evenings, would congregate on the roof. *"Let fashion assemble at Saratoga,"* Harrigan wrote, but in the ghetto:

> The heat is intense, and the crowd is immense. /
> All praying and whistling for wings, / To get up
> and fly to the clouds in the sky, / The Boarders of
> Mulberry Springs.

"Sunday Tan" was written by lyricist Ira Gershwin for *The Ziegfeld Follies of 1936*, but the lyrics were not used and it was probably never set to music. Nevertheless, it is a wonderful snapshot of urban life in the mid-1930s, and Gershwin's poetic genius shines in his ability to (almost) rhyme such pairs as "comics/stomics" and "raspberry/Asbury":

> When the city is sweltering, / The temp'rature
> high— / People go helter-skeltering / To Coney and
> Rye. / One and all, / Let them fall / For their Sunday
> at the beach. / If it's hot / We've a spot / That is just
> in reach. / Really haven't far to go, / Climbing up
> three flights or so.

> Refrain: In a chimney setting, / With you I'll be getting /
> My Sunday tan. / Through with daily labors, / Up
> there with the neighbors— / The rooftop clan. / We
> can give the raspberry / To Newport and Asbury /
> The minute we plan / Parading in our undies— /
> Getting our Sund'y's tan. ~ ~ ~ Reading Sunday
> comics, / Exposing our stomics / The rooftop clan.

Another great roof song comes from Moss Hart and Irving Berlin's Depression-era musical *Face the Music* (1932). The same show also contained such hits as "Let's Have Another Cup of Coffee," and "Manhattan Madness," as well as "On a Roof in Manhattan" in which two lovers imagine they are on the ramparts of a Spanish castle:

> We'll build a castle in Spain / On a roof in
> Manhattan, / And in our lofty domain, / We'll pretend
> to be Latin. / You'll sing a sweet little tune, / While I sit
> and strum my guitar, / We'll be so close to the moon, /
> I'll reach up and pluck you a star, / And thru the night
> we'll remain, / Wrapped in velvet and satin, / And
> dream of Castles in Spain, / On a roof in Manhattan.

Possibly the greatest, and certainly the most successful of all New York roof-related songs is Carole King and Gerry Goffin's 1962 classic "Up on the Roof," which was made famous by the Drifters. Its lyrics talk about a place of refuge, *"When this old world starts a-getting me down"*:

> I'll climb 'way up to the top of the stairs / And all
> my cares just drift right into space / On the roof it's
> peaceful as can be / And there the world below don't
> bother me—Up on the roof.

Right in the middle of town, the roof is *"far away from the hustling crowd / And all that rat-race noise down in the street."* Even better, at night the stars *"put on a show for free,"*

> And, darling, you can share it all with me / I keep
> a-tellin' you / Right smack dab in the middle of
> town / I found a paradise that's trouble proof / And
> if this world starts getting you down, / There's room
> enough for two—Up on the roof.

Although many city summer songs mention beaches and roof tops, arguably the best song about summer in New York City is the 1966 Lovin' Spoonful hit, cowritten by John Sebastian, Mark Sebastian, and Steve Boone, which succinctly sums up both the tension and the magic of "Summer in the City":

> Hot town, / Summer in the city. / Back o' my neck
> gettin' dirty and gritty. / / Been down / Isn't it a
> pity; / Doesn't seem to be a shadow in the city. / All
> around / People looking half-dead / Walkin' on the
> sidewalk hotter than a matchhead / / But at night,
> it's a different world. / Go out and find a girl. /
> Come on, come on and dance all night; / Despite
> the heat, it'll be all right. / And babe, don't you know
> it's a pity / The days can't be like the nights ~ ~ ~
> Cool town, evening in the city . . . Running up the
> stairs / Gonna meet you on the rooftop.

Open Spaces: The Parks

For a giant metropolis, New York is surprisingly green. In fact, with twenty-six thousand acres of parkland, and 1,500 parks, playgrounds, and monuments, New York has by far the largest urban park system in the country. Early on, New Yorkers' love of open spaces was reflected by their patronage of "pleasure gardens," private parks where, for a modest entrance fee, one could listen to bands, stroll flower-bordered paths, have a lemonade or sherbert, and at night, marvel at fireworks.

Although early Manhattan had numerous squares and monuments, as early as the 1840s city planners recognized the need for a large, centrally located park. Agreeing upon its location, however, was another matter. For years, there were two major contenders: the first was an undeveloped ninety-acre swatch of woodlands along the East River that extended from 66th to 75th Streets and inland to Third Avenue. Originally owned by Samuel Provoost (New York's first Episcopal Bishop, whose cousin, David, a notorious smuggler, hid contraband goods in "Smugglers' Cave" near the present corner of 71st Street and York Avenue), and then the country seat of the Jones family, it was already a favorite picnic spot. Although bypassed for the city's main park, it remained a favorite destination until the area was developed in the 1890s. In 1880, J.L. Fenny was inspired to write a song about being "Up at Jones' Wood":

Myself and Lizzie Rodgers, / Who is my steady company, / Attended a moonlight picnic, / Of the Peerless Coterie. / The girls with smiling faces / Were in a happy mood, / And every one went in for fun, / Up at Jones' Wood. ~ ~ ~ To please the charming creatures / The boys did all they could. / But they got on their ear [drunk] a-drinkin' beer / Up at Jones' Wood.

The privately owned Palace Garden pleasure garden was located on 14th Street and Sixth Avenue.

THE PALACE GARDEN POLKA
(WITH ACCOMPANIMENT OF SINGING BIRD)

Performed at the PROMENADE CONCERTS with the greatest success
and dedicated to the LADY PATRONS
BY
THOMAS BAKER.
NEW YORK.
PUBLISHED BY HORACE WATERS 333 BROADWAY.
BOSTON MASS.
PUBLISHED BY OLIVER DITSON & Cº 277 WASHINGTON St.

In 1853, after years of debate, the state legislature authorized the city to use its right of eminent domain to acquire 843 acres in the center of the island running from 59th to 110th Streets. Pushed by leading citizens, who admired the great public parks of London and Paris, it was to be the first landscaped public park in the United States. In 1857, following a design competition, Frederick Law Olmsted and Calvert Vaux were selected to construct the city's new "Central Park." It was one of the largest public works projects ever undertaken by the City of New York, and when the twenty thousand workers finished, they had created one of the masterpieces of American landscape architecture. It opened to the public in the winter of 1859 to rave reviews—some of them musical.

By 1865, more than seven million people visited Central Park each year. It was the fashionable place to see and been seen. (In its first decade, it was estimated that more than fifty percent of the park's visitors arrived by private carriage, at a time when only five percent of New Yorkers owned carriages.) As the city moved uptown and public transportation improved, the park's visitors began to diversify. Still, strolling in Central Park remained a fashionable New York thing to do.

Composer-about-town George Cooper, who also gave us "Mistress Jinks of Madison Square," "Strolling on the Brooklyn Bridge," and "I Never Go East of Madison Square," wrote the lyrics for several Central Park songs, including "Twilight in the Park" and this 1869 hit, "Walking in the Park":

The "style" of things for me, / When every thing looks gay, / Is up in Central Park / To pass the time of day! ~ ~ ~I patronize the "Mall," / I stroll around the "Lake," / I watch the dashing teams, / And try to keep awake; / My very languid air, / The people remark: / They'd ought to pay me well / To ornament the Park!

Over the years, songwriters have found plenty to sing about in Central Park: There was "Pretty Little Flora or Listening to the Music Up in Central Park" (1869), "On the Benches in the Park" (1896), "Sailing on the Lake" (1874), and Jerome Kern and Oscar Hammerstein's "Winter in Central Park" (1929). And, of course, there were always songs about the great New York preoccupation—meeting members of the opposite sex, including "I'll Meet You in the Park" (1874), "In the Park (On the Mall)" (1948), and "In Central Park" (1905), which began:

There's a spot in New York, In the heart of town / That is dear to all. . . . // Chorus: Come, dear, to Central Park for a stroll with me. / While stars are peeping and cops are sleeping, oh come with me. / Down, dear, in lover's lane, none but the moon will see. / And I'll be your lovey, if you'll be my dovey / in Central Park.

From the east side a belle, from the west side a swell / Who will spoon all day; / And forgetting all pride in the swan boat they'll ride. / You will hear them say. / Coney Island is fine, but the free park for mine / When I want a lark: / So a seat that is shady for me and my lady / In Central Park.

In the 1870s, Arthur French and W.S. Mullaly (a well-known minstrel of the period), wrote two hit songs: "Flirting on the Mall" and "Flirting on the Ice":

To Central Park one day, / I took my love with me, / To pass the time away / In skating merrily, / When on the gliding steel / She whispered once or twice— / Oh! George, my George, pray don't reveal / Our flirting on the ice.

There are literally dozens of other Central Park songs, not to mention several musicals, not the least of which was Rodgers and Hart's "A Tree in the Park" (1926) from the show *Peggy-Ann;* and Dorothy Fields and Sigmund Romberg's 1945 *Up in Central Park,* a musical about New York political boss William M. Tweed featuring the songs "Carousel in the Park," "Close as the Pages in a Book," and "April Snow." It would be remiss not to

CENTRAL PARK AND THE GONDOLA

One of New York's great folk tales concerns the purchase of gondolas for Central Park's rowboat lake. As more and more money was spent on the park, the city councilmen began to get fidgety. Going over park expenses with a fine-toothed comb, one not terribly well-educated councilman was aghast to find that park designers Olmsted and Vaux had ordered six Venetian gondolas for the lake. At the next council meeting he denounced this as a waste of public money: "Instead of buying six," he demanded, "why didn't they just order two and breed them?"

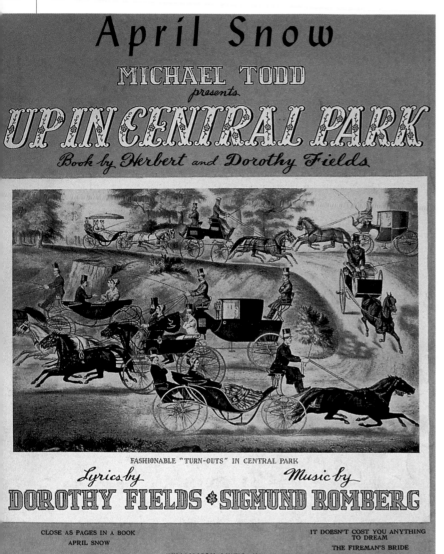

April Snow

MICHAEL TODD
presents

UP IN CENTRAL PARK

Book by Herbert and Dorothy Fields

FASHIONABLE "TURN-OUTS" IN CENTRAL PARK

Lyrics by
DOROTHY FIELDS

Music by
SIGMUND ROMBERG

CLOSE AS PAGES IN A BOOK
APRIL SNOW

IT DOESN'T COST YOU ANYTHING
TO DREAM
THE FIREMAN'S BRIDE

WILLIAMSON MUSIC, INC.
R K O BLDG · RADIO CITY · NEW YORK

ABOVE: Sheet music from *Up in Central Park* featured an older print of "Fashionable 'Turn-Outs' in Central Park."

RIGHT: Union Square in 1912.

mention that many classical composers have also been inspired by Central Park—most notably Charles Ives, who wrote both "Romanzo di Central Park" (1900) and "Central Park in the Dark" (1907).

Central Park was not the only park in the city. Brooklyn's Prospect Park, also by Olmsted and Vaux, was completed in 1868, and many New Yorkers considered it the designers' finest work. Prospect Park has been celebrated by a number of pieces, including Luigi Conterno's "Prospect Park" (1874), Rick Rench and Danny DiMinno's "Prospect Park in Brooklyn" (1949), and Edward Edelson's march, "Prospect Park Parade" (1968).

Smaller city parks were also celebrated in song. Union Square on 14th Street (the heart of New York's theatre district from the 1860s to the 1890s) was particularly popular, inspiring songs such as the "Union Park Schottish" (1852), and Harrigan and Braham's "On Union Square" (1886), which told how *"On warm summer days the actors of plays assemble to gossip and stare / And grandly posé in a statuate way at the plaza on Union Square."* Although it was originally called Union Square because it was where the Bowery (now Fourth Avenue) intersected Bloomingdale Road (now Broadway), since the Civil War, Union Square has been the site of many of New York's union meetings, workers' rallies, and political protests. This fact was noted by George and Ira Gershwin in their song, "Union Square" from the 1933 musical *Let 'Em Eat Cake.* A follow-up to their Pulitzer

Prize—winning musical *Strike Up the Band* (a satire on war), and *Of Thee I Sing* (a satire on politics), *Let 'Em Eat Cake* was a satire on life in general. The song starts in peace and unity: *"Our hearts are in communion / When we gather down on Union / Square, heigh ho!"*

> *Tis here we discover all the tonics / That cure all the problems of the race. / Oh, on boxes they put soap in, / How we love it in the open / Air, heigh ho! / We may not fill our stomics, / But we're full of economics / Down on Union Square! / Down here on Union Square!*

Soon, agitators, led by a character named Kruger, interrupt the singers and segue into a new chorus demanding "Down With Everyone Who's Up!" Their eclectic list of denunciations include:

> *Down with one and one make two! Down with ev'rything in view! / Down with all majorities, / Likewise all minorities! / Down with you and you and you! ~ ~ ~ Down with books by Dostoyevsky! / Down with Boris Thomashefsky![4] / Down with Balzac! Down with Zola! / Down with pianists who play "Nola!"*

Weekends in the City

A few songs concern themselves with weekdays in the city, such as "Monday in Manhattan" (1935), which begins by complaining about the booming traffic, confirming the narrator's fears that he is back in Manhattan and his vacation days are over. But most songs about city days celebrate the weekend, such as "Saturday Night in Central Park" (1947), and "Uptown Saturday Night" (1974). Sundays were particularly inspiring, perhaps because until the 1960s, many New Yorkers worked half-days on Saturdays, so Sunday was their only real day off. Sunday songs include Harry Von Tilzer's 1902 hit "On a Sunday Afternoon" (*"Take a trip up the Hudson or down the bay / Take a trolley to Coney or Rockaway"*); "On the Proper Side of Broadway on a Sunday P.M." (1902); Harrigan and Braham's "Sunday Night When the Parlor's Full" (1877); and classical composer Elie Siegmeister's piano suite *Sunday in Brooklyn* (1946), with movements such as "Prospect Park," "Sunday Driver," "Family at Home," and "Coney Island." Portia Nelson's "Sunday in New York" (1959) as well as Peter Nero and Carroll Coates's similarly entitled hit "Sunday in New York" (1964), and Harold Rome's "Sunday in the Park" from the 1937 landmark musical revue *Pins and Needles*, are all classic

descriptions of how New Yorkers spend their weekends. *Pins and Needles* presented by the "Labor Stage," performed by members of the International Ladies' Garment Workers' Union (ILGWU), and written by an undiscovered talent named Harold Rome, was an unexpected success; the politically conscious revue ran for over two years. Among the show's hits was "Sunday in the Park," which began:

> *All week long I work in the shop, / I work and work and never stop / Get up at six and go to bed at nine. / But the day I think is the best, / Is Sunday that's my chance to rest, / The only day that you might say is mine / / We leave our hot and stuffy flat, / There's one place that we know; / And subway to the public park / oh, that's the place to go. / On Sunday in the park.*

From the ILGWU's show *Pins and Needles*, the song's cover art reflects a wishful labor-management relationship.

EASTER PARADE
by IRVING BERLIN
PRICE
50¢
IRVING BERLIN
Music Corporation
1650 BROADWAY, NEW YORK 19, N. Y.

Holidays and Parades

Holidays give New Yorkers a chance to vary their routines, relax, and reconsider life. Although some New Yorkers do go away, many more "stay in town" and enjoy the relative peace and quiet that descends on their city. Since 1924, the Christmas season in New York traditionally begins with R.H. Macy's Thanksgiving Day Parade. (Macy's was one of the first New York stores to commercialize Christmas: it introduced illuminated window displays and an in-store Santa as early as the 1870s.) It's not surprising, then, to discover a song entitled "Santa on Parade!" by Claude Lapham (1939) *Inspired by the R.H. Macy & Co. Thanksgiving Day Parade.*" Other Christmas-in-New York songs include Harold Rome's "Yuletide, Park Avenue" (1946), "Rockefeller Plaza Christmas Tree" (1954), the rap hit "Christmas in Hollis" (Queens) by Russell Simmons and Daryl McDaniels (1987), and a number of work-for-hire carols like Billy Butt's 1991, "It's Christmas in New York," written for the annual Radio City Music Hall pageant. (These songs might be one of the reasons that people come to see the Rockettes dance, not sing.)

Despite all the New Year's Eve hoopla in Times Square—which few native Manhattanites ever attend—there are surprisingly few pieces that mention New Year's Eve, except for Werner Janssen's 1929 symphonic jazz poem *New Year's Eve in New York.*

One of New York's unique holiday traditions is the Easter Parade—which is not really a parade at all, but rather an informal procession that starts about noon every Easter Sunday on Fifth Avenue after services end at several of the city's largest churches. When the parade began in the 1880s, Fifth Avenue from 50th to 59th Streets was still "millionaires' row." The parade grew out of the ancient custom of promenading to and from church to show off the new clothes that were traditionally worn at Easter to celebrate the arrival of spring. It soon became the city's annual fashion parade and attracted both well-dressed strollers and those anxious to see (and copy) the latest fashions. Hats were particularly important. Today, thousands of New Yorkers, many of them wearing elaborate headgear, still stroll Fifth Avenue every Easter Sunday. George M. Cohan wrote a song about "The Easter Sunday Parade" in 1927, but it is Irving Berlin's 1933 song, "Easter Parade," from the revue *As Thousands Cheer,* that most people remember:

In your Easter bonnet / With all the frills upon it, / You'll be the grandest lady in THE EASTER PARADE . . . On the Avenue, Fifth Avenue, The photographers will snap us / And you'll find that you're / In the rotogravure.

Years later Berlin recalled how he had struggled to find just the right song for Moss Hart's story. "I'd written a couple of old-fashioned-type songs," he said, "but they were lousy. So I reached back to something I'd written in 1917. It went *'Smile and show your dimple, / you'll find it very simple . . .'*" He kept the tune, but changed the lyrics, and the rest, as they say, is musical history.

Ethnic parades provide New Yorkers with more than a chance to dress up and go for a stroll with their friends. Parades are a way to demonstrate the power and strength of your group in a public way. Today, there are dozens of ethnic parades throughout metropolitan New York. The oldest and still one of the largest is the Irish Saint Patrick's Day Parade, which marches up Fifth Avenue each March 17th. Founded in 1766 by Irish servicemen in the British Army, almost all of whom were Protestants, the parade still annually draws hundreds of thousands of marchers and supporters. Of course, this quintessential New York Irish event was fair game for the songwriting team of Edward Harrigan and David Braham to satirize. For their 1874 musical, *The Day We Celebrate,* they wrote "Patrick's Day Parade," a descriptive song that purported to list the parade's marching order when it was still held downtown:

The ancient Order of Hibernians, Father Matthews' Temperance men, / The Sprig of Shamrock and Fenians too, on the seventeenth of March fall in. / The longshoremen are next in line, all hardy, stout and tough, / Their hearts are made of Irish oak, although their hands are rough, / The music blaring sweet "Garry Owen" or "Killarney's Lakes" so fair, / To the City Hall we make a call, To be review'd by the Mayor.

A relatively recent but wildly successful addition to New York's parade calendar has been the annual Greenwich Village Halloween Parade. Founded by performance artist Ralph Lee in 1974, the nighttime parade invites New Yorkers to create their own outrageous costumes and join in the fun. Lou Reed, one of today's finest musical commentators on New York, wrote "Halloween Parade" for his 1989 album, *New York.* In it, he describes some of the parade's participants:

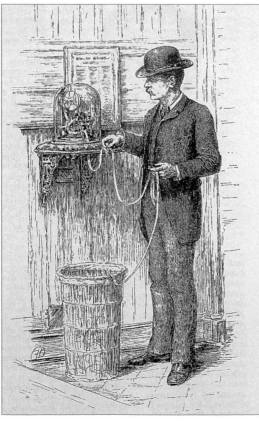

ABOVE: A bedraggled Edward "Ned" Harrigan (left) and Tony Hart (right) ready to step off in their own two-man "Patrick's Day Parade."

RIGHT: Investor checks early ticker tape in 1885.

There's a downtown fairy singing out "Proud Mary" as she cruises Christopher Street / And some Southern Queen is acting loud and mean where the docks and the badlands meet . . . There's a Crawford, Davis, and a tacky Cary Grant / And some Homeboys lookin' for trouble down here from the Bronx. . . . There's the Born Again Losers and the Lavender Boozers and some crack team from Washington Heights / The boys from Avenue B and the girls from Avenue D / Tinkerbell in tights . . .

Finally, it would be remiss not to mention that most distinctive of all New York processions, the ticker-tape parade. Created spontaneously by Wall Street office workers on October 29, 1886, during festivities marking the dedication of the Statue of Liberty, ticker-tape parades were inspired by a unique combination of reams of used financial paper (which could serve as impromptu confetti), tall buildings from which to throw it, and the narrow streets of lower Manhattan. They soon became a local tradition and were officially sanctioned by the city. Even the sanitation department got into the act by carefully measuring the amount of paper collected after each parade so it could be compared to previous ones. To date, the largest was the 1981 parade celebrating the release of American hostages by Iran (1262 tons of paper); the silliest was probably the 1938 parade for Douglas "Wrong Way" Corrigan, who flew halfway around the world in the wrong direction. Once fairly common, today ticker-tape parades are held only on special occasions, and ticker tape has been replaced by computer paper, canceled checks, and hastily shredded phone books. One of the largest of all the ticker-tape parades took place in 1927 in honor of Charles Lindbergh. Years later, the talented singer/songwriter Al Stewart captured both the event and the era in his 1995 song "When Lindy Comes to Town":

When Lindy comes to town / And all the bands are playing / When Lindy comes to town / And all the flags are waving / Mr. Coolidge he will say / It's a public holiday / You can see them ride down Wall Street / In a ticker-tape parade.

City Sports

New Yorkers have always enjoyed sports and have long been enthusiastic, if demanding sports fans. Songs and instrumental pieces were written to celebrate famous boat races off the Battery in the 1830s; commemorate sledding along Broadway in the 1850s; and mark the opening of the Jerome Park race course in 1867.

William Vincent Wallace (1812–1865), an Irish-born virtuoso on both the piano and the violin (he was called "The Irish Paganini"), and longtime fixture on the local musical scene, was inspired by a New York winter sport to compose "Winter Polka or Recollections of a Merry Sleigh Ride" (1853). In the nineteenth century, sleigh riding along Broadway was a popular activity. Gene Schermerhorn, writing about his New York childhood, recalled that in the 1840s, public sleighs

all had at least four horses and sometimes six, eight, or ten. People used to crowd in and hang on the outside. . . . Someone would shout "Come right up here by the stove." Of course, there was no stove but they would crowd up all the same. On the [coach] box were sometimes men dressed in fancy costumes or like old women. I remember once seeing some men with huge tin trumpets eight or ten feet long Every small boy who could not ride, seemed to feel like taking it out on those who could by pelting them with snowballs; but no one seemed to mind it much.[5]

When bicycles appeared on city streets in the 1890s, it was inevitable that composers would take note of the new craze. Soon, there appeared such gems as the "New Cycle Path March," commemorating the 1895 opening of a dirt bicycle path along Brooklyn's Ocean

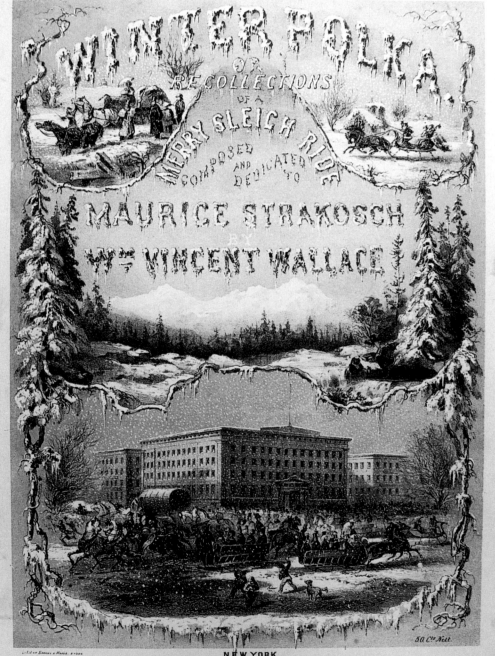

This elaborate sheet music cover matches Gene Schermerhorn's memories of sleighing—right down to the young gentlemen in the foreground throwing snowballs. Pictured in the rear is the Astor House, the city's first luxury hotel on the west side of Broadway between Barclay and Vesey Streets. Erected 1834–1836, it was razed in 1913 during construction of the subway.

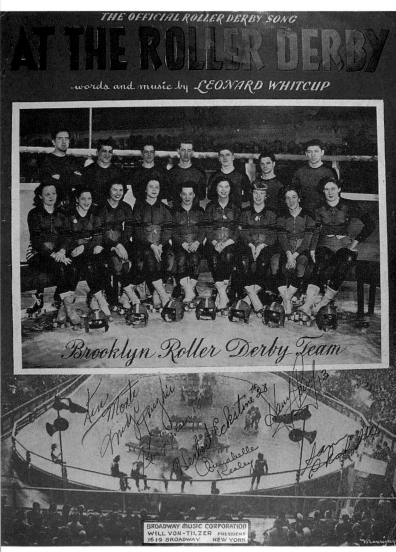

Parkway, and the marvelously illustrated 1898 "New York and Coney Island Cycle March Two-Step" by E.T. Paull, marking the fad for multi-day bicycle races. Years later, Brooklynites could musically celebrate another local sport with "At the Roller Derby."

Baseball

If there is one sport that is musically identified with New York, it is baseball. Although the birthplace of baseball is still hotly debated, Alexander J. Cartwright's 1846 rules for the "New York game," as played by members of the New York Knickerbocker Club, was one of the earliest and most influential tracts in modern baseball. New York baseball fans were among the first to eat hot dogs (introduced by Harry M. Steven at the Polo Grounds, circa 1900) and to hear "Take Me Out to the Ball Game," a song composed in 1908 by New Yorkers Albert Von Tilzer and Jack Norworth.

During the first half of the twentieth century, the Giants, the Yankees, and the Dodgers inspired large and enthusiastic local followings. The Giants, who left the Polo Grounds of upper Manhattan for San Francisco in 1957, seem to have had little musical impact. And despite their repeated championship performances, the Yankees as well as the more recently arrived Mets, have inspired only occasional musical accolades: for example, Paula Lindstrom's "I Love the New York Yankees" (1981), or Ruth Roberts and Bill Katz's "Meet the Mets" (1963).

However, the Brooklyn Dodgers, or "De Bums" as they were frequently called, inspired a wealth of musical tributes. Beloved by the citizens of Brooklyn, the (Trolley) Dodgers' 1957 decision to leave for some town west of the Mississippi—which shall remain nameless—is still deeply regretted. Not only was it seen as a betrayal of local fans (which it was), but it also coincided with other economic and social setbacks for New York's largest borough, as postwar America shifted its attention to the suburbs.

Songs inspired by the Dodgers included "Dem Flatbush Bums" (1949), and "Leave Us Go Root for the Dodgers, Rodgers" (1942). The latter featured Murgetroyd Darcie, *"the belle of Canarsie, who went 'round with a fellow named Rodge."* Although a good dancer, Rodge was really a phoney from Coney, who *"for baseball and such had no use,"* so Murgetroyd hit him with her *"handbag as big as a sandbag and to him these hard woids Murgy said":*

Leave us go root for the Dodgers, Rodgers / That's the team for me— / Leave us make noise for the boisterous boys on the B.- M.- T.- / Summer or winter or any season / Flatbush Fanatics don't need no reason. / Leave us go root for the Dodgers, Rodgers. / That's the team for me—

In 1941, lyricist Michael Stratton and composer George Kleinsinger (who later gained fame as the composer of the children's cantata *Tubby the Tuba*) wrote a short but delightful musical fantasy entitled the *Brooklyn Baseball Cantata*, which relates how the Brooklyn Dodgers play and win a game against the New York Yankees. In addition to "The Brooklyn National Anthem," the cantata contains a number of great choruses, including "Kill the Umpire," in which the umpire tells of his unhappy childhood, how he sold his soul to the devil, and attended umpire school where he *"learned to be wrong nine times out of ten"* and *"shattered ties with all decent men."* In the end, the narrator awakes to find that the Dodgers' victory was only a dream; but, as the piece closes, other voices assure him that *"it's bound to happen soon."* When the cantata was recorded in the late 1948, renowned opera singer and passionate baseball fan Robert Merrill sang the lead.

In 1957, local pride in the Dodgers and their imminent departure inspired musical pleas like Roy Ross, Sam Denoff, and Bill Persky's "Let's Keep the Dodgers in Brooklyn," recorded by radio personality Phil Foster:

Say, did you hear the news about what's happenin' in Brooklyn / We really got the blues about what's happenin' in Brooklyn. / It ain't official yet. We hope official it don't get, / But beware, my friend, and let me warn ya,— / they're thinkin' a takin' the Bums to California.

The song goes on to implore *"don't let them leave our premises, / L.A. would be their nemesis,"* so:

We offer our bridges. / You can take 'em wid yez, we have a couple we could spare; / But we'd all feel so glum—widout the Duke and Gilliam, / We'd need one left to jump off in despair.

Sophisticated Rhythms: High Life in New York

Some New Yorkers' idea of well-spent leisure time involves movement up (and occasionally down) the social ladder. Perhaps because many songwriters were "cultural refugees" coming to New York from small-town and rural America, they were particularly interested in writing about the sophistication of city life. No one better exemplified the out-of-town migrant who could out–New–York–the–New-Yorkers than Indiana-born Cole Porter, whose music is the epitome of mid-twentieth-century urban chic. Porter's nuanced musical descriptions of New York life, with those of his contemporaries George and Ira Gershwin, Richard Rodgers, and Lorenz Hart, set the standard for elegance and sophistication. But they were not the first to take note of the subject: New York's high society had been inspiring songwriters since the mid-nineteenth century.

New York did have an established high society, one that had little to do with the arts. Made up primarily of the descendants of old Dutch and Anglo-American families, New York's "society" never had the amount of power or influence that they did in such cities as Boston or Philadelphia. Nevertheless, they fought hard to hold back the tide of the nouveau riche and the foreign-born who were increasingly important in the life of the city. In the late 1860s, an obsequious lawyer and socialite named Ward McAllister helped Mrs. William Astor draw up the famous "A-list" of four hundred local elites—coincidentally, just the number that could comfortably fit into her newly built ballroom. McAllister crowed about the success of "The Four Hundred" list in his self-serving book *Society as I Have Found It* (1890); but songwriters merely used it as fodder for a new round of comic songs. For example, a song giving an overview of New York's upper, middle, and lower classes and entitled the "Broadway Opera and Bowery Crawl" was interpolated into the 1872 production of *The Black Crook*:

The afternoon's the time to see, / The fashionable gent or belle, / The morning's for the bus'ness man, / The afternoon is for the swell, / He struts on Broadway gaily decked / In beaver [hat], broad cloth, gloves, and all / And while the lads with envy smile / He takes his usual Broadway crawl. / / Chorus: The Broadway crawl, The Broadway crawl / The quizzing [of] darlings or making a call. / The Broadway crawl, The Broadway crawl / I'll show you the Broadway crawl.

Another style I'll try to show, / Through Bowery he often goes; / With pantaloons stuck in his boots, / And beaver pushed up on his nose, / He's already ready for a "muss," / And loudly boasts his want of fear; / But oftentimes he finds his match, / And then he "crawls off on his ear." / /

The Bowery crawl, The Bowery crawl / For smoking, or drinking, or raising a brawl. / The Bowery crawl, The Bowery crawl, / I'll show you the Bowery crawl.

But in my song I'll not forget the dandy of Fifth Avenue, / Leave out the swell of "Upper Ten"? By Jove! 'twould never do. / He dotes upon the Opera, / And all that sort of thing, you know. / For promenading afternoons / He's just the fellow for a beau. // The opera crawl, / The opera crawl / Escorting the ladies to party or ball, / The opera crawl, the opera crawl, / I'll show you the opera crawl.

In 1890, Edward Harrigan and David Braham devoted a whole musical to mocking the pompous Ward McAllister in *Reilly & The Four Hundred*. Songwriter J.S. Cox also contributed a song entitled "New York Society" (1889), which began:

I've seen society in every shape and form— / I've watched the tide of fashion rise and fall; / I've viewed it in its calm, I've seen it in its storm, / And this is my conclusion after all: // Chorus: Baden Baden Spa, France and Germany, / Liverpool or London,

Spain or Italy; / In such society there's much variety, / But nothing equals New York society. // It dabbles in the water or perhaps upon the shore, / It yawns and wishes it was back in town. / And though it maybe nice to drink the nasty waters, / And loose your money gambling at the spa . . . the New York season I prefer by far.

But if you really wanted recognition *"by a rapid transit route,"* songwriters Cobb and Edwards suggested in their 1902 song "On the Proper Side of Broadway on a Sunday P.M.," that *"with a crowd you must be seen"*

On the proper side of Broadway on a Sunday P.M. / Where the clothes and diamonds do not care who may be wearing them. / You may not be such a mucher but you'll be as much as such. / On the proper side of Broadway on a Sunday P.M. // Let your tailors be your teachers, advertise your form and features, / On the proper side of Broadway on a Sunday P.M.

For many, 1930s films visually crystallized the image of sophisticated New York. Perhaps no film star was more closely associated with New York high life than dancer Fred Astaire.

BELOW LEFT: High society in New York was not confined to Manhattan.

BELOW RIGHT: This 1892 song made fun of an attempt to narrow "The Four Hundred" to an even more exclusive core of 150 socialites.

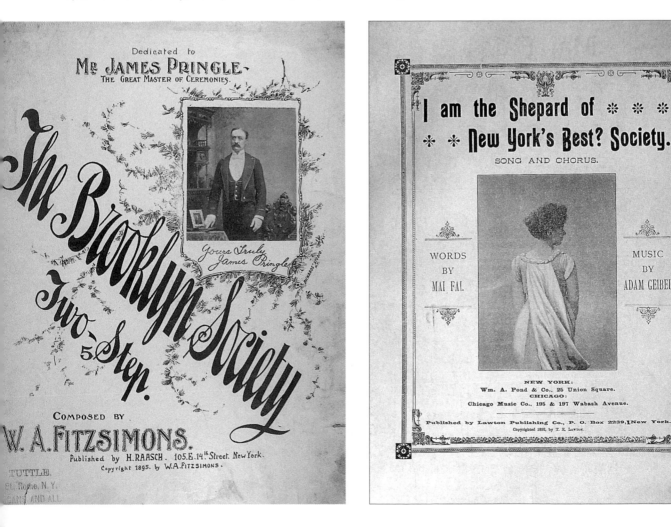

THE LOWLIFE

Although not nearly as popular as the city's high life, there have been some remarkable songs about New York lowlife. Examples range from the 1853 tear-jerker "The Dying Words of Little Katy or Will He Come?" based on the Dickensian exploits of a long-suffering hot-corn girl,[6] to the 1895 Harry Dillon and Nat Mann song "What Right Has He on Broadway?," in which a Bowery bum explains, *"I always stop at good hotels for I've a need of rest / I stay until the porter says, 'These seats are for the guests,'"* but complains, *"If you're not dressed complete they'll say, / What right has he on Broadway?"*

More disturbing are modern ballads that expose the misery of New York's poor and defenseless. In this genre, no contemporary writer is stronger or more compelling than Lou Reed. In his 1988 classic "Dirty Boulevard" he deals with homelessness, drugs, and a doomed childhood:

> *Pedro lives out of the Wilshire Hotel / He looks out a window without glass / The walls are made of cardboard, newspapers on his feet and / His father beats him 'cause he's too tired to beg. . . . No dreams of being a doctor or a lawyer or anything / They dream of dealing on The Dirty Boulevard . . . He's going to end up on The Dirty Boulevard.*

Barefoot and dressed in rags, hot-corn girls sold corn-on-the-cob on the streets of New York.

In the 1940 film *Blue Skies*, Astaire had a major hit performing Irving Berlin's song "Puttin' on the Ritz." Actually, the song had been revised for the 1940 film. The original 1928 version was set in Harlem and began:

> *Have you seen the well-to-do up on Lenox Avenue / On that famous thoroughfare with their noses in the air / High hats and colored collars, white spats and fifteen dollars / Spending ev'ry dime for a wonderful time.*

For the 1940 film, Berlin revised the lyrics to:

> *Have you seen the well-to-do up and down Park Avenue / On that famous thoroughfare with their noses in the air / High hats and Arrow collars, white spats and lots of dollars / Spending ev'ry dime for a wonderful time*

"Uptown," New York's society is still heavily based on money and bloodlines; on the other hand, "Downtown," society is ruled by artists and intellectuals. At least in songs, people successfully cross back and forth between the two worlds. Take, for example, Billy Joel's "Uptown Girl" (1983), or the *"dame named Harriet"* in the Stephen Sondheim song "Uptown, Downtown" from *Follies* (1979), who *"climbed to the top of the heap from the bottom,"* but from time to time she would cross the city's social divide to visit her former life:

> *Uptown, she's steppin' out with a swell. / Downtown, she's holding hands on the El. / Hyphenated Harriet, The nouveau from New Rochelle // Uptown, she's got the Vanderbilt clans, / Downtown, She's with the side-walk Cezannes . . .*

> *She sits at the Ritz with her split of Mumm's / And starts to pine for a stein with her Village chums, / But with a Schlitz in her mitts downtown in Fitzroy's Bar, / She thinks of the Ritz / Oh, it's so schizo.*

Dancing the Night Away

There is no end of things to do in the big city, but over the years, nothing has been more popular than dancing. In the early days, balls, waltz, and cotillions were extremely popular. They were held in private homes, clubs, pleasure gardens, parks, and public dance halls. Most dance music was instrumental and lacked lyrics, but to stimulate sales, composers often selected a title that celebrated a specific location. Publishers cooperated by creating beautifully lithographed covers that reflected the titles.

Take Brooklyn, for example. Over the years dance music celebrating Brooklyn has included "The Brooklyn Polka" (1847), "The

Brooklyn Trio" (1877), "Brooklyn's March" (1898), "Brooklyn Bridge Waltz" (1875), "The Brooklyn Boogie" (1946), "The Brooklyn Mambo" (circa 1940), "The Brooklyn Beguine" (1958), and another "The Brooklyn Polka" (1944)—by Zeke Manners, who also wrote "The Pennsylvania Polka." Then there were dozens of pieces like "The Coney Canter" (1913), "The Coney Island Dip" march (1901), "The Coney Island Glide" (1911), and "Steeplechase Rag" (1917), many of which commemorate specific Coney Island attractions. Other New York–related dance titles celebrate long-forgotten dance fads, from the "Gothamite Quick Step" (1853), to "The Metropolitan Polka Redowa" (1852), and "The St. Nicholas Schottish" (1853).

By the late nineteenth century, public dance halls were flourishing throughout the city. As Hutchins Hapgood noted with disapproval in his 1910 book *Types from City Streets*:

> *The dance-hall is truly a passion with working girls. The desire to waltz is bred in the feminine bone. It is a familiar thing to see little girls on the East Side dancing rhythmically on the street, to the music of some band organ, while heavy wagons roll by unheeded. When those little girls grow older and become shop-girls . . . some of them dance every night, and are so confirmed in it that they are technically known as "spielers." Many a girl, nice girl, too, loves the art so much she will dance with any man she meets, whatever his character or appearance. Often two girls will go to some dance-hall, which may or may not be entirely respectable, and deliberately look for men to dance with. . . . When carried to an excess, [spieling] is as bad as drink or gambling.[7]*

As public dance halls became more popular, so, too, did songs about public dancing. "My Little Battery Queen," an 1896 song by Walter Crane and J. Morningstar, is typical of many songs that celebrated the joys of dancing, or, as it was then called, "spieling":

> *My love is a jolly First Warder, the prettiest girl ever seen, / And I am her mother's star boarder in their home by the old Bowling Green; / We're shy of a piano and parlor, so dancing is done on the green, / I'm proud as a cable [car] conductor when I spiel with the Battery Queen . . .*

In addition to outdoor dances in public parks such as the Battery, German dance halls were extremely popular in late-nineteenth-century New York. Perhaps that was because at places like "Old Walhalla Hall" (1897):

ABOVE: **Waltzing to a band at a Broadway nightclub in 1923.**

LEFT: *"Cordially Inscribed to the Citizens of Brooklyn,"* **this 1898 march also served to advertise the availability of this local band leader and his ensemble.**

You need no introduction, you just ask the girl to dance, / And if you're good at spieling she will gladly take a chance. / And when the dance is over and you ask the little dear, / If she would have a glass of wine, she'll say, "no—lager beer."

According to Bert Grant and A. Seymour Brown's "Broadway Glide" (1912), even average citizens danced their way through the city's streets:

Strolling on the corner, Forty-second Street, / Notice ev'rybody shuffling their feet; / Even if you go into a swell café, / See how all the people at the tables will sway. / See the old tragedian and young soubrette; / There's a Dutch comedian and suffragette. / Over here, over there, see them do it ev'rywhere, / And ev'rybody seems to want to throw their shoulders in the air.

Ira Gershwin and Harry Warren also found rhythm in New York's streets in their 1948 hit "Manhattan Downbeat," a song introduced by Fred Astaire and Ginger Rogers in the film *The Barkleys of Broadway:*

Listen to those seven million voices! / The Town of Babel merely was a toot! ~ ~ ~ There's no beat has Manhattan Downbeat beat! / Battery Park to Spuyten Duyvil, / Manhattan has no rival— / No beat has Manhattan Downbeat beat.

Some famous songs are set in New York dance halls. In addition to classics such as "Stompin' at the Savoy" (1936) are more recent narratives like the catchy 1978 Barry Manilow hit "Copacabana" (a.k.a. "At the Copa"), which tells the tale of a 1940s show girl named Lola, who worked at the famous nightclub with her true love, a bartender named Tony. Even though Tony is killed in a barroom fight in the 1940s, and the Copa has become a disco, thirty years later the mentally unhinged Lola continues to show up nightly at the club to relive her past.

OPPOSITE: An elegantly dressed couple stepping out for a night on the town in 1897.

THE BIG APPLE

AS INTRODUCED AND FEATURED BY *TOMMY DORSEY*
THE BIG APPLE
LYRIC BY BUDDY BERNIER
MUSIC BY BOB EMMERICH
A.S.C.A.P.

Featured by TOMMY DORSEY

CRAWFORD MUSIC CORPORATION
Music Publishers   1619 Broadway, New York

New York has had many nicknames over the years. "The Big Apple" seems to have originated among Southern stable-hands who used it when referring to New York racetracks. It was popularized in the 1920s by John J. FitzGerald, a reporter for the *Morning Telegraph*, and was widely used by black jazz musicians in the 1930s before it became passé. In 1971, it was revived as part of a publicity campaign by Charles Gillett, president of the New York Convention and Visitors Bureau.

In 1937, bandleader Tommy Dorsey introduced a New York–inspired dance "The Big Apple" by Buddy Bernier and Bob Emmerich. According to the lyrics, if you couldn't learn this easy dance your name would be *"mud"* and you would be a *"social dud."*

Chapter 10

NEW YORKERS IN LOVE

C onsidering how many people live in New York, it can be surprisingly difficult to find just "the right one" to love—not that New Yorkers don't put considerable time and effort into looking. Many songs about New York manage to celebrate the city without even mentioning

romance, in others love is lurking just below the surface, and in still more, it is the whole point of the song. This stroll down urban lover's lane starts by exploring how songwriters have portrayed the women and men of New York City.

Women

During the nineteenth century, the term "belle" was frequently used to describe attractive women. Not surprisingly, there is a spate of songs touting local belles, many of them dedicated to individual women. For example, there were "Les Belles de New-York: Valse de Concert" (1858), "The A1 Belle of Madison-Square" (1870), "A Fifth Avenue Belle" (1895), "The Belle of 14th Street" (1868), "The Belle of Murray Hill" (1899), "The Belle of Broadway" (1879), and "The Belle of Greater New York" (1897).

Not all the belles were found in upscale neighborhoods either: songwriters celebrated "The Belle of Avenoo A" (1895); "The Belle of Avenue B" (circa 1895); and "East Side Belles" (1895). "The Belle of Avenoo A," written by Safford Waters and introduced in the 1895 musical comedy *Tommy Rot*, is particularly interesting because of its heavy use of New York slang and local accent to tell the story of a tough young woman or "chippie" (*"my name's Sadie, I can polish any lady / What is anxious fer ter have a serap [scrap?] wid me . . ."*) from the East

Side and her beau, Billy McNeil, a bouncer at Clancy's Bar. The song was vaudevillian songstress Blanche Ring's first hit:

> *I am de belle dey say ov Avenoo A, and if yer strollin'*
> *down dat way / Yer pretty sure ter see me*
> *on de street; / 'Cos I'm somethin' of a walker, and*
> *de fact dat I'm a corker, / Is de talk ov ev'ry copper*
> *on der beat . . . Git off de earth and don't attempt to*
> *stay / 'Cos I'm a queen! de belle ov Av'noo A. / /*
> *Chorus: I am de belle of Avenoo A / And yez can*
> *bet your stuff dat I'm up to de snuff / It fairly makes*
> *me smile to tink ov my style, / 'Cos I'm de belle,*
> *dey say, ov Avenoo A . . .*

Shortly after the success of "Belle of Avenoo A," some local wit wrote a parody called "The Belle of Avenue B" which contained the lines: *"Now I'm sad and dejected, for my Rosa is gone away / On a trip to Blackwell's Island [a city prison], the summer months to stay; / But she sent me a letter and she wishes she was here / Where she could eat the sauerkraut and drink the lager beer . . ."*

Despite a successful 1952 Fred Astaire musical film entitled *The Belle of New York* (which was actually a remake of an 1897 stage musical), by the turn of the century the term "belle" had been overexposed and was ripe for ridicule. "Broadway Belle," a 1908 song by Ted Snyder and Julian Eltinge describes a self-absorbed young woman who is a far cry from the demure young things of the 1850s. (Julian Eltinge, by the way, was America's leading female impersonator and one

ABOVE: Two fashionably attired belles go for a stroll on the cover of Gustave Satter's 1858 "Les Belles de New-York: Valse de Concert."

OPPOSITE: A contented man sings the praises of local women.

of the most famous stage personalities of his time. He was so successful that he eventually owned his own theatre on Forty-Second Street.)

I'm the newest thing on Broadway, I'm the girl you've read about . . . For I am a Broadway belle, a raging, bowling swell, / A Venus, don't you know, a poet told me so; / My beauty and my grace, my perfect form and face, / All these, it may be seen, make me a Broadway belle.

When I take a stroll down Broadway, just to take the morning air, / And the chappies trail behind me, and the cabmen stop and stare, / And when I take my seat at Rector's with a very haughty air, / They will look my way and then they'll whisper: She's the talk of the town / In her new sheath gown, and she's got a Pittsburgh millionaire.

But not all turn-of-the-century New York women were as self-centeredly assured as "Broadway Belle." The city was filled with

"good" women who were untouched by the evils of urban life. The heroine of "Just Around the Corner From Broadway," a Blanche Merrill and Gus Edwards song from 1914, falls in this category:

She lives just around the corner from Broadway / In the shadow of Long Acre [Times] Square; / But tho' she lives next door to Broadway, / You never see her there. / A little slow, perhaps that's so, / But just the kind of girl your mother likes you to know . . .

And then there was the woman lauded in the "dainty waltz song" written by Pierce Kingsley and Herman Berl, "A New York Girl Is Good Enough for Me" (circa 1910). Among her attributes:

She's ev'ry inch a lady, / And it's hard to find her mate; / So faithful, fond and loving, / Just as jolly as can be, / She's just a plain New Yorker, / But she's good enough for me.

Of course, over the years most New York women have been more interesting than the proper, straight-laced damsels serenaded above. Those women could live anywhere—but real New York women were outspoken, street smart, and *"not the kind that's slow."* Readers have already been introduced to "Rose of Washington Square," and "Moitle From Toity Toid and Toid." Songs about some of their sisters included "My Pearl's a Bowery Girl" (1894); Bert Kalmar's "I'm a Vamp From East Broadway" (1920), which was made famous by comedian Fanny Brice; "She's a Bombshell From Brooklyn" (1943); and John Stomberg's song "My Best Girl's a New Yorker" (1895), popularized by the comedy team of Weber & Fields:

My best girl's a corker, not the kind that's slow. / Born and bred a New Yorker, I would have you know; / You may sing about your Mollie, your Mamie or your Pearl; / They're all back numbers when compared with my best girl.

One of the greatest of all songs celebrating New York women remains Phil Spector and Jerry Leiber's 1960 hit about a young Hispanic woman who lived in East, or "Spanish Harlem." The lyrics compare her to a red rose that flourishes in the street despite the concrete, and that comes out only when the moon and stars are on the wane. Although raised in the ghetto, she remains soft and desirable: ready to be plucked and transplanted to the singer's own garden.

Other songs celebrated women who only dreamed of being Hispanic. For example, there was the "Señorita From the Bronx"—a 1930s

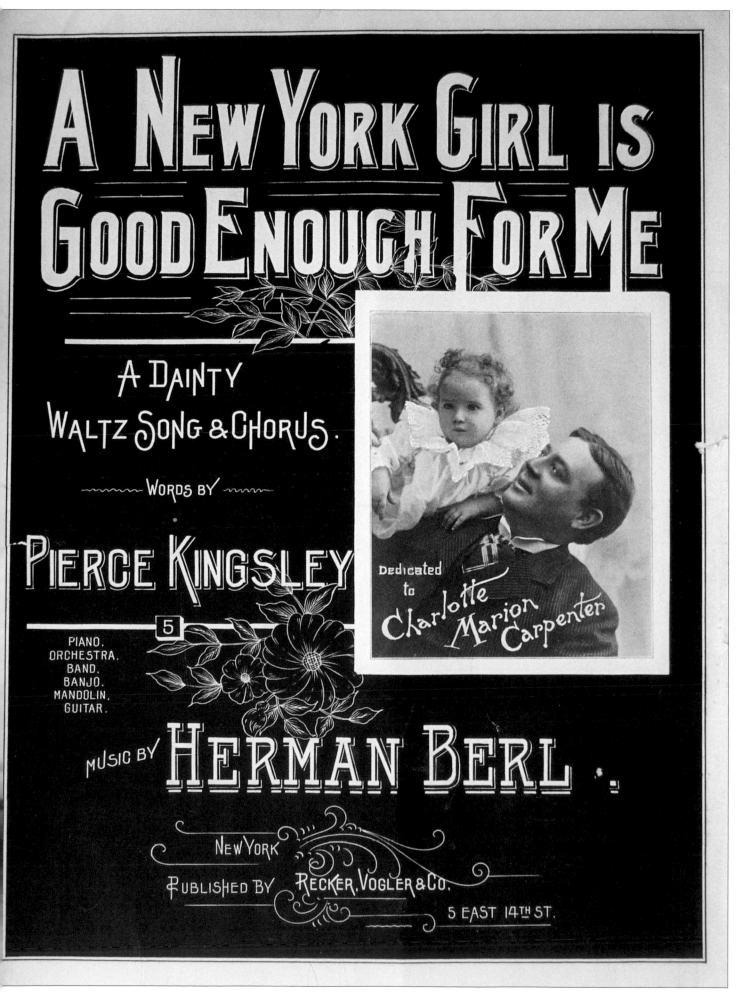

Yiddish novelty song recorded by the Sholom Secunda Orchestra, and "She's a Latin From Manhattan," a 1935 Al Dubin and Harry Warren song made famous by Al Jolson:

She's a Latin from Manhattan, you can tell her by her "Manyana." / She's a Latin from Manhattan and not Havana. // Tho' she does the rumba for us, and she calls herself Dolores, / She was in a Broadway chorus, known as Susie Donahue. // She can take a tambourine and whack it, / But with her it's just a racket, / She's a "hoofer" from Tenth Avenue // She's a Latin from Manhattan / She's a "forty-second streeter," / She's a Latin from Manhattan, Señorita Donahue.

Fairly early on, songwriters and singers recognized that not all New York women fell into the historically narrow category of "respectable." Actually, while we are on this culturally dated topic, it should be noted that two of the nineteenth century's most popular "fallen women" songs were set in New York. The first was William B. Gray's enormous hit "She Is More to Be Pitied Than Censured: A Story From Life's Other Side" (1898). Gray, who also wrote "The Volunteer Organist," was the kind of composer whose work helped define the term "maudlin." On the cover of the "She Is More to Be Pitied" he careful noted that the song's story was "Taken from an Actual Occurrence," and offered a disclaimer: "The theme of this song is indeed a delicate one to handle, and is offered in sympathy, not defense, for the unfortunate erring creature, and life of one who suggested its construction." The first verse describes an incident *"at the old concert hall on the Bowery,"* where a *"crowd of young fellows carousing"* make fun of *"a girl who had fallen to shame"* seated at the next table until *"they heard an old woman exclaim"*:

She is more to be pitied than censured, / She is more the helped than despised, / She is only a lassie who ventured, / On life's stormy path ill-advised. / Do not scorn her with words fierce and bitter, / Do not laugh at her shame and down-fall; / For a moment just stop and consider / That a man was the cause of it all.

Another popular Victorian-era song was the Tin Pan Alley smash "My Mother Was a Lady or If Jack Were Only Here" (1896). The songwriters, Edward Marks and Joseph Stern, claimed it was based on an incident at the little German restaurant on 20th Street where they regularly ate lunch. Some of the customers were giving the new waitress a hard time. The young working woman, who had only recently arrived from Lancashire in the north of England, was not amused by what passed for wit at a men's bar.

Eventually, she burst into tears, declaring that "they wouldn't dare speak to her like that if her brother Jack were only there." And, she added for good measure, "My mother was a lady." Inspired, Marks and Stern immediately repaired to a nearby basement saloon at 28 East 20th Street (where Theodore Roosevelt's Birthplace National Monument now stands) and wrote the song "My Mother Was a Lady or If Jack Were Only Here." It sold more than a million copies—a phenomenal success at the time. Despite the stilted story and trite ending (it turns out that one of the wits knows her brother, apologizes, and marries her), it does offer a glimpse of the difficulties faced by young immigrant women working in turn-of-the-century New York:

Two drummers [salesmen] sat at dinner, in a grand hotel one day, / While dining they were chatting in a jolly sort of way, / And when a pretty waitress brought them a tray of food, / They spoke to her familiarly in manner rather rude; / At first she did not notice them or make the least reply, / But one remark was passed that brought the tear drops to her eye, / And facing her tormentor, with cheeks now burning red, / She looked a perfect picture as appealingly she said: // Chorus: "My mother was a lady, like your own you will allow, / And you may have a sister, who needs protection now, / I've come to this great city to find a brother dear, / And you wouldn't dare insult me, Sir, If Jack were only here."

For the most part, however, New York's song women took a much more cosmopolitan approach to the facts of life. In "A Little Birdie Told Me So" from the Rodgers and Hart musical *Peggy-Ann* (1926), a flapper relates that her mother told her, *"My darling, if you're going to New York, / I must tell you of the mysteries of life. / In towns like that, a little friendly visit from the stork / Is rather awkward if you're not a wife!"* The song "Flutter on by, My Broadway Butterfly" (1919) describes a socially active local woman by saying: *"You give your honey sips to, oh so many lips / Flutter on by, my Broadway butterfly."*

Many New York women were not shy about developing their interpersonal skills. Take, for example, the Fifth Avenue debutante who moves to Brooklyn and discovers that "She's Got a Great Big Army of Friends Since She Lives Near the Navy Yard" (1929):

Once there was a wealthy girl from swell Fifth Avenue lonesome as she could be . . . Putting on the Ritz and staying in society, She never got a thrill, / Living near the Navy Yard she's happy as can be, / 'Cause now she gets her fill, / For down with the hoi pol loi / She always meets some sailor boy . . .

She's Got A Great Big Army Of Friends
Since She Lives Near The Navy Yard
with
UKULELE
Arrangement
by
Bob Nelson,
Billy Frisch and
Monty Siegel
NAVY YARD
GENE AUSTIN, inc.
MUSIC PUBLISHERS
745 SEVENTH AVE. NEW YORK

FALL IN LINE

SUFFRAGE MARCH

COMPOSED FOR THE PIANOFORTE
by
ZENA S. HAWN

Price 50 Cents

Copyright 1914 by The New York State Women's Suffrage Association. International Copyright Secured.

The ARTHUR W. TAMS MUSIC LIBRARY, Inc.
1600 Broadway,   New York.

ABOVE: Women suffrage marchers and accompanying bands march up Broadway past the Flatiron Building in 1914.

OPPOSITE: "Don José From Far Rockaway" in action.

There are a number of songs about New York prostitutes, but none comes close to Cole Porter's 1930 classic "Love for Sale." Written for *The New Yorkers*, the sketch was originally set in front of Reuben's midtown Madison Avenue restaurant and sung by the show's white leading lady, Kathryn Crawford. Because of the enormous moral outcry against the song, the sketch was rewritten and the song assigned to a black performer; the site of the sketch was changed from Reuben's to the "Cotton Club, Lenox Avenue, Harlem." Said to be Porter's favorite Porter song, it was banned by radio stations for decades after it was written:

> When the only sound in the empty street / Is the heavy tread of the heavy feet / That belong to a lonesome cop, / I open shop. / When the moon so long has been gazing down / On the wayward ways of this wayward town / That her smile becomes a smirk, / I go to work.

By the turn of the century, in addition to those New York women in the world's oldest profession, there were an increasing number anxious to explore a much newer undertaking—

voting and equal rights. Ever since the New York City Women's Suffrage Association was formed in 1840, the city has been a center for the struggle for women's rights. By 1913, the largest suffrage parades in the country took place along Fifth Avenue. Composer Zena S. Hawn even set the struggle to music in 1914 when, under the auspices of the New York State Women's Suffrage Association, she published the "Fall in Line Suffrage March":

Recent years have seen a host of songs about independent women, including "Native New Yorker" (1977), which became a major disco hit:

> You grew up riding the subways, / Runnin' with people—up in Harlem, down on Broadway / You're no tramp, but you're no lady. / / Talkin' that street talk—you're the heart and soul of New York City.

> And love—love is just a passing word / It's the thought you had in the taxicab that got left on the curb, when he dropped you off at East 83rd . . .

Men

The number of songs about male New Yorkers has not kept pace with their female neighbors, but nevertheless there have been many significant ones—despite Paul Simon's claim the he is "The Only Living Boy in New York" (1969). Early on, songwriters contributed such musical insights into the habits of the fashionable young male population as "I'm a Perfect New York Dude" (1883), "What New York Swells Are Coming To" (circa 1868), and "Chappies on Broadway" (1895)—"*They cut a swell at each hotel, eat free lunch all the day, / And each one dotes on full-length coats, / The chappies on Broadway . . .*"

New York men were frequently targets of musical humor. In response to the 1921 Rudolph Valentino–inspired hit "Sheik of Araby," Tin Pan Alley songwriters Bert Kalmar and Harry Ruby drew on Lower East Side references to produce the parody "The Sheik of Avenue B," which was introduced by Fanny Brice in 1922. Another novelty song, "He's a Latin From Staten Island" (1941), is a parody of the earlier hit "She's a Latin From Manhattan" (1935). Other Hispanic "wannabes" were the subject of such songs as the "Bronx Caballero," "The Bronx Casanova," and Harold Rome's "Don José From Far Rockaway" from the 1952 musical *Wish You Were Here*. Like many of the New York men celebrated in song, this Casanova did not lack self-confidence:

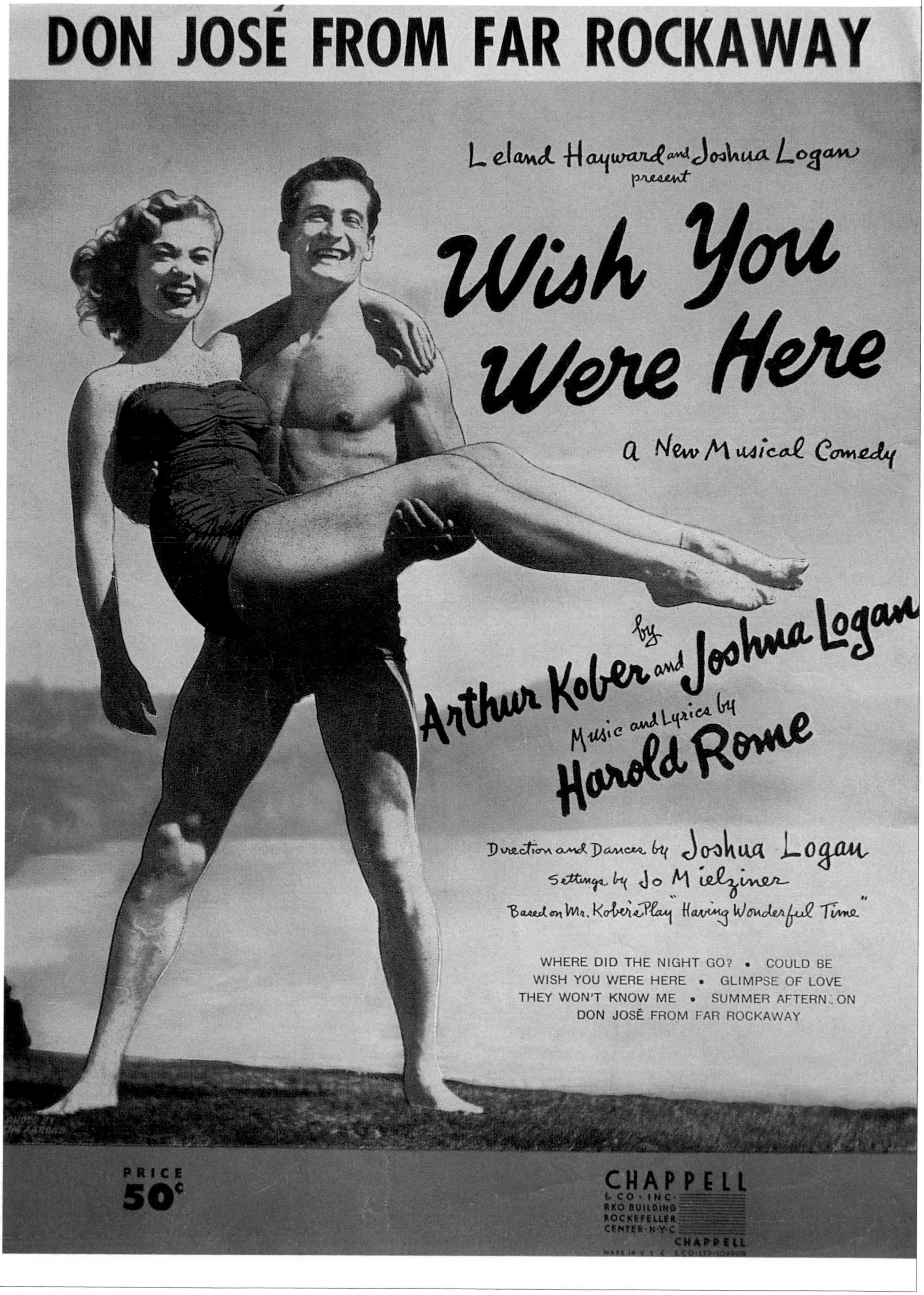
DON JOSÉ FROM FAR ROCKAWAY
Leland Hayward and Joshua Logan present
Wish You Were Here
A New Musical Comedy
by Arthur Kober and Joshua Logan
Music and Lyrics by Harold Rome
Direction and Dances by Joshua Logan
Settings by Jo Mielziner
Based on Mr. Kober's Play "Having Wonderful Time"
WHERE DID THE NIGHT GO? • COULD BE
WISH YOU WERE HERE • GLIMPSE OF LOVE
THEY WON'T KNOW ME • SUMMER AFTERNOON
DON JOSÉ FROM FAR ROCKAWAY
PRICE 50¢
CHAPPELL
& CO · INC ·
RKO BUILDING
ROCKEFELLER
CENTER · N · Y · C
CHAPPELL

I'm passion's flame. / When girls hear my name / They faint from upper Bronx to Queens. / When you love me / You're loving far beyond your means. / Comes the dawn / Don't look for me. / I'll be gone. / On the B.M.T. // Chorus: I'm Don José from Far Rockaway, / The man that women whisper of. / Don José from Far Rockaway, / The Joe DiMaggio of love!

Most songs about masculine New Yorkers concern younger men, but a notable exception is Kurt Weill and Maxwell Anderson's "September Song," a thoughtful and reflective piece about growing older from their 1938 musical about seventeenth-century New Amsterdam, *Knickerbocker Holiday*. Only real Broadway buffs will recall that the character who wistfully sings about the long while between May and December is none other than Peter Stuyvesant.

Returning to more contemporary men, there is John Taylor's 1964 Motown hit "The Boy From New York City," which celebrates a wealthy, sophisticated, young man-around-town who's kind of tall and really fine. The narrator, "cool, cool Kitty," also expresses interest in the boy's more material attributes—including a fine penthouse, a mohair suit, and pockets full of *"spending loot."* And transcending the usual playboy stereotype, Billy Joel wrote a song for the 1986 film *Moonlighting* about a would-be big shot in Manhattan's Little Italy who spreads money and attitude around his neighborhood in an attempt to become a "Big Man on Mulberry Street."

Dating and Mating in the Big City

Meeting that "special person" has always been difficult in New York. Actually, most New Yorkers are usually ready to strike up conversations with one another on the street, at bars, or in subways. But when it comes to giving out personal information—names, addresses, phone numbers—to casually met strangers, many city dwellers tread the line carefully. The 1911 song "I Live Up-Town" revolves around how a street-smart New York woman handles the not terribly original line, "Haven't we met somewhere?" Contemporary New York women will empathize with her polite but evasive answer:

Subway station, fellow gay. / Meets a girlie on her way. / "I've seen you before," he sighs. / Little

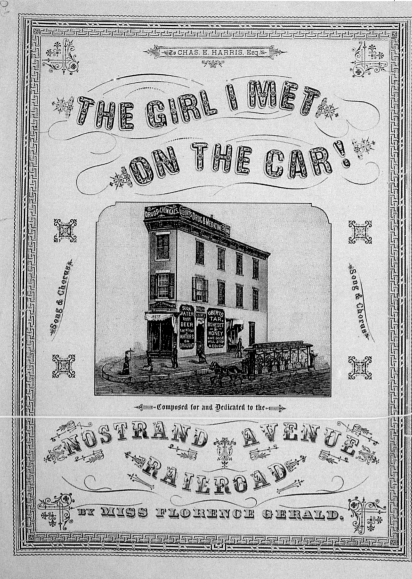

girlie only smiles and answers wise / "Your face looks familiar, too. / Think I saw it at the Zoo, / I'm delighted, you're invited, / Call around and see me, do!" // Chorus: I live up-town, when lonely, / Just call around, you only, / Never mind the address, it's an easy place to find. / There's a sidewalk out in front, a little yard behind. / Look for a girl named Floie, / Someone you meet will know me / Johnny look around, look around, till you find me, / I live up-town.

Meeting, and sometimes losing, the person of your dreams on New York's mass transit appealed to generations of New York songwriters. About 1870, a Miss Florence Gerald wrote a song entitled "The Girl I Met on the Car!," which she *"Composed for and Dedicated to the Nostrand Avenue Railroad"* in Brooklyn.

ABOVE: Years before the arrival of the subway, New Yorkers were eyeing each other on horse-drawn trolleys; in this case, on the Brooklyn's Nostrand Avenue line.

OPPOSITE: A well-dressed young woman meets a "masher" on a subway platform.

Sometimes picking up strangers was remarkably easy, but there was often a catch. Like any major city New York had its share of "fast" women, prostitutes, petty criminals, and con men. "Oh, You New York Girls, Can't You Dance the Polka?," an early sea chanty, warns sailors about New York women. The song, which dates from the 1830s when the polka spread from Bohemia to become an international dance sensation, is still well-known and frequently sung by folk musicians:

> As I walked down through Chatham Street [or the Broadway], / A fair maid I did meet, / Who kindly asked me to see 'er safe home, / She lived on Bleecker Street. // Chorus: To me way, you Santee, my dear Annie, / Oh, you New York gals, can't you dance the polka?

> When we got up to Bleecker Street / We stopped at No. 44 / Her "mother" and "sister" was there / To meet us at the door. . . . When we got inside of the house, / The drinks were passed around. / The liquor was so awful strong / My head went round and round!

To make a long story short, Jack is drugged, relieved of his gold watch and purse, and awakes "stark naked in the bed."

> On looking round this little room, / Nothing could I see, / But a woman's shift and apron, / Which were no use to me. So, / With a flour barrel for a suite of clothes, / I went down to Cherry Street / There Martin Churchill took me in / And sent me around Cape Horn.[1]

Some variants of "Oh, You New York Girls" include the verse: "To Tiffany's I took her, / I did not mind expense, / I bought her two gold earrings / An' they cost me fifteen cents."

Several generations later, Will R. Anderson wrote a song about a similarly employed New York woman named Marie who he met "one evening while strolling Broadway." Entitled "She Was One of the Working Girls" (1900), the narrator tells how "We went to a restaurant quite near by, ten dollars I had at the most, / She said: I'd like some Mumm's Extra Dry and some quail on toast. . . ." By the end of the song, Marie, after dining elegantly at his expense, runs off with his watch and jewelry, leaving him to reflect that "she was one of those working girls, and she worked on me." And then there was George Little and Jack Stanley's 1914 song "Broadway Love," which cautioned lonely men that "dangers lurk with strangers so be careful who you pick. / She may be neat and pretty but a scheming little trick. / Now of old Broadway's dangers you are old enough to know and I am too."

On a much less cynical note, there are any number of songs about people who found true love on the streets of New York, ranging from Cole Porter's "When Love Beckoned (In Fifty-Second Street)," to "Blossoms on Broadway." One of the most interesting is Gordon Jenkins's *Manhattan Tower*, a cantata-like mélange of songs, narrative, and instrumental interludes about a man who comes to New York to follow his dreams and finds true love. Composed by orchestra leader Gordon Jenkins, who claimed to be "the only left-handed

BROOKLYN'S BIGGEST SEX SCANDAL

One of the most scandalous episodes in city history occurred in 1874 when Theodore Tilton, a respected newspaper publisher, accused the distinguished minister and moral crusader Henry Ward Beecher of having an affair with his wife, Elizabeth Tilton. Spiritualist, reformer, and "free love" advocate Victoria Woodhull exposed the case to the public, and in the lurid court case that followed, Beecher, minister of Brooklyn's prestigious Plymouth Congregational Church in Brooklyn Heights (and brother of *Uncle Tom's Cabin* author Harriet Beecher Stowe), was thoroughly discredited. Although he was eventually acquitted by the court, local songwriters had no trouble convicting him. In 1875, one local "free-and-easy" entertainer named Chris Malone was winning applause with his song "Beecher'o":

> In Brooklyn town there lives a man, / A celebrated preacher'o, / Who preached the gospel on an improved plan, / Did the Rev. Henry Ward Beecher'o. / In Plymouth Church he used to preach, / The way to glory he did teach, / Tho' for other men's wives would oft-times reach, / The Rev. Henry Ward Beecher'o.[2]

POPULAR SONG EDITION

Manhattan Serenade

MUSIC BY
LOUIS ALTER
LYRIC BY
HAROLD ADAMSON

Featured by
DINAH SHORE

ROBBINS MUSIC CORPORATION
799 SEVENTH AVENUE • NEW YORK

conductor on radio and television" and who also scored such 3-D film classics as *Bwana Devil*, it was premiered in 1945 and proved extremely popular. By the time Jenkins recorded it for Columbia with his orchestra and the Ralph Brewster Singers in 1964, the piece had tripled in length. The published score suggested that the piece could be presented as a play, a ballet, or a concert piece by any school or concert group. Today, the darkly dramatic voice-over narration and the overwrought score give the piece a dated, film noir feel, but also offers an interesting musical glimpse of romance in post–World War II New York.

Billed as "Americana full of the life and . . . love of a big city," *Manhattan Tower* begins as the narrator, Steven, newly arrived in New York, first enters the tower and views the *"Magical City."* He is thoroughly impressed (*"the elevator operator was Merlin"*) and opens the window to enjoy street noise (*"a strange music, it is an orchestra conducted by the Statue of Liberty"*). Later, he visits Billy's Bar & Grill—a *"men's only"* establishment. In the background of the 1964 recording, listeners hear ethnic voices complaining about their wives; yet when he looks up, he finds that Billy's has been invaded by an independent young woman named Julie, who orders a *"Happiness Cocktail"* and proceeds to charm the male stronghold with song. Steven picks up Julie and in a series of songs they go dancing ("I'm Learnin' My Latin"); fall in love ("Once Upon a Dream"); take a pre-dawn ride in Central Park ("This Close to Dawn"); spend the "Morning in Greenwich Village"; visit an outdoor art show ("The Magic Fire"); and watch a wedding party leave a church. Given the theatrical conventions of the 1950s, modern listeners might jump to the conclusion that the couple will marry and live happily every after. However, just as you begin to brace yourself for the inevitable saccharine ending, an interesting twist occurs. Julie, in the best urban feminist tradition, announces "Married I Can Always Get":

> It's not for me with all its smug connubiality, boys /
> I'll live the life that I'm used to . . . Businessmen
> are always tired / I'll take a cruise into a more
> adventurous clime / Stick to romantic roulette /
> Married, I can always get, but not yet . . .

Steven is crushed. After several more songs— "A Party in the Tower" and "New York's

My Home"—he decides to leave, but not before vowing that *"someday the tower would be mine forever . . . I knew that someday I would return, that I must return, for I left my heart behind in that tower, that tower in Manhattan."*

Finally, while on the subject of love, some mention should be made of the difficulties facing urban romance in a sprawling city. Since most city residents do not own cars, getting to the other end of town can be a daunting challenge. In ages past, when men were expected to call for women and see them home, falling in love with someone from the opposite side of New York could be disastrous. The challenge of inter-borough dating was addressed by several songwriters, such as J.D. Kelly's 1880s song "Broadway Swell and Brooklyn Belle," and years later in Arnold Horwitt and Richard Lewine's "Subway Song" from the 1947 revue *Make Mine Manhattan*:

> I'm in love with a girl, / And she loves me too, /
> But our love is hardly complete / 'Cause she lives
> in Brooklyn on New Lots Avenue / And I live
> in the Bronx, on Two hundred and forty-second
> street . . . / / You can tell the conductor and the
> motorman, too / Mister Cupid went down to
> defeat / Somewhere between Brooklyn on New Lots
> Avenue / And my little grey home in the Bronx . . .

> You may think of pretty things to whisper in her
> ear, / But the train is making so much noise that
> she can't hear, / Tho' you may not know the fellow
> standing at your right, / You can tell exactly
> what he had to eat that night . . .

> I'm beginning to wonder / What Romeo would
> do / Would he think Juliet was so sweet / If she
> lived in Brooklyn on New Lots Avenue / (spoken):
> And then he took the Lexington Avenue Local
> to Queens Plaza and waited for the Broadway
> 7th Avenue Local, which runs only once every
> thirty-five minutes after midnight and takes an
> hour and a half to get to the Bronx, On Two
> hundred and forty-second Street!

Despite all the impediments to urban romance, New York men and women have successfully managed to find each other for almost four hundred years. Their ability to persevere in the face of an increasingly complex cityscape has produced generation after generation of new New Yorkers who, like their parents before them, share both a deep love of their hometown and a need to celebrate their urban lives in song.

OPPOSITE: Published primarily for school performances, this *Manhattan Tower* score left out all the suggestive songs as well as the heroine's decision not to marry.

NOTES

CHAPTER 1

1 See "Manhattan" in Jackson's *The Encyclopedia of New York City*, p. 718.
2 See Stokes, *The Iconography of Manhattan Island*, I:70.
3 After the Civil War, New York's broadside ballad trade was controlled for many years by Michael Cregansteine, "King of the Song Sheet Men." A picaresque multilingual Dublin-born character whose alcoholism had interfered with earlier attempts at religious and military careers, Cregansteine wrote, printed, and distributed hundreds of broadsides from his flophouse hotel at 25 Bowery. He had an amazing accent—a mixture of French, German, and English with a touch of Irish brogue. At night, he would occasionally dazzle fellow Bowery bar patrons by reciting passages by Sallust, Caesar, or Virgil in Latin. See Gilbert, *Lost Chords*, pp. 40–42.
4 See Slobin, *Tenement Songs*, p. 164.
5 John Pendleton's firm was bought out in 1834 by the piano-maker Adam Stodard and his young partner, a lithographer named Nathaniel Currier. Although their music publishing firm, Stodard & Currier, at 1 Wall Street, only lasted one year (1835), Currier went on to establish a more successful partnership with James Merritt Ives. As Currier & Ives, they created iconic images that continue to shape our perceptions of nineteenth-century American life.
6 For information on Tin Pan Alley, see Chapter Four.
7 See Chapter Two, "The Skyline and Skyscrapers," for a discussion of the Flatiron Building and windy corners.
8 Although the "schottische" was a popular dance form in the nineteenth century, the spelling varied and seems to have been a matter of individual choice.

CHAPTER 2

1 The *Oxford English Dictionary* defines "masher" as a term popular in the 1880s for "a fop of affected manners and exaggerated style of dress who frequented music-halls and fashionable promenades and who posed as a 'lady killer.'"
2 The colors of the New York City flag.
3 "Anschluss" refers to the German annexation of Austria in 1938. I am indebted to Dr. Martin Burke, a Brooklyn native, for bringing the use of this term to my attention.

CHAPTER 3

1 As quoted in Lazare's informative recording, *Folk Songs of New York City*, Vol 1.
2 *Jim Jam Jems* was a theatre magazine. Cartoonist Rube Goldberg (1883–1970) moved to New York City in 1907 to work for the *Evening Mail*. Although his cartoon strip "Boob McNutt" ran for twenty years, he is best known for his drawings of ridiculously complicated machines designed to accomplish extremely simple tasks. He received a Pulitzer Prize for his editorial cartoons in 1948.
3 A reference to *Abie's Irish Rose*, a long-running Broadway play about a Jewish-Irish marriage, which opened in 1922.
4 Fashionable uptown restaurants.

CHAPTER 4

1 *The Black Crook* was denounced by all the moralists of its day. One New York minister complained that it was luring away the male members of his congregation. Instead of listening for "the pealing of bells," he stated, the men were now more interested in observing "the peeling of belles." See Marks, *They All Had Glamour*, pp. 1–12.
2 "Chickens" was a turn-of-the-century slang term for women. It was later shortened to "chicks."
3 See Ewen, *The Life and Death of Tin Pan Alley*, pp. 205–212.

CHAPTER 5

1 Madame C.J. Walker (1867–1919) was a successful beauty salon owner and businessperson who developed and marketed a line of beauty care products designed for African-American women. She was said to be the first black woman to become a millionaire, and her daughter, A'lelia, was an important patron of the Harlem Renaissance.

CHAPTER 6

1 See Jay, *Learned Pigs and Fireproof Women*, p. 215.
2 See *The Rough and Ready Songster* (New York: Nafis and Cornish, circa 1848), pp. 195–196.

CHAPTER 7

1 Translated by Mark Slobin in *Tenement Songs*, pp.156–157. © 1982 by the Board of Trustees of the University of Illinois. Used with permission of the University of Illinois Press.
2 For an excellent review of calypso and calypsonians in New York see

Donald Hill's essay, "I Am Happy to Be in This Sweet Land of Liberty," in Allen and Wilcken's *Island Sounds in the Global City*, pp. 74–92.
3 For a thoughtful overview of how Hispanic composers have addressed the city see Peter Manuel's essay, "Representations of New York City in Latin Music," in Allen and Wilcken's *Island Sounds*, p. 297.
4 Translated by Mark Slobin in *Tenement Songs*, pp. 159–160.
5 See Manuel in Allen and Wilcken's *Island Sounds*, pp. 32–33.
6 Ibid., p. 28.
7 Ibid., p. 30.

CHAPTER 8

1 See Robert W. Snyder's article, "Crime," in Jackson's *The Encyclopedia of New York City*, p. 297.
2 See Manuel in Allen and Wilcken's *Island Sounds*, p. 37.
3 Sing Sing Prison is located thirty miles north of the city on the Hudson River in Ossining, New York. Getting there inspired the expression to be "sent up the river" for going to jail.
4 People who remember the invective from the 1960s may be surprised to learn that New York police were called "pigs" as far back as the 1840s. See Allen, *The City in Slang*, p. 213.
5 Delaney was a colorful local character who for more than two decades printed inexpensive chapbooks containing the lyrics to hundreds of popular contemporary songs. Years later, Edward Marks, in his delightful book of reminiscences, *They All Sang*, wrote: "Delaney had a remarkable habit of never coming directly to the point. . . . He would just hang around the office looking absent-minded, as if he wandered in by mistake, until you said, 'Hello, Will, guess we rang the bell with that waltz, huh?' Then he would say, 'Tain't so bad. How much do you want for it? Remember, I ain't got too much money.'" See Marks, *They All Sang*, p. 24.
6 A ward heeler is someone who "heels" problems on a local level.
7 *Plunkitt of Tammany Hall: A Series of Very Plain Talks on Very Practical Politics* was first published as a series of newspaper articles and then issued as a book by McClure, Phillips & Co. in 1905. Although not meant to be a comedy, it is, without a doubt, one of the funniest books ever published on American political history and a must-read by anyone interested in New York history.

8 For an excellent article on this song and Harrigan's relation to the New York Irish community see Don Meade's "The Life and Times of Muldoon, the Solid Man" in *New York Irish History: Journal of the New York Irish History Roundtable*, Vol 11, 1997.
9 Lazare, *Folksongs of New York City*, Vol. 1, Album Notes. For an engaging recording of this and other folk songs about New York City, see Lazare's, *Folksongs of New York City*, Vols. 1 and 2.
10 Quoted in Gilbert, *Lost Chords*, pp. 90–91.

CHAPTER 9

1 See Ewen, *The Life and Death of Tin Pan Alley*, p. 41.
2 For La Guardia's own explanation of his actions see Fiorello La Guardia, *The Making of an Insurgent, An Autobiography: 1882–1919* (Philadelphia, Pa.: J.B. Lippincott Company, 1948), pp. 27–29.
3 Morris Rosenfeld's *Selected Works* (New York: Forverts,1912) quoted and translated by Mark Slobin in his insightful study of Jewish music in turn-of-the-century New York, *Tenement Songs*, p. 70.
4 By throwing in the name of Yiddish theatre star Boris Thomashefsky, Ira Gershwin demonstrates his uncanny ability to rhyme just about anything.
5 See Schermerhorn, *Letters to Phil*, pp. 33–34.
6 Barefoot and dressed in rags, hot-corn girls selling corn-on-the-cob were once a common sight on New York streets. As Luc Sante noted in his important and fascinating study *Low Life*, hot-corn girls "stood for virtuous striving not unmixed with a sexy aura of availability." See Sante, *Low Life*, p. 61.
7 See Hutchins Hapgood, *Types from City Streets* (New York: Funk & Wagnalls Company, 1910), pp. 134–136.

CHAPTER 10

1 This compilation version is based on variants from William Main Doerflinger's *Shantymen and Shantyboys* (New York: The MacMillian Company, 1951) and Stan Hugill's *Shanties from the Seven Seas* (New York: Routledge & Kegan Paul, 1961). The story itself is older than the 1830s, and probably dates back to the very beginnings of shore leave.
2 Quoted in Gilbert, *Lost Chords*, p. 95.

Selected Bibliography

Allen, Irving Lewis. *The City in Slang: New York Life and Popular Speech.* New York: Oxford University Press, 1993.

Allen, Ray, and Lois Wilcken. *Island Sounds in the Global City: Caribbean Popular Music and Identity in New York.* Ithaca: New York Folklore Society and Institute for Studies in American Music, Brooklyn College, 1998.

Batterberry, Michael, and Ariane Batterberry. *On the Town in New York: A History of Eating, Drinking, and Entertainments from 1776 to the Present.* New York: Charles Scribner's Sons, 1971.

Bodkin, Benjamin A., ed. *Sidewalks of America: Folklore, Legends, Sagas, Traditions, Customs, Songs, Stories, and Sayings of City Folk.* Indianapolis: The Bobbs-Merrill Company, Inc., 1954.

Cohan, George M. *Twenty Years on Broadway.* New York: Harper & Row, 1924.

Comical, Topical and Motto Songs. New York: Richard Saalfield, 1887.

Delaney, William W. *Delaney's Song Book.* 89 vols. New York: William W. Delaney, 1882–1921.

Doerflinger, William Main. *Shantymen and Shanty Boys.* New York: MacMillan Company, 1951.

Dunshee, Kenneth Holcomb. *As You Pass By.* New York: Hasting House, 1952.

Erenberg, Lewis A. *Steppin' Out: New York Nightlife and the Transformation of American Culture, 1890–1930.* Westport, Conn.: Greenwood Press, 1981.

Ewen, David. *The Life and Death of Tin Pan Alley: The Golden Age of American Popular Music.* New York: Funk and Wagnalls Co., Inc., 1964.

_____. *New Complete Book of the American Musical Theater.* New York: Holt, Rinehart & Winston, 1970.

Geller, James. *Famous Songs and Their Stories.* New York: The MaCaulay Co., 1931.

Gershwin, Ira. *Lyrics on Several Occasions: A Selection of Stage and Screen Lyrics Written for Sundry Situations; and Now Arranged in Arbitrary Categories.* New York: Alfred A. Knopf, 1959.

_____. *The Complete Lyrics of Ira Gershwin.* Edited by Robert Kimball. New York: Alfred A. Knopf, 1993.

Gilbert, Douglas. *Lost Chords: The Diverting Story of American Popular Songs.* New York: Doubleday, Doran and Co., 1942.

Green, Stanley. *Ring Bells! Sing Songs!: Broadway Musicals of the 1930s.* New Rochelle, N.Y.: Arlington House, 1971.

Groce, Nancy. *Musical Instrument Makers of New York: A Directory of Eighteenth and Nineteenth-Century Urban Craftsmen.* Stuyvesant, N.Y.: Pendragon Press, 1991.

Guiheen, Anna Marie, and Marie-Reine A. Pafik. *The Sheet Music Reference and Price Guide.* Second edition. Paducah, Ky.: Collector Books, 1995.

Guiterman, Arthur. *Ballads of Old New York.* New York: Harper & Brothers Publishers, 1920.

Harlow, Alvin F. *Old Bowery Days.* New York: D. Appleton & Co., 1931.

Hart, Lorenz. *The Complete Lyrics of Lorenz Hart.* Edited by Dorothy Hart and Robert Kimball. New York: Alfred A. Knopf, 1986.

Harrigan, Edward. *The Famous Songs of Harrigan and Hart.* Edited by Richard Moody. New York: Edward B. Marks, 1938.

Henderson, Mary C. *The City and the Theatre: New York Playhouses from Bowling Green to Times Square.* Clifton, N.J.: James T. White & Company, 1973.

Jackson, Kenneth T., ed. *The Encyclopedia of New York City.* New Haven: Yale University Press, 1995.

Jay, Ricky. *Learned Pigs and Fireproof Women.* New York: Villard Books, 1987.

Kahn, E.J. Jr. *The Merry Partners: The Age and Stage of Harrigan and Hart.* New York: Random House, 1955.

Karmen, Steve. *The Jingle Man.* Winona, Minn.: Hal Leonard, 1980.

Landauer, Bella C. *My City, 'Tis of Thee, New York City on Sheet-Music Covers: Selections from the Music Collection of Bella C. Landauer at the New-York Historical Society.* New York: New-York Historical Society, 1951.

_____. *Striking the Right Note in Advertising: Selections from the Music Collection of Bella C. Landauer at the New-York Historical Society.* New York: New-York Historical Society, 1951.

Lawrence, Vera Brodsky. *Strong on Music: The New York Music Scene in the Days of George Templeton Strong, 1836–1875.* Vol. 1, *Resonances, 1836–1850.* New York: Oxford University Press, 1988.

_____. *Strong on Music: The New York Music Scene in the Days of George Templeton Strong, 1836–1875.* Vol. 2, *Reverberations, 1850–1856.* Chicago: University of Chicago Press, 1996.

Lazare, June. *Folksongs of New York City.* Vol. 1 (1966) and Vol. 2 (1981). Folkways Records; reissued by Folkways, Center for Folklife Programs and Cultural Studies, Smithsonian Institution. Washington, D.C.: Folkways Cassette Series, 1992 and 1993.

Levy, Lester. *Grace Notes in American History: Popular Sheet Music from 1820 to 1900.* Norman: University of Oklahoma, 1967.

Loesser, Arthur. *Humor in American Song.* New York: Howell, Soskin, Purl, 1942.

Moody, Richard. *Ned Harrigan: From Corlear's Hook to Herald Square.* Chicago: Nelson-Hall, 1980.

Marks, Edward B. *They All Sang: From Tony Pastor to Rudy Vallée.* New York: The Viking Press, 1934.

_____. *They All Had Glamour: From the Swedish Nightingale to the Naked Lady.* New York: J. Messner, Inc., 1944.

Odell, G.C.D. *Annals of the New York Stage.* 15 vols. New York: Columbia University Press, 1927–1949.

Porter, Cole. *103 Lyrics of Cole Porter.* Edited by Fred Lounsberry. New York: Random House, 1954.

_____. *Cole.* Edited by Robert Kimball. New York: Holt, Rinehart & Winston, 1971.

Riordon, William L. *Plunkitt of Tammany Hall.* New York: E.P. Dutton & Company, 1963.

Sante, Luc. *Low Life: Lures and Snares of Old New York.* New York: Vintage, 1991.

Schermerhorn, Gene. *Letters to Phil: Memories of a New York Boyhood, 1848–1856.* New York: New York Bound, 1982.

Shay, Frank. *More Pious Friends and Drunken Companions.* New York: MaCaulay Co., 1928.

Slobin, Mark. *Tenement Songs: The Popular Music of the Jewish Immigrants.* Urbana: University of Illinois Press, 1982.

Smith, Carleton Sprague. "Folk Songs of Old New York." *Musical America,* Vol. 9 (1939).

Snyder, Robert W. *The Voice of the City: Vaudeville and Popular Culture in New York.* New York: Oxford University Press, 1989.

Spaeth, Sigmund. *Read 'Em and Weep: The Songs You Forgot to Remember.* Garden City, N.Y.: Doubleday, Page & Company, 1926.

_____. *Weep Some More, My Lady.* Garden City, N.Y.: Doubleday, Page & Company, 1927.

Stokes, Isaac Newton Phelps. *The Iconography of Manhattan Island, 1498–1909.* 6 vols. New York: Robert H. Dodds, 1915–1928.

Williams, William H.A. *'Twas Only an Irishmen's Dream: The Image of Ireland and the Irish in American Popular Song Lyrics, 1800–1920.* Urbana: University of Illinois, 1996.

Zellers, Parker. *Tony Pastor, Dean of the Vaudeville Stage.* Ypsilanti: Eastern Michigan University Press, 1971.

Song Index, Credits, and Permissions

The author has tried to include basic bibliographic information for each piece. All the songs mentioned in the text are listed below alphabetically by title with credit information and page numbers where the songs appear in the book. Page numbers in *italics* refer to illustrations. Songs without page numbers do not appear in the book. (Abbreviations: M = musical or revue; F = film; w. = lyrics; m. = music.)

Second Hand Rose (From Second Avenue) (w. Grant Clarke/m. James F. Hanley: 1921) M: *Ziegfeld Follies of 1921*, page 64.

Seeing New York in the Rubber-Neck Hack (w. Paul West/m. John W. Bratton: 1904), page 23.

Señorita From the Bronx (w./m. Sholom Secunda: 1930s), pages 168, 170.

September Song (w. Maxwell Anderson/ m. Kurt Weill: 1938) M: *Knickerbocker Holiday*, page 175.

Seventy-Six Polka (m. Charles Weisheit: circa 1852), page 118.

She Is More to Be Pitied Than Censured: A Story From Life's Other Side (w./m. William B. Gray: 1898), page 170.

She Lives on Murray Hill (w. Edward Harrigan/m. David Braham: 1882) M: *Mordicai Lyons*, page 66.

She Reads the New York Papers Ev'ry Day (w. Paul West/m. John W Bratton: 1902), page 140.

She Was One of the Working Girls (w./m. Will R. Anderson: 1900), page 175.

She Will Still Be Standing in the Harbor (w./m. Carmen Lombardo & John Jacob Loeb: 1943), page 46.

She's a Bombshell From Brooklyn (m. James V. Monaco/w. Al Dubin: 1943) F: *Stage Door Canteen*, page 168.

She's a Latin From Manhattan (w. Al Dubin/m. Henry Warren: 1935) F: *Go Into Your Dance*, pages 111, 170, 171.

She's Got a Great Big Army of Friends Since She Lives Near the Navy Yard (w./m. Bob Nelson/Billy Frisch/Monty Siegel: 1929), pages 170–171.

Sheik of Avenue B, The (w./m. Bert Kalmar/Hary Ruby/Friend/Downing: 1922), page 172.

Shopping: A Comic Song (w./m. E.C. Riley: 1848) "Published for A.F. Stewart's Department Store," page 36.

Sidewalk Waltz, The (w. Joe Young/ m. J. Fred Coots: 1933), page 31.

Sidewalks of New York, The or East Side, West Side (w. James W. Blake/ m. Charles B. Lawlor: 1894), pages 9, 31, 113, 136, 142, 143–144.

Since I Joined Tammany Hall (w./m. Lou Edmunds: 1893), page 136.

Sing a Little Love Song (w. Sidney D. Mitchell/m. Con Conrad/Archie Gottler: 1929) F: *Broadway*. Copyright 1929. De Sylva Brown Henderson, page 72.

Sky City (w. Lorenz Hart/m. Richard Rodgers: 1929) M: *Heads Up*. © 1929 Warner Bros. Inc. Rights for Extended Renewal Term in U.S. controlled by Warner Bros. Inc. o/b/o the Estate of Lorenz Hart and the Family Trust U/W Richard Rodgers and the Family Trust U/W Dorothy F. Rodgers. (Administered by Williamson Music.) All Rights Reserved. Used by Permission WARNER BROS. PUBLICATIONS U.S. INC., Miami, FL 33014, page 32.

Skyscraper (w. Sammy Cahn/m. James Van Heusen: 1965) Musical. ©1965 (Renewed) Cahn Music Company & Van Heusen Music. All Rights o/b/o Cahn Music Company administered by WB Music Corp. All Rights Reserved. Used by Permission WARNER BROS. PUBLICATIONS U.S. INC., Miami, FL 33014, page 32.

Slaughter on Tenth Avenue (m. Richard Rodgers: 1936) M: *On Your Toes*. Illustration Courtesy of The Rodgers and Hammerstein Organization and Williamson Music. Used by Permission, pages 124–125.

Slumming on Park Avenue (w./m. Irving Berlin: 1937) F: *On the Avenue*. © Copyright 1937, 1958 by Irving Berlin. © Copyright Renewed. International Copyright Secured. Used by Permission. All Rights Reserved, page 67.

Solid Men to the Front (m. C. S. Grafulla: 1870), page 136.

Song of the City (Trylon and Perisphere) (w./m. William Grant Still: 1939), page 48.

South Fifth Avenue (w. Edward Harrigan/m. David Braham: 1881) M: *Mulligan's Silver Wedding*, page 83.

Spanish Harlem (w./m. Phil Spector & Jerry Leiber: 1960), page 168.

Sparkling Polka, The (m. Thomas Baker: 1855).

Staten Island, The Gem of New York Bay (w. Charles Edwin Lyman/ m. George S. Dare: 1935), page 101.

Staten Island Gentleman, A Comic Ballad, The (w. Champion Bissell/m.Thomas Baker: 1859), page 121.

Staten Island Polka-Mazurka, The (m. Karl Merz: 1854), page 101.

Statue of Liberty Is Smiling, The (w./m. Jack Mahoney & Halsey K. Mohr: 1918), page 46.

Steeplechase Rag (m. Johnson: 1917), page 163.

Stompin' at the Savoy (w. Andy Razaf/m. Benny Goodman/Chick Webb/Edgar Sampson: 1936) Copyright © EMI Robbins Catalog, Inc, pages 88, 89, 165.

Streets of New York, The (w./m. Liam Reilly: circa 1981) Copyright © Liam Reilly and Bardis Music/River Music. International Copyright Secured. All Rights Reserved. Used by Permission, page 104.

Streets of New York, The (w./m. Dr. William Jarvis Wetmore: 1865), page 29.

Streets of New York, The (w. Henry Blossom/m. Victor Herbert: 1906) M: *The Red Mill*, page 30.

Streets of Old New York, The (w. Jeff Branen/m. Arthur Lange: 1914), page 28.

Strolling on the Brooklyn Bridge (w. George Cooper/m. Joseph P. Skelly: 1883), pages 41, 42, 151.

Subway Directions (w. Betty Comden & Adolph Green/m. Jule Styne: 1961) M: *Subways Are for Sleeping*, page 120.

Subway Dream (w./m. Helen Miller & Eve Merriam: 1971), page 121.

Subway Express, The (w. James O'Dea/m. Jerome Kern: 1907) M: *Fascinating Flora*, page 120.

Subway Glide, The (w. Arthur Gillespie/m. Theodore Norman: 1907), pages 112, 118.

Subway Rag (w. James B. Carson/ m. Don Heath: 1912), page 120.

Subway Rag (w./m. Buster Davis & Steven Vinaver: 1958).

Subway Rider (w./m. Micki Grant: 1980), page 121.

Subway Song (w. Arnold Horwitt/ m. Richard Lewine: 1947) M: *Make Mine Manhattan*. Copyright © 1947 PolyGram International Publishing, Inc. Copyright Renewed. International Copyright Secured. Used by Permission. All Rights Reserved, page 179.

Subway Squeeze, The (w. Paul West/ m. Nat D. Ayer: 1912) M: *Let George Do It*, page 121.

Subway Sun, The (w. Max Lief & Nathaniel Lief/m. Ray Perkins: 1928) M: *The Greenwich Village Follies*, page 121.

Subways Are for Skiing (w./m. Michael McWhinney: 1964) M: *. . .And in This Corner*, page 121.

Sugar Hill Penthouse (m. Duke Ellington: 1945), page 33.

Summer in the City (w./m. John Sebastian/Mark Sebastian/Steve Boone: 1966) © 1966 (Renewed) Trio Music Company, Inc. Alley Music Corp., Mark Sebastian Music. All Rights Reserved. Used by Permission, page 148.

Sun March & Two Step, The (m. Monroe H. Rosenfeld: 1894), page 140.

Sunday in Brooklyn (m. Elie Siegmeister: 1946), page 153.

Sunday in New York (w./m. Portia Nelson: 1959) M: *Demi-Dozen*, page 153.

Sunday in New York (w. Carroll Coates/m. Peter Nero: 1964).

Sunday in the Park (w./m. Harold Rome: 1937) M: *Pins and Needles*. © 1937 (Renewed) Chappell & Co. All Rights Reserved. Used by Permission. WARNER BROS. PUBLICATIONS U.S. INC., Miami, FL 33014, page 153.

Sunday Night When the Parlor's Full (w. Edward Harrigan/m. David Braham: 1877), page 153.

Sunday Tan (w. Ira Gershwin: 1936) M: *Ziegfeld Follies of 1936*. (Cut prior to opening.) © 1993 Ira Gershwin Music. All Rights Reserved. Used by Permission. WARNER BROS. PUBLICATIONS U.S. INC., Miami, FL 33014, page 148.

Sunny Side of Thompson Street, The (w. Edward Harrigan/m. David Braham: 1893) M: *The Woolen Stocking*.

T

Take a Ride Underground (1904) M: *Trip to Chinatown*, page 118.

Take a Trip Down to Luna With Me (w. William Cahill/m. S.R. Henry: 1908).

Take Me Back to Manhattan (w./m. Cole Porter: 1930) M: *The New Yorkers*. © 1930 (Renewed) Warner Bros. Inc. All Rights Reserved. Used by Permission. WARNER BROS. PUBLICATIONS U.S. INC., Miami, FL 33014, page 27.

Take Me Back to Old Broadway (w. Milton Nobles, Jr./m. Robert Kelly: 1911), page 126.

Take Me Back to New York Town (w. Andrew B. Sterling/m. Harry Von Tilzer: 1907), pages 8, 25.

Take Me Down to Coney Island (w. Hugh Morton/m. Gustave Kerker: 1897) M: *The Belle of New York*, page 98.

Take Me 'Round in a Taxi Cab (w. Edgar Selden/m. Melville J. Gideon: 1908) M: *Ziegfeld Follies of 1908*, page 123.

Take Me to New York, Take Me to the Fair (1964) Jingle from "Official New York World's Fair Album," page 51.

Take Plenty of Shoes (w. Will B. Cobb/m. Melville J. Gideon: 1908) M: *The Boys & Betty*, page 23.

Take the 'A' Train (w./m. Billy Strayhorn: 1941) Copyright © 1941 (Renewed) by Music Sales Corporation (ASCAP) and Tempo Music, Inc. All Rights Administered by Music Sales Corporation. International Copyright Secured. All Rights Reserved. Reprinted by Permission, pages 9, 84, 85, 120.

Talkin' New York Blues (w./m. Bob Dylan: 1961), page 65.

Talking Subway Blues (w./m. Woody Guthrie: 1930s), page 121.

Tammany: A Pale Face Pow-Wow (w. Vincent Bryan/m. Gus Edwards: 1905) M: *Fantana*, pages 134, 135–136.

Taxi (w. Harry D. Kerr/m. Mel. B. Kaufman: 1919), page 123.

Teatime on Fifth Avenue (w./m. Margaret Neas: 1940) M: *Two Weeks, With Pay*, page 65.

Ten Million Men and a Girl (w./m. John Redmond/Jim Cavanaugh/Jake Edwards: 1942), page 46.

Tenderloin, The (w. Joe Flynn: 1895), page 126.

Tenth and Greenwich (w./m. Melvin Van Peebles: 1971), page 63.

Terrible Disaster-Boiler Explosion on Board a Staten Island Ferry Boat With Dreadful Loss of Life (w. A.W. Harmon: 1871), page 132.

Texas, Brooklyn and Heaven (w./m. Ervin Drake & Jimmy Shirl: circa 1940) F: *Texas, Brooklyn and Heaven*, page 96.

Texas, Brooklyn and Love (w. Ogden Nash/m. Vernon Duke: 1946) M: *Sweet Bye and Bye*, page 96.

That Man Could Sell Me the Brooklyn Bridge (w. Paul Francis Webster & Sammy Fain: 1958) F: *Mardi Gras*, page 44.

There Wasn't Any Broadway on Robinson Crusoe's Isle (w./m. Bobby Jones & Iva Willis: 1913), page 79.

There's a Boy in Harlem (w. Lorenz Hart/m. Richard Rodgers: 1938) F: *Fools for Scandal*. © 1938 (Renewed) Warner Bros. Inc. All Rights Reserved. Used by Permission WARNER BROS. PUBLICATIONS U.S. INC., Miami, FL 33014, page 89.

There's a Broadway up in Heaven (w./m. Edward J. Lambert & Gerald Dolin: 1935), page 75.

There's a Broken Heart for Every Light on Broadway (w./m. Fred Fisher & Howard Johnson: 1915), page 79.

There's a Little Street in Heaven That They Call Broadway (w./m. A. Baldwin Sloane & James Waldron: 1903) M: *Chinese Honeymoon*, page 75.

There's No Room for a Dead One on the Great White Way (w. Joseph H. Herbert/m. Raymond Hubbell: 1905), page 79.

They Never Proved a Thing (w./m. Bill Jacob & Patti Jacob: 1969) M: *Jimmy*, page 138.

Third Avenue El (w./m. Michael Brown: 1956) M: *Four Below*, page 118.

Thirtieth Street Murder, The (w. Henry Bachus: 1858), page 124.

INDEX